- Please return items before closing time on the last date stamped to avoid charges.
- Renew books by phoning 01305 224311 or online www.dorsetforyou.com/libraries
- Items may be returned to any Dorset library.
- Please note that children's books issued on an adult card will incur overdue charges.

Dorset County Council
Library Service

DL/2372 dd05450

Authors' Note

The author has, with the exception of names that are in the public domain, protected the identities of those individuals encountered through Officer A's work (witnesses, informers, police officers, solicitors, etc.) by changing names and altering some background details and chronologies. Those cases that are a matter of public record are reported in their original detail.

THE CRIME FACTORY

The Shocking True Story of a Front-Line CID Detective

OFFICER 'A'

MAINSTREAM
PUBLISHING

EDINBURGH AND LONDON

First published in Great Britain in 2012 by
MAINSTREAM PUBLISHING COMPANY
(EDINBURGH) LTD
7 Albany Street
Edinburgh EH1 3UG

ISBN 9781780575254

A catalogue record for this book is available
from the British Library

Printed in Great Britain by
CPI Group (UK) Ltd, Croydon, CR0 4YY

1 3 5 7 9 10 8 6 4 2

'The percentage of respondents who feel that Surrey Police deal with the crime issues that matter is the highest nationally, first out of 43.'
– Her Majesty's Inspectorate of Constabulary website, 2010 police report

'Surrey has the second-lowest crime detection rate (21 per cent) in the country; 42nd out of 43.'
– Her Majesty's Inspectorate of Constabulary website, 2010 police report

*

'The difference between the psychological profile of a good detective and the psychological profile of a successful criminal is paper thin.'
– CID induction lecture

Contents

Foreword

WHEN I WAS GIVEN A DRAFT of this book to read, I was not sure what to expect. I knew from talking to Officer 'A' that he loved the Job (for those who serve, it is not *a job* but *the Job*). I also knew that his fall from grace had been hard and painful.

What I found was a thoroughly good read. I was intrigued; I laughed and I cringed, but I also found myself deeply disturbed by it. The book is not penned for entertainment and the point is made that policing is not like it is on television. His recollections are 'warts and all' and he does not pull any punches. His self-deprecating comments and open admissions about his own mistakes do him credit. I doubt that all the police officers referred to in this book can say the same.

I know for certain that some of what he has written about is true. I wish some of it were not so. Some may criticise him for even thinking of writing such a book: I do not. At the end of the day, I would urge everyone to keep an open mind and to understand that there are officers serving now who face the same pressures, the same challenges and the same problems. If you add into that caustic mix falling police budgets – Surrey Police has even disbanded its occupational health department – fewer officers and worsening pay and conditions of service, then I, for one, would not be surprised to find more Officer As waiting in the wings.

As one of his former colleagues is quoted as saying: 'We're great at sorting out other people's mess, but when it comes to our own, we're bloody useless.' Sad, but true.

The police are not perfect and have human frailties like everyone else. Whilst the public have the right to expect the best from the police, surely the police also have the right to expect the best support for what they have to do in return?

Kevin Morris, QPM
Police officer, superintendent,
Head of the Superintendents Association
for England and Wales (retd)

Preamble

'I MEAN, WHAT'S THE MARKER HERE? How bad was your worst day at work?'

'Ian' and I were on our . . . well, I suppose it might have been our third bottle of wine on what was a school night.

Ian, a detective sergeant on a covert unit, was stabbing his finger into a newspaper story about a supermarket worker who had ended up suing his bosses for stress-related ill health.

We laughed – at first. Until we read that his employers then coughed up a £140,000 compensation hairball.

We were wondering just what kind of stress could lead to a £140,000 payout, about five years' salary. A shortage of Toblerone in the choccy aisle just before a Swiss national holiday? A frustrated customer who'd punched an automated checkout after it had asked him to scan the same item 33 times before demanding he verify his age?

I'm sure the supermarket worker deserved his payment; Ian was just finding it particularly hard to accept since at the time he was sleeping on a mattress on the floor next to the marital bed because his constant thrashing and sweating, along with the occasional 'stress-related' yell, was keeping 'Lou', his fiancée, awake every night.

'Really! Come on!' Ian said, the red wine in his glass dangerously close to spilling as he gesticulated. 'What was *your* worst day?'

I shrugged, not wanting to go there.

'Well, I'll tell you mine. That guy who got stabbed in the leg.'

I looked blank.

'Don't tell me you don't remember?'

I've been told I have a photographic memory. I'm not sure that such a condition exists, but it is true that I never needed to refer to my notebook in court, made interviews a nightmare for suspects and could not forget a face, crime or clue. Badge numbers, car registrations, court cases, names and faces are all stored neatly on my mind's infinite box of index cards and I usually have little trouble recovering them when needed.

To Ian's amazement, I told him I'd not heard this story before.

It was a typical Saturday in a busy Surrey town. A young man got into an argument with a nightclub doorman and produced an insult so exceptional that the doorman felt justified in breaking the base of a beer bottle and plunging it into the victim's thigh, severing his femoral artery.

Two things happen here.

The first is that the heart's astoundingly powerful pump pushes the artery's top half up into the thigh, forcing it through the flesh towards the groin, while the lower half is drawn down, in the opposite direction, towards the ankle.

The second is that blood starts spraying out of the wound with about the same power as a garden hose on medium.

For a cop, strolling through any British town centre on a Saturday night is a bit like a game of roulette. On this occasion, it was Ian and John, another constable, who walked straight into this double-zero.

Three kindly lads, who were between pubs, held the victim down – he was thrashing about quite a bit, in a lot of pain. Then, while John pulled the wound open, Ian reached into the man's leg and began a desperate search for the upper end of his artery, to pinch it with his thumb and forefinger.

He couldn't find it – it's not easy when blood is being pumped into your eyes. The young man died there and then on the pavement in a twitching, vomiting mess.

Ian is still searching that wound in his nightmares.

Once it had been called in and a detective inspector had arrived, he said, 'Good effort, bad luck. Now, if you don't mind, start copping witness details. And that club? No one comes out until their pars [particulars] are down and confirmed, so throw a cordon double-quick.'

Even after trying to clean up, Ian and John looked like two extras from *Dawn of the Dead* as they stumbled through the rest of that night, covered in a dead man's drying blood.

Ask me – or any other CID detective – what our worst day was and we're spoiled for choice.

I have seen a foot poking out of a wheelie bin, rotten green with age; a junkie long dead, swollen with maggots, alone in his flat – apart from his dog on a string. I have been at the unrolling of a five-week-old corpse wrapped up in a carpet. I have seen a man's freshly decapitated head staring up at me from a railway track, with eyes that I could have sworn were still alive.

I have come to, lying with my face on a patio, pressed into a congealing puddle of my own blood after falling through a plate glass window – drunk from trying to forget about the girlfriend who'd just slept with a friend because, she said, of the long hours I spent at work. I have been dumped by a girl who said she couldn't take any more after I'd spent six months working undercover as a smelly junkie and was almost force-fed crack cocaine.

I've seen a man walk free with the £50k he'd conned out of a little old lady; I've seen a Crown Prosecution Service prosecutor agree with a drug dealer who explained that the 4 kg of coke I'd busted him with was for personal use.

I've watched my sanity slowly slip away like water through my fingers.

I've listened to a paedophile tell me that one Christmas he'd fucked a turkey – and that's not a euphemism. I've seen the results of someone being hit 30 times in the head with a brick. I've placed a noose around my neck and stepped off a chair. I've seen a man with a knife in his chest, lying dead in a children's play area, swings swaying spookily in the wind, as if the murderer had just run away. I've seen senior officers (note the plural) crash their cars while drunk and get away with it. I've been picked up by the throat by a paratrooper I've just pepper-sprayed and told I'm about to die.

I've had to explain to rape victims why the man who attacked them has walked free. I've arrived at work to hear that yet another colleague has had a breakdown and committed suicide, or has tried and failed to commit suicide, or gone off the rails in some spectacular fashion, like leaving a live hand grenade left over from his army service days on a superintendent's desk with a goodbye note attached.

I've stood my ground as 20 travelling folk steamed towards me, ready to stab and beat me to death with kitchen knives and cricket bats. I've listened as a corrupt officer told me that my name has been passed on to a biker gang who already have the name of my informant (who has disappeared).

All CID officers have their own version of the above. For my dad, also a CID man, it was the psychopathic murderer he'd nicked for killing and then raping a 15-year-old girl on New Year's Eve. As he was taken down to the cells, the psycho said, 'I'll fucking kill you.' Yeah, yeah, yeah, we've heard it all before. Dad waved him bye-bye.

But then the psycho escaped from prison on the Isle of Wight, where Dad happened to be sailing at the time. And then, not knowing he was so close to the man he wanted to wreak vengeance upon, he was eventually captured a mile from our Sussex home, carrying a large knife. Overtly, Dad took it in his stride. 'Nothing to worry about, son,' he told me, tousling my hair as I looked at him, eyes wide.

The best day you have as a police detective? The day you become one. The day you crack a murder. The day where nothing *too* bad happens and you make it home physically and mentally unscathed.

The job is not like it's portrayed on TV. We do not solve murders in forty-five minutes (my best was four hours). We swear a *lot*. Our livers and lungs are, after our deaths, used to scare kids into not smoking and drinking. I suspect that some brains of some long-term police officers may look a little different, too. We get to see the worst crimes you can imagine and then some, so we have no taboos: we take the piss out of anything without mercy.

There have been many books written about life in the police, from action-packed tales of specialised squads to the long and successful careers of Metropolitan Police Commissioners; from plain old bobbies on the beat to stories of corruption, robbery and murder. These all have their place and many are excellent, but no one has yet captured what life is really like in the Criminal Investigation Department (CID), the oldest and best investigating body in the world, to which everyone – from the SAS and MI5 to foreign agencies and governments – comes for advice and assistance.

I am immensely proud to have spent the past decade as a CID detective. I love the police and, like many others, I've given the job everything I've got to offer – and have paid the price.

I've watched over the years as the police has changed from being a crime-fighting force to a crime-management system built on a business model. We're lost in the stats game; in trying to give the government the vote-winning figures they want, we've lost the plot and the criminals are the ones who have benefited.

Consider this: In 2010, Surrey, my manor, had the second-lowest crime-clearance rate in the country at 21 per cent (42nd out of 43 police forces), yet had the highest customer satisfaction in the country.[1] How can this be possible? Are the people of Surrey really happy that we're crap at our job?

As we now catch and prosecute so few criminals, who wouldn't be tempted to commit to a life of crime in our present society? Putting morals aside for one minute, consider the financial benefits of becoming a drug dealer. There are plenty of people who've already made that choice. I could find someone selling an ounce of heroin in any town in the UK within two hours.

From an ounce, you can sell 286 £10 bags. I've seen teenagers sell two ounces of heroin a day, making about £5k profit for two days' work. Minus expenses and time off, they could make £15k a week, £780k each year. If they lived off £30k a year, in five years and three months they'd have saved £4 million, enough to live the rest of their lives in comfort. What young person on a council estate with only the hope of a poorly paid job to look forward to wouldn't be tempted?

Many senior cops above the rank of chief inspector are more concerned about surviving their careers than preventing and reducing crime. They play the stats game, create initiatives and avoid controversy so they can continue on the promotional trail and collect bonuses

---

[1]   Surrey slipped to No. 43 in 2011.

and full pensions at the end of the last few (hopefully) uneventful years of their career. This is known, aptly enough, as the Gravy Beat. As a result, during the first decade of the twenty-first century, detectives like myself have watched, mouths open, as the police descended into an Orwellian madness.

Detectives today often find themselves paying for the past crimes of their police forebears, and so it will be for the detectives of the future. Our slip-ups, mistakes and abuses always come back to us in the end, whether it's a young man falsely arrested for drug dealing, or someone on the receiving end of racism or verbal abuse, or someone whose cries for help are ignored.

What hurts good police officers more than anything and exacts the largest public cost are the cover-ups and corruption, as well as the collusion of senior officers with media and politicians, and those officers who milk the job for every possible bonus, perk and sinecure.

Police officers should be morally bound to do what is true and right, and accept that while they're not going to get rich, the rewards – not least of which is the privilege of doing the job itself – are ample.

So, with that in mind, do join me on my own very personal, extremely raw and very real tour of today's Criminal Investigation Department, aka the *Crime Factory*.

1

The 42 Blues Brothers

SURREY: A PLEASANT GREEN LAND OF picture-perfect villages, cricket, tea parties, cute commuter stations and more four-by-fours than the US Army.

Picture one such village, home to several sites of special scientific interest and situated just outside Guildford, on a quiet weekday afternoon, just after lunch.

Villagers are napping as Grieg's Morning Suite plays from radios tuned to Classic FM.

An elderly gent with a terrier on a leash crosses the village green, heading towards the B247, beyond which lies open parkland.

He looks left and then right and then starts to cross when he stops, head cocked.

Was that a car engine? He looks to the east, where the road dips into a slight hill; his dog strains at the leash, pulling the old gent towards the open parkland.

Yes, that's definitely an engine, coming at high speed, judging from the revs.

And was that a siren?

Suddenly, a marked police car breaks the bow of the hill and launches into the air, causing the siren to slow and simultaneously rise in pitch as the vehicle leaves the ground.

Aaaand freeze-frame.

* * *

Inside the car, I'm at the wheel, in the middle of screaming, 'FUUUUUUUCK!'

Behind me, in the backseat, is one of Surrey's most prolific drug dealers, a 6 ft 4 maniac, a gypsy by the name of Jake. Even though he's cuffed, he's managed to get his hands in front of him and is trying to strangle me.

His face is bright red, covered in blood and bruised, as is mine. I am in the middle of thrusting my right elbow back into Jake's nose.

Next to Jake is Lee, aka 'The Cowboy', a fellow police officer. Jake's booted foot has just connected with Lee's chin and he's lying sprawled on the back seat.

All of us are crying from the effects of CS gas and can barely see.

* * *

All I ever wanted was to be a detective. It's in my blood. Dad was a detective sergeant on the Regional Crime Squad; Mum was a detective sergeant in the CID. I had an uncle who was a chief superintendent, an aunt who was one of the first female officers to be made a detective; one grandfather was a Guard in Ireland and bodyguard to the Taoiseach, whilst the other was a constable during the Blitz in the Second World War. He was awarded the long service and good conduct medal for just five years' service, as it was deemed being a constable during the Blitz raids was the equivalent, in terms of stress and exposure, of a full thirty-year career. He proved them right by dying of a heart attack at 47. My great-grandfather, also a cop, was shot dead in an IRA ambush.

Growing up, I was exposed to police life through the stories my parents told each other when they came home. Dad telling Mum about a fatal plane crash on his first late shift: he called one guy 'India Rubber Man' because outwardly there was little injury but every bone had been smashed, so he felt like rubber when he was picked up. Mum telling Dad about her night spent acting as a decoy on Brighton seafront, dressed up as a prostitute to catch a serial sex attacker.

My dad was part of the Regional Crime Squad operations of the 1970s and 1980s that are now police folklore. The old 'my dad could have your dad in a fight' discussion at school was no contest. My mum was harder than most other dads.

I spent a lot of time in police stations, meeting coppers, who always had a kind word and who sat me in their cars or introduced me to their horse before an emergency call interrupted us. I watched as they scrambled, all blue lights, fast cars, action and go, go, go. I dreamed of joining them.

I applied at 18 and a half, the earliest possible age, but was knocked back, being told I was still too young. I worked as an apprentice mechanic and auto electrician and reapplied when I was 21. I was appointed on 21 September 1998.

My best friend Paul became a police officer at the same time and my dad took us both out for a curry. We talked about the job non-stop, asking Dad to tell us my favourite stories. Towards the end of the meal, Dad gave us a short and unforgettable speech, words of advice, and I wish that every police officer could hear them and live and work by them.

'I can't give you what it is you came looking for when you decided to become a police officer. You have to discover it for yourself. While belief and opinion may be bullied into you, never forget you always have the warranted and true individual right to exercise your intuition and evaluate the evidence.

'For others to understand that evidence – to be convinced by what you know to be true – is not easy. To remain resilient requires strength, both physical and mental, and a great deal of good fortune. Remember also that you are part of a body; value the men alongside you because you will need friends in the right places.

'That is police work, pure and simple. Good luck!'

* * *

Aaaand go.

Sailing through the air, I see the old gent out of the corner of my eye. We make startled eye contact a split second before the car hits the tarmac and, in time with the impact, I throw my elbow back into Jake's nose with all my strength.

The car's suspension makes an incredible *doing* sound as we bounce back up, the force of which makes the siren sound like a cat in mid-castrato. I keep control and floor the accelerator, taking us towards Guildford town centre.

The old gent watches us disappear. The road is empty, silent. He then turns at the sound of other engines, as three cars full of screaming gypsies, armed with knives and sticks, all determined to rescue Jake before we get him to Guildford nick, bomb past as fast as their engines will allow.

* * *

My dad hadn't been wrong. Joining the police had led to action from day one.

At 9 a.m. on this particular morning, the inspector had introduced me to Lawrence and said: 'This is Lawrence. He's a chief inspector here from Northern Ireland on a fact-finding mission. He wants to see how we do things, so I suggested you show him around.'

As Lawrence went to get his kit, the DI leaned over and said, 'Do try not to break him, won't you?'

'I'll try, guv.'

As we climbed into the car, Lawrence, who looked like everyone's favourite uncle, asked me in a soft Derry accent where the worst area for crime was. Easy.

'Park Barn.'

'Take me there.'

Park Barn was a warren estate, as bad as anything the UK had to offer. You might find anything from kids trashing a stolen car to drug dealers making a drop or setting up shop in one of the empty flats. It was unusually quiet, however, and as we drove in our unmarked car, a voice suddenly piped up on the open channel.

'Bored, bored, bored.'

Another voice came on. Chief Inspector Witcher, aka 'Witcher the Twitcher', had been monitoring.

'Identify yourself now!' he yelled.

There was a pause.

'I said I was bored,' the voice answered, 'not fucking stupid.'

Turning down the radio, I said, 'Ahem. Erm, anyway, this is the estate.' Lawrence smiled at this little 'insight' into UK police 'humour'.

We drove around for a few more minutes before I spotted Jake Michaels, a 6 ft 4 gypsy and bullyboy who loved to fight (as long as the other guy was smaller than him). He was also one of the county's most notorious drug dealers. Every single cell in my body screamed at me to pull his Peugeot 309Gti over.

Although he was personable enough, I'd dismissed Lawrence as a bit of a wet rag. He was babbling about some initiative when I cut him off.

'STFU², Lawrence. This is about to get interesting, so look sharp.'

As I drew close, Jake floored it and seconds later we were white knuckles, doing 60–70 through 30–40 zones.

This was a high-risk pursuit – Jake was forcing people off the road – but my inspector, who wanted Jake as much as I did (his dodgy gear had helped a few young local people end their lives prematurely), let me continue the chase. Besides, hell-raising Jake and his crew had been taking the piss out of the police for so long that we simply had to get him put away, if only to win back our self-respect and bring some peace and quiet to Guildford and the surrounding area.

If Jake was running for it, then that meant he had to be carrying, so this was a real golden chance for me to grab a great collar.

We were on our own, however; I'd asked for back-up but no traffic officers were close by, so we roared out of Guildford on our tod. I hoped the idiot would crash into a hedge.

'Just stay on him,' Lawrence said. 'He's going to crash at that speed.'

I didn't say anything. I already had a sinking feeling, but, like a terrier down the rabbit hole, I couldn't stop myself when I had the scent.

Sure enough, Jake led us straight into his travellers' camp. He swung the car to a halt, throwing up a wave of dust that half-obscured him as he ran, package under his arm, beyond the trailers that ringed the site.

I pulled up outside and Lawrence immediately started to run in after him. I grabbed him.

'No way! I admire your spirit, but if we go in there, there's no way we'll come out in one piece.'

---

²   Shut the Fuck Up

There was a standing order that no police entry was allowed into this site without a PSU – a Police Support Unit: one inspector, three sergeants and eighteen PCs in riot gear.

'We'll seize the car, though, right?'

'Yeah, but be really alive on this one, OK?'

I called in a tow truck and we waited. The camp was quiet, which I thought was a bit odd. At the very least I expected a barrage of police-related insults.

Two other officers, Jim Churchill, a gentle Mancunian, and Lee aka 'The Cowboy', appeared in another car.

'You do realise it's going to kick off the moment you touch Jake's car, don't you?' Lee asked.

'Yup,' I replied, nodding.

Then the tow truck arrived. The driver turned white when he saw what we were about to do. As I went over to help hook it up, I heard a growl and saw Jake charging towards us. He was ripping off his T-shirt as he ran – his veins were so bulged they looked like wires wound over the surface of his skin. It was obvious he'd just had a huge hit of crack – he looked ready to kill.

I dived back, raising my left arm just in time to push aside his massive fist, and drew and flicked open my asp (collapsible baton) with my right hand, but he charged straight past and thumped the driver, knocking him to the floor. Still moving fast, Jake then ran up to Jim, who stood his ground and tried to shove Jake back. Jake bent down about a foot to get into Jim's face. He yelled something and unleashed two mighty punches, knocking Jim out cold.

I then emptied half a can of CS spray in Jake's direction, but this had no effect, apart from making him angrier, if that were possible. I chucked the spray as he marched towards me. I felt movement from behind and turned just in time to see Lawrence, asp drawn, leap like a ninja with the metal baton raised above his head. He brought it down on Jake's crown with all of his strength. The skin split, from Jake's hairline to the back of his head. That's it – game over, I thought. He's killed him.

But no, Jake was standing. And now we'd made him *really* angry.

'Fucking help me!'

I turned to see Lee facing a wall of gypsies, armed with baseball bats and two-by-fours. Lawrence shoved me. 'Go! I got this.' I watched as Lawrence ducked a punch and swung the asp into Jake's legs. As Jake fell, Lawrence said, 'Not so fucking hard now, are you, laddie?' and started to beat him over and over and over again on the legs and body.

Then I heard the roar of an engine. Jake's dad had driven his lorry across the entrance, blocking our escape.

I looked behind me and saw about 20 gypsies coming towards us, with bricks and bats. Lawrence was still beating Jake, who was fighting back. Jake grinned, his face red and swollen.

'You're fucked, copper.'

I had to admit he was right.

'Red one. Red one. Officers need urgent assistance!'

I screamed it over and over into my radio, as a man darted forward from the crowd. Jim was still lying prone and I grabbed his CS gas and sprayed it at the yelling mob. It just made them angrier.

We were between the mob and Jake, whom Lawrence was now trying to cuff. Lee and I swung our asps furiously back and forth, like a pair of high-speed Samurai, trying to keep the mob that wanted to rip us to pieces at bay.

There is perhaps nothing that unites the police like a cry for help from one of their own. We rush to any emergency as fast as we can, but when it's one of our 'family', the rush can take on a manic dimension.

Seven uniformed officers had abandoned the pub they were lunching in and piled into an unmarked green Vauxhall Astra. They were driving Keystone Kops-style through Guildford to the camp, which was about five miles from the town centre, when they wrote off the car by grounding it on a central reservation (it was simply too heavy).

A riot-training exercise was taking place nearby when a sergeant heard the call. He relayed the message, and an inspector, three sergeants and eighteen constables in riot gear dropped what they were doing and leapt into two police transport vans. About three other units left judges and solicitors hanging, as they scrambled out of a courtroom.

'Everyone's coming!' Nick, my detective sergeant, screamed back over the radio. 'Forty-two units! It's like the fucking Blues Brothers!'

I'd never been so scared. No witness would testify to what had happened to us should we have been killed. Even so, some crazy part of me still wanted to get out of there with Jake in cuffs. What we didn't know was that a young, fast-tracked and inexperienced chief inspector (he had to be shown how to put on a stab vest) was already at the scene but had decided to set up a Rendezvous Point and ordered everybody to form up 100 m from the camp.

Steve and Chris, two bulldog detectives, ignored him and jumped into a Land Rover, ordered four PCs inside and roared up to the camp.

I'd never seen such a beautiful sight.

Once inside, they didn't hold back.

'We can do this!' I yelled to Lee, as more cops stormed over the barricade.

Together, as the others held the mob back, we grabbed Jake.

'Coming?' I asked Lawrence, as Jake tried to writhe free from our grip.

Lawrence was breathing but looked almost ecstatic. 'No way! I'm not leaving this – this is the most fun I've had in weeks!'

Our eyes were streaming from the CS gas as we manhandled Jake into the back of the car. As soon as he was in, Lee screamed, 'Go, go! Fucking go!'

I spun the wheels and we shot off. Even though we had him cuffed to the rear, Jake wasn't done; he was still kicking Lee and the back of my seat as I drove, and spitting and biting. Blood was spurting all over the interior, and Jake was covered in CS spray, so I opened all the windows.

'We're being followed!' Lee screamed. Three carloads of gypsies were right behind us.

It was 3 p.m. on a weekday afternoon.

'I hope Guildford's ready for this,' I thought and then we sailed over the hill, bounced past the old man, bound for Guildford town centre.

There's a scene in the Robert De Niro film *Ronin* where the camera pulls back from the car chase to reveal the narrow labyrinthine streets of Nice. I'd be the first to say Guildford cannot compete – except in one important way: the chaos of the streets and the nonsensical one-way system, surely created by Lucifer himself.

Once we entered the town, our pursuers caught up with us – we simply couldn't go fast enough. We then wound our way through the town, Jake fighting us, while I radioed ahead demanding that the 'reception committee' be ready to meet us.

The station had a rolling door that wasn't quick enough to stop the gypsy snatch team from crashing in behind us, so we rushed Jake through into the yard at the back of the station as another battle erupted in the car park. The yard was overlooked by the courts, which happened to be full of Jake's cousins, who were there for the trial of one of his siblings.

When they saw Jake, who was still fighting, they climbed the wall and tried to tear the wire roof off so they could join in. Jake finally calmed down when Dave, an ex-Royal Marine, arrived with a set of keys for the cuffs.

They faced each other in the yard for a long moment. Jake, a bloodied monster of sweat, muscle and popping veins, with eyeballs practically popping out of his head. Dave, a good few inches shorter but clearly a fighting man, in his pristine uniform. Dave clenched his fists and said, 'We can do this the easy way or the hard way.'

'Easy way,' Jake said, his body sagging in defeat.

'Good man,' Dave replied, as he stepped forward and undid the cuffs. The moment they were off, Jake turned into a Tasmanian devil and did his best to take on all-comers before he realised that the continued arrival of reinforcements meant his only option really was surrender. So, bruised and bloodied, we won the day.

One of Surrey's most persistent drug dealers was behind bars and this time – because he had assaulted several police officers – he was going to stay there.

When we visited his home, his six-year-old son – well trained to hate the police – swore at us until an enterprising officer asked him if he'd like to sit in a police car and play with the lights.

'Really? Can I?'

By the time the search was done, Jake's boy wanted to be a police officer. I can think of no better revenge.

I was in shock afterwards. I was locked on alert; I simply couldn't switch off, as I replayed the day's events and thought about how close we'd come to being seriously injured or worse.

Jim's jaw had a lump on it the size of an orange; Lee and I quickly lost count of our bruises. We were exhausted.

Lawrence returned to the station with a spring in his step and a smile on his face. 'How you boys doing?' We could barely answer. 'Well, that was grand. I'm off to my physio appointment now, I'll see you later.'

'How come you're so fresh?' I asked.

'I've policed the streets of Belfast. That was nothing.'

Mark Rowley, then a chief superintendent (at the time of writing, he's Assistant Commander in the Met), gave Jim a bottle of Scotch. He then bought beers in the police bar for me and Lawrence, and eventually everyone else.

Just about every rota from Woking and Guildford was there and we got completely smashed as we exchanged war stories from the day.

The nightly news simply said a man had been arrested for assaulting police officers (we lost the drugs in the melee). It's a phrase we hear all too often – it understandably doesn't occur to most people that several officers had faced serious injury and possibly even death to make that arrest.

The best thing of all was that our actions that day really made a difference. Sometime later, it was near midnight on New Year's Eve and the people of Guildford were gathered near the Town Hall clock. Mark Rowley was on the balcony, keeping an eye on events. Rowley spotted Jake, who was between court appearances, and a gang of gypsies 30-strong. They started jeering at Mark, flicking the Vs and generally starting a bit of aggro in the crowd.

Mark turned to me and said, 'I want you to deal with him.'

Fifteen of us, including the same guys who had dug us out of the crap on the day we fought Jake, removed our helmets and marched into the crowd, which parted like the Red Sea. We lined up in front of Jake and stared at him. It went very quiet and Jake and his 30-strong gang walked away like puppies. We didn't hear a peep for the rest of the night. I did it again with Jake when I happened to be there when he kicked off in a courtroom and he backed down immediately.

The painful memories had stuck with Jake – as had the scars. As Lawrence said after the Battle of Guildford: 'Don't EVER give them an inch, show them a moment of weakness – or the back of your head.'

Along with Lawrence, Jim and Lee, I received a commendation for my actions that day. I was delighted because I knew that this news would reach the ears of the hallowed Criminal Investigation Department. What I wanted more than anything else in life was to become a CID detective and to achieve this I needed to make an impression.

POLICE RANK, PURPOSE AND STRUCTURE
(AN UNOFFICIAL GUIDE)

The Patrol Constable

And so you begin. Here you will learn vital skills such as pre-emptive phlegm avoidance drill (one step back as the scrote gargles up a phlegm-gem) and how to tackle unhinged, pissed-up rugby players in the high street (a giant bundle charge made up of as many police officers as you can find). You will also learn how not to screw up an accident report book (ARB) or statement, as the God of the Red Pen (Sergeant) will quickly and ferociously stamp out your errors.

There are three main types of Patrol Constable:

The Rookie or Probationer, aka 'All the Gear and No Idea': Fresh out of training school and still thinks that effective verbal communication will diffuse the samurai sword incident unfolding in front of them. At this point, a good rookie has about seven years of natural and optimistic enthusiasm left.

The Uber-Cop, aka (to detectives) lids, woods, woodentops, shinies or plod: The shiniest, most good-looking and slick officer that's ever patrolled the streets of Anytown. They've been trained in tactical pursuit, use of stingers to stop fleeing cars, have reached the level of a Class 1 driver, have a physique to die for and are generally an all-round good egg. They manage to make directing traffic look like the ultimate recruitment ad and are able to address individual detectives as 'mate' and make it seem appropriate *and* genuine. Most likely they are a good thief-taker and are dying to make the jump into the firearms unit or the CID. On average the Uber-Cop has around four years' service and therefore about three years of enthusiasm left.

The 20-Year Service PC: These guys are seriously NFI[3]. Seen it all, twice, and would not blink an eye if Oswald Mosley appeared before them leading an army of Nazis down Anytown High Street on a Thursday afternoon. They can knock out the solution to any situation with their eyes closed whilst employing the sarcastic complaint that if policing

---

[3] Not Fucking Interested

were an Olympic sport the gold and the world record would be theirs.

They're counting the days until their index-linked pension kicks in. They despair of Uber-Cop ('We didn't have fancy pepper sprays and asps in my day, Mr Flash Harry. Back then, it was all fists and wooden sticks.') and quietly feel sorry for the probationer (they will never admit this) who ends up crying after attending their first fatal RTA (Road Traffic Accident) or similarly distressing event.

Their enthusiasm has been replaced by an extremely hard squinty-eye view of the world. Think Judge Dredd with a truncheon. Definitely on the endangered species list.

The Detective Constable, aka 'Tech' or 'Techie'

There are three basic types of DC:

The Learner: Recently graduated, shiny, in awe of stepping into the hallowed offices of the CID. Keen as mustard but incredibly naive about the world they've just entered. They've yet to learn basics, such as 'Detectives' detect (also known as solving crimes) while 'Traffic' deal with road accidents. They look uncomfortable in double-cuffs and fall for the most obvious of gags, e.g.

El CID (see below): 'I'll start and you finish. P, Q, R, S . . .'
Learner: 'T?'
El CID: 'Thanks, don't mind if I do. Milk and two sugars.'

El CID: Epitomises the core beliefs of the CID. Generally will submit an overtime bill each month, the type of which is believed to have contributed to the downfall of Lehman Brothers. This officer eats, sleeps and shits crime (and is polite in public, so pardon me).

They are on first name terms with prolific offenders *and* their families. If not already divorced and developing an alcohol problem (occasionally drug addiction), they will be soon.

Many of these officers are used as test subjects for insomnia surveys, fill the church halls used by Alcoholics Anonymous and are considered the pinnacle of a Relate counsellor's career. After death, their internal organs are shown to schoolchildren to put them off smoking and drinking. Without exception, all El CID officers have many eccentricities and often turn the CID office into something more fantastical than Hogwarts. For example, one rare afternoon when things were a bit slow, within an hour *Police: The Musical* was born in the style of Queen meets Abba.

Squad: For the El CIDs who manage to avoid disciplinary actions, marital and career implosion and political infighting, and don't annoy the Detective Inspector (too often), the shiny world of squads awaits (murder, robbery, covert, surveillance, corruption, etc., etc.)

Here you can wear street clothes and must start every phone conversation with, 'Free to speak?' and play with the shiniest and Gucciest kit, as well as utter those immortal words when about to be dicked with an SJ (Shit Job): 'Sorry, but that particular task is not in my squad's remit.'

The Uniformed Sergeant

Could have come from anywhere on promotion because it actually makes sense to send a highly trained detective back to uniform after ten years in the CID. Otherwise it's a case of the blind leading the blind. There are two distinct types.

White Stripes: Newly promoted and so woefully out of their depth that a scuba set won't save them. They're still in shock and reeling from the sergeants' course, which has no bearing whatsoever to the real world of rotas, time sheets, vehicle maintenance, inter-rota relationships that have gone tits-up and 'performance development and strategy meetings'. Those skilled enough to understand the concept behind the phrase 'bullshit baffles brains' will eventually become quite useful.

Uncle or Auntie Sarge: These God-like (in the style of Morgan Freeman) officers have been in rank years and use the same parenting approach with constables and senior officers alike. They've seen everything, possess more political savvy than the entire House of Commons and are the station's lynchpin.

In the good old days, they would have used 'sergeant's humour' in performance reviews, real examples of which include: 'This officer should not be allowed to breed,' and 'Somewhere a village is missing its idiot.' They mellow as they close in on pension and in their twilight years they tend to take a kindly approach to everyone.

The Detective Sergeant

No multiple types here, just the one. Can be found anywhere, usually in two different places at the same time. They are the station ringmasters, wheeling murderers, rapists, robbers, various specialist officers and senior managers on and off as and when they need to deal with them. These human lie detectors don't miss a trick. As the old police saying goes: 'Chuck Norris once attempted to become a DS but was turned down on the grounds of not being mentally or physically tough enough to cope with no sleep for 14 years and all the psychopathic juveniles [the DCs].' In their spare time, they hold 'Use the Force' classes for aspiring Jedi and I don't mean Section 3 of the Criminal Law Act.[4]

The Inspector, Uniformed and Detective

This is the rank where resemblance to police officer starts to fade. Now referred to as managers. Regardless of the department, there are two types of inspector.

The Boss/Guv: This inspector is widely respected as an officer who has slugged through the ranks and genuinely recognises that if police headquarters were to disappear tomorrow, the only inconvenience caused to the troops would be where to send their overtime claims.

Arguably, you only need good inspectors like this to achieve a smoothly run and effective police force. The Boss resents being promoted, as all the fun of the job disappears at the next rank. They have a habit of humorously (to them) slinging your overtime sheets out of the window, as they are on a fixed salary and can no longer claim overtime. Every detective hopes that the Boss will be the next Detective Chief Inspector because the other option is our worst nightmare (see below).

The Sir/Ma'am: This inspector is most likely on the Accelerated Promotion Scheme (APS) and is about as useful as a toothpick in a gunfight. This officer genuinely thinks that being called Sir or Ma'am is a mark of respect. In any case, they'll only be with you for six months until they are promoted upwards to a position where they can cause no more damage. Perhaps Staff Officer to the Chief Officers Group (COG) or Chief Inspector, Stationery and Provisions.

---

[4] Apologies for the police in-joke and I won't do it again. This refers to the use of reasonable force.

The Chief Inspector

Again, the department doesn't matter. There are two types.

God: Fair, all-knowing and all-powerful beings. They apply their power in a meaningful and compassionate fashion whilst shielding their people (rank and file) from the Dark Side (Senior Management Team and COG). DCIs in the God category are reverently referred to as 'The Guv'.

Dr Evil or Smiling Assassin: Total tosser by-product of the Accelerated Promotion Scheme or, worse still, acting as a remora fish to their sponsors (sponsors are more senior officers who act as mentors and who tend to use this in a Stalinist way by placing acolytes in strategic locations). They are, therefore, in league with the Dark Side, which consequently means they are not to be trusted. Their performance review might read: 'Must try harder to forget all this cop stuff and focus on being a manager.'

The Superintendent and Chief Superintendent

Sightings are rare, but we know they exist due to the relentless torrent of policy and procedure that spews from their offices with their signature attached. Unashamedly prostitute themselves to the COG, local government and the Police Authority in order to obtain that vital jump to Assistant Chief Constable so they can join in the ACPO foxtrot.[5]

There are one or two exceptions, particularly in units like the Flying Squad and Murder Teams who don't know how they got to this rank and are damned if they won't be at the head of a Method of Entry Team, charging headfirst into a crack house to deliver the immortal line: 'You're nicked, sunshine/Johnny/young feller-me-lad/you bastard, etc., etc.

N.B. It is now possible to stay at this rank after a serious PFU[6] and/or committing a criminal offence. For example, the press caught out a superintendent who forged and lied on an application form to compete in a high-profile sports event. This offence might have landed a lesser

---

[5] ACPO: Association of Chief Police Officers, a forum for the chiefs to meet and share ideas. The ACPO foxtrot: Dancing between jobs and forces in a short space of time so that no one has time to notice that you're not actually doing any work. Their preferred choice of music is Groucho Marx's 'Hello, I Must Be Going'.

[6] Public Fuck-Up

rank with two to four years in prison. This superintendent was docked ten days' pay.

It is also possible to move on from this rank after similar errors to the Chief Officers Group, where it is likely that you will not take part in the ACPO foxtrot. You may, however, partake in the COG two-step, where you hop from assistant chief constable to acting deputy chief constable and back, skipping your way towards the pension. Another example might be arriving from the Met into the Shires as an assistant chief constable, despite having failed the Strategic Command Course three times in a row. Normally, you're only allowed one attempt, but rules are there to be broken if you are in the right club, lodge or circle.

Chief Officers Group (COG)

You've cracked it! Six-figure memoir deals, medals, knighthoods, Lordships and fame (or infamy) are yours for the taking. This is the elite group of every force that is answerable to the Chief Constable and contains the Chief Constable and Assistant Chief Constables. All you have to do is manipulate the force performance figures and come up with new and interesting ways to make the force look good to the public (this, of course, involves annoying the hell out of the rank and file).

As a member of COG, you are now blessed with the power to do whatever you wish (within the law, of course). Perhaps the best way to use this power is to endear yourself to the troops forever. For example, former Surrey chief, Sir Dennis O'Connor, pitched up at a 5 a.m. briefing on a multiple drugs warrant operation. When handed the cold and stale pre-raid breakfast roll by catering, Sir Dennis asked who had arranged the food. Furnished with the relevant Chief Inspector's details, Dennis located him, told him off and then gave the nearest sergeant the following immortal order:

'Sergeant, take my credit card. The pin number is ****. You are to go to the nearest McDonald's and purchase 150 McMuffin breakfasts and distribute them to the teams. Thank you.'

Sir Dennis was well known for arriving unannounced on shift and getting in amongst it, and most of us loved him for it. Sadly, although there are other outstanding chiefs out there, the majority are not so well loved amongst the ranks for a number of reasons.

You really, really have to work hard to get fired, as former Commissioner Ian Blair proved while in charge of the Met (and previously of the Parish of Surrey) and then Paul Stephenson. But, as they say, despite the corruption and mismanagement scandals surrounding them, they resigned or 'retired' – and I quote Stephenson on this – with their 'honour intact' (as well as their bonus, pension and, waiting in the wings, cushy job offers for advisory roles across the globe).

Ian Blair secretly taped telephone conversations, most notably with the Attorney General, Lord Goldsmith; this was legal but described by the chairman of the Metropolitan Police Authority as 'totally unacceptable'. He referred to the murders of Holly Wells and Jessica Chapman by publicly stating that 'almost nobody' understood why it became such a big story. He sought a £25,000 performance bonus during criminal proceedings over the shooting of Jean Charles de Menezes – while on a salary of £228,000 and with rank-and-file officers facing the prospect of pay cuts. Blair also continued to be paid his full salary for a year after his resignation in December 2008, as per the terms of his contract, which ran until February 2010.

On 17 July 2011, Paul Stephenson – whose reign lasted a little over two years – announced his intention to resign from the post of Commissioner as the result of speculation regarding his connection with Neil Wallis, who'd been arrested three days earlier on suspicion of involvement in the News International phone-hacking scandal. Wallis's company Chamy Media had provided 'strategic communication advice and support' to the Met. Early in 2011, Stephenson received £12,000 worth of free hospitality from a Champneys health spa, where Wallis was working at the time.

I admit I've smashed the senior ranks in this, but I wouldn't be doing our tour around the Crime Factory enough justice if I didn't. Treachery and double-dealing in the police extends to all officers of any rank the moment the thought of career advancement enters their heads. Police stations are often more dangerous environments for officers than the streets we patrol.

Policing should be about making the good guys feel good, the bad guys feel bad, bodies in the bin and convictions in hand. It is that simple and no one can make a case for anything otherwise. Every copper who remembers that is doing well. Those who don't remember it, repeat after me:

'I am a copper. Nothing else matters, not even my own political agendas. It is not a job. It is an appointment. It is unacceptable for me to neglect the public in pursuit of a personal career. I must fight crime whilst supporting my colleagues in ALL matters.'

And finally:

The basic mission for which the police exist is to prevent crime and disorder.

The ability of the police to perform their duties is dependent upon the public approval of police actions.

Police must secure the willing cooperation of the public in voluntary observation of the law to be able to secure and maintain the respect of the public.

The degree of cooperation of the public that can be secured diminishes proportionately to the necessity for the use of physical force.

Police seek and preserve public favour not by catering to public opinion but by constantly demonstrating absolute impartial service to the law.

Police use physical force to the extent necessary to secure observance of the law or to restore order only when the exercise of persuasion, advice and warning is found to be insufficient.

Police, at all times, should maintain a relationship with the public that gives reality to the historic tradition that the police are the public and the public are the police; the police being only members of the public who are paid to give full-time attention to duties that are incumbent upon every citizen in the interests of community welfare and existence.

Police should always direct their action strictly towards their functions and never appear to usurp the powers of the judiciary.

The test of police efficiency is the absence of crime and disorder, not the visible evidence of police action in dealing with it.

Any objections? I didn't think so. These are the Peelian principles, developed by the founder of the modern police, Sir Robert Peel – perhaps even more relevant today than they were in 1829.

2

Turning Tech

AS SOON AS I BECAME A cop, I wanted to become a detective. Of course, you didn't just transform into one overnight, but I didn't want to waste any time and applied as soon as I was sure I had most of the necessary skills, which remain:

Encyclopedic knowledge of the law

Street experience

Stamina that would make a student doctor look like a part-time worker

Ability to understand and interact with street patois but be able to switch to scholastic court language in an instant

Authoring skills that compact major incidents into evidential files

Constitution of Herculean proportions

Cunning

Ability to moralise heavily for a victim and abandon any morals when dealing with a criminal whom you've made a deal with before, then breaking it

Unswerving commitment

Razor-sharp humour

Ability to work on no sleep and no relaxation for extended periods

Most importantly, never miss anything and follow the ABC: Assume Nothing. Believe No One. Check Everything.

It takes a certain kind of person to become a detective, someone slightly odd – if not totally maladjusted. In fact, the job quickly shoves the mildly maladjusted over the edge of their mental precipice.

As a uniformed constable, the best way to get into the CID was to build a reputation as a prolific and consistent thief taker backed up by accurate and meaningful report writing. Report writing should take the form of a clear and detailed guide (with decent grammar and few spelling mistakes) to the *modus operandi* (MO) of both thief and thief taker.

If you nailed a burglar prolific enough to get noticed by the CID, then you were going places. As we will see, burglars cost the taxpayer a fortune, so putting a stop to the busiest of them was a high priority.

Once I'd been 'noticed', I was offered a cuppa by a detective sergeant from CID during a prisoner handover and invited into the holyland of the CID office. This was a big deal, as uniforms didn't get let in very often. Until very recently, all uniformed coppers had to knock before entering.

One question new recruits to CID are always asked is: 'Are you sure you're ready for this?' Becoming a detective is a huge step. You could be the first investigator on the scene after a murder with older, more experienced uniformed officers of senior rank asking you what to do.

As the DS put it: 'So, you want to live and work amongst the worst that humanity has to offer, to see things no human should have to see on a daily basis, sights and incidents that will stay with you until your dying day – and get paid less than a McDonald's manager for doing it? Are you sure you're ready – or even want – to do this?'

My mental response was simple: 'I was born ready.'

Although I started confidently, as the DS looked at me over the cup of tea, I started to burble, trying and failing not to talk too much, knowing he was reading me, studying me to see whether and how I might fit, whether I carried myself like a detective and had the mental strength and self-belief for the job.

My one advantage was that, thanks to my family history, I knew the way detectives talked, the sort of behaviour that was expected – and what you could get away with.

Sure enough, I just about made it through and the DI invited me to work as an 'aide' on CID for three months. In reality, I made tea (38.5 degrees, stirred five times clockwise, five times anti-clockwise and two sugars for my detective sergeant), answered the phones and took enquiries no one else wanted whilst keeping the day/night book up to speed for the shift handover.

Then it was back to uniform, where I waited and prayed like an auditioning actor for a 'callback', a summons by the DCI for a 30-minute 'chat' (i.e. grilling). The detective inspectors and detective chief inspector were terrifying men – scarred officers who'd fought their way up through the ranks over many years.

The meeting wasn't exactly a sales pitch. Five of us were taken into the office and we were told once again about the horrendous hours, terrifying and exhausting court battles, all the trouble we would end up in and how it was much harder to get promoted once you were in CID.

Then we were told to learn the law (PACE, CPIA and RIPA in detail, things like the Locard Theory of Transference[7], and about a dozen other topics) in our own time. The CI would let us know if and when we got a board (interview), before adding: 'And think on what you wear to the boards, should you be chosen. I might like to see you in a suit, I might not. I might like to see you in a tunic [uniform], I might not.'

On the day of the boards, half of us were in suits, half in tunics. Of course, he didn't care which clothes we wore, he was just toying with us.

'Board' means to face a board of senior officers, which in my case was the Detective Chief Inspector and two detective inspectors from separate specialist operational units. CID detectives kick off a great many investigations that are later passed on to specialised units, so the bosses of those units are keen to check that you aren't some kind of fuck-up.

In the board, I was hit with scenario after scenario. They would write down my answer and come back with more specific questions.

---

[7] Locard's principle: When a perpetrator(s) enters and leaves a crime scene, they bring something into and out of the scene.

Even when I was certain I'd given the most comprehensive answer possible, that it wasn't possible to do anything else, one of them would ask, 'Anything else you want to tell us?' Think of a menacing Chris Tarrant asking, 'Sure that's your final answer?'

I sat there, flicking through my mind's index, before finally saying, 'I've nothing more to say about that.' Grimaces all round. Each time I thought I'd blown it. But there was little time to reflect, as a new and more convoluted scenario was quickly thrust before me.

I'd given the correct answer to each question, but it was a test of character, to see how I'd cope under pressure, particularly from more experienced and far more senior-ranking officers.

Most CID detectives had been with the same department for at least ten years and the majority rarely moved on, so slots didn't open up that often. In my case, fifteen constables had applied for three positions. I was the youngest, with half the usually accepted service of five years.

I came second.

Three months later, the DCI called me up and told me I was starting Monday.

As I already knew, the official way of doing things in the police rarely matched reality. I was supposed to go on an eight-week training course for baby detectives, where we'd learn interviewing, how to deal with crime scenes and forensics, handling informants and so on. Instead, I learned on the job and I was finally sent on the course three months later.

Learners were supposed to be assessed by their CID tutor and detective sergeant every four weeks, but after seven months of no assessments I was signed off and, boom, I was a real, grown-up detective, ready to be let loose on society.

This was heady stuff for a 22 year old. Being a detective is not much more financially rewarding than being a uniformed PC (PCs and DCs take home the same basic salary) and has fewer promotional prospects (it's much harder for DCs to rise up the ranks due to the smaller size of the department and the many experienced techs with lots of experience and dazzling skill sets).

Therefore, cops who were drawn to apply for the CID had a

genuine sense of duty and really, really loved a challenge. We got the most interesting and difficult jobs: burglaries, bank robberies, murders, rapes, drug dealing and so on.

My skipper[8], Detective Sergeant 'Uncle' Bill Keagan was a legend. Think Gene Hunt's older, wiser brother from down south. His motto was *Deprehendo Deprehensio Vitum*: 'Overtime Solves Crime'.

'Surrey is a huge area,' Bill told me when I first started. 'It borders London and covers parts of the M25, M4, M3, A3, Heathrow and Gatwick – all the major drugs routes – and plenty of London crims use Surrey as a base. Unfortunately, we are but poor cousins to the Met. While they call on a team of 30 detectives for every murder, we send a CID man and a couple of PCs. There's about 400 new crimes in Surrey every day. We might have two DSs and two DCs on call for the whole county. There used to be an inspector, two sergeants and sixteen PCs at my nick and now we haven't got that many on duty in the whole division [county] tonight.'

This sounded great to me. Action all the way.

The CID was packed full of very strong characters – all with differing specialities. The other detective constables included Tim, aka 'Posh Tim' because he had the accent and bearing of a lord.

Matt also came from a regal family. He wore Harris tweed suits and Brylcreemed his hair, even though he was only 25.

Hilary, 'Hills' was much loved; a proper mother figure to our office, although she could be very ferocious when required.

Bart, a northern lad, had already been in the CID three years, and James was a city boy turned cop who could turn his hand to anything.

Bill, James, Bart and I formed a bit of a clique, as we shared a similar style.

Tim, Hilary and Matt would never be down with the kids, but when it came to dealing with barristers and judges they were way better than me. I felt more at ease dealing with the slags; I could speak their lingo without thinking. James and Bill were utterly at home on both sides of the criminal fence.

---

[8] As a rule, sergeant = 'skipper', detective inspector = 'boss', detective chief inspector = 'guv', although 'guv' and 'boss' are sometimes interchangeable.

Working alongside Bill was Nick, a redheaded 5-ft-8 Inspector Clouseau lookalike and possibly the sharpest DS I ever encountered. He wore a Clouseau mac and hat to jobs just to confuse the uniform officers. They didn't know whether to take him seriously or not. He was utterly mad and dangerously intelligent.

Our other DS was Jim, a former paratrooper with 20 years in as a detective, who took great delight in winding people up. He was 6 ft 5, bald, had a goatee and wore diamond earrings. He looked like a genie.

Bill had a God-given ability to read people and he knew to let me get on with it, although he always stepped in if I was about to make a mistake. Making mistakes was part of the job – the worst thing to do was to hesitate or not make a decision because you were scared to.

I was so passionate about the job that I'd have tears in my eyes whenever Bill gave me the 'not only have you let me down, you've let your team down and you've let yourself down' speech after I'd screwed something up.

Our detective chief inspector, Steve Rodhouse, had a fresh-faced RAF fighter pilot look about him (some called him Tintin behind his back) and he went beet red whenever he had to talk in front of an audience.

One of the most important aspects of the Job was teamwork. Not Police Competency Framework-imposed teamwork but natural team spirit. The unwritten rule was that no one went home if the on-call detective picked up a job that was going to run late into the night. Or, if we had prisoners in the bin, no one went home until it was done, even if it wasn't your job. One DC took the case summary to write, another the remand application. Two other DCs interviewed and so on. You wrapped the job up for the common good of the office.

Similarly, if someone on the team was divorcing or had been bereaved, then they were sent home while the remainder carved up their workload and filled out their time sheets as if they were there.

Our divisional commander, a chief superintendent, was a former detective who had gone up the ranks in the department and she unofficially signed off on this. That's leadership and common sense policing because whilst we were covering extra work for someone, we knew when our time came we would be looked after. We loved her for that and worked all the harder for it.

Every week I joined the hunt for drug dealers, burglars, murderers, paedophiles and rapists. There was tremendous freedom to progress our investigations as we saw fit but with that came tremendous responsibility. Anything went wrong, we saw it as a reflection on our department and we took it very personally. More than anything, we hated letting victims down.

We dealt with the most appalling aspects of human life. We often worked shifts far in excess of 16 hours, and there were plenty that lasted 24. On those rare occasions it did fall quiet, no one said the 'Q' word.

Once, when a DC did say it, Nick threw a stapler at him. Ten minutes later there was a major gas explosion, killing two people, quickly followed by a stranger rape, an attempted murder, a child abduction, another rape, two serious robberies involving weapons and a blinded victim, and then a seven-handed violent disorder with a sprinkling of stabbings. We didn't go home for nine days. When things finally quietened down, Bill called time and, exhausted, we all went down to the Albert and got thoroughly smashed before heading home.

It felt like I'd only just put my head on my pillow when the persistent ringing of my mobile woke me.

'Not sleeping in, are we, my dear chap?' Bill said. 'The on-call team that's supposed to be covering for us has picked up a very nasty attempted murder on the other side of town, so I need you here an hour ago.'

I mumbled incoherently, hung up and looked at the time: 5 a.m.

'Ooooargh.' I was on my bed, fully dressed; the aroma of lager and kebab had filled the room. I recalled a 'Viva Las Vegas' karaoke moment and a 'blue light taxi' home and cringed.

I staggered to my feet, threw open the window, belched and grabbed a lungful. I then went to the bathroom, stuck my head under a tap, drank as much water as I could without being sick, swallowed four ibuprofen and, twenty minutes later, rolled up at work with a slight sway.

Youth was on my side, then. I could see older members of the team were much worse, grey-skinned and swaying steadily throughout the briefing, all the while trying to control their stomachs.

'A fishing rod burglary gone wrong,' Bill announced.

This is where the thief aims to hook the car keys through the letterbox using a home-made fishing rod.

'The owner saw what was going on, chased the would-be thief and received a knife to the stomach that nicked the liver; he may or may not pull through.

'We have some excellent CCTV images of the suspect for once, buying cigarettes from a nearby petrol station, so take a good look, and note the distinctive cross-shaped earring in the left ear. I know we were expecting a quiet day in the office, but let's pull ourselves together, OK?'

I hit the streets with Posh Tim. After a few futile hours, dying for the fry-up hangover cure, we dipped into the Prince of Wales, where they served all-day brekkies.

I'd just lifted my first forkful loaded with Irish sausage, egg and fried toast when Tim nudged me in the ribs, causing my carefully stacked fork to drop its load.

'What the—'

'That's our man,' Tim said.

Sure enough, there he was, earring and all, at the bar, digging out his wallet.

'I don't believe it,' I said. 'Well, if he buys a pint, we'll keep discreet observations while we finish our breakfasts and *then* nick him.'

Hardly appropriate perhaps, but none of us would be going anywhere and at least we'd be fuelled for the lengthy shift that was still to come.

As it turned out, he was getting change for the meter.

We nicked him, and so began another 24-hour day, during which we were out and about in the CID car when we spotted a Saab soft-top blasting down the road, far exceeding the speed limit.

We popped on the siren and pulled it over.

John, a strapping Irishman and excellent cop, went to the driver's window to talk to the driver and stopped in surprise.

We'd only pulled over a well-known newspaper columnist, with two delightful-looking young ladies reclining on his backseat.

'Good afternoon, sir, ladies,' John said. 'Do you know why we pulled you over, sir?'

The columnist was extremely sarcastic, and perhaps trying to maintain the image for which he is so renowned – maybe he was showing off to the young ladies – he asked us the time-honoured question: 'Haven't you got any rapists or murderers you should be chasing?'

He really did ask us this. I kid you not. There are witnesses.

'Just a moment, sir,' John said, stepping back from the car and lifting his radio to his mouth.

'Control, Yankee 51. Have we any outstanding rapists or murderers we should be chasing?'

'Yankee 51, Control. Just a moment, I'll check.'

There was a pause. John mouthed, 'Won't keep you a moment, sir.'

'Yankee 51, Control. No, no, there's no outstanding rapists or murderers. Why do you ask?'

'Well, I've just pulled over a gentleman for travelling, oh, almost two-thirds over the speed limit on the Guildford Road.'

'I see,' said Control. 'That's the stretch of road where the little girl was run over and killed three days ago, wasn't it?'

'Yes, that's correct, Control. It's the stretch of road where the little girl was run over and killed three days ago.'

'Roger Yankee 51. Please carry on with your vital road safety duties to prevent any more deaths on the road.'

'Roger that, Control. OK sir, now that's been cleared up, where were we?'

Inexplicably, the journalist's celebrated bluster evaporated into acquiescence.

I had hoped that the illustrious columnist might write up the story, urging his millions of readers to slow down, perhaps even use his unique and influential position to start a campaign to try and reduce the number of children killed or seriously injured (5,000, according to the AA Motoring Trust) on our roads every year.

Alas, he did not.

3

The Off-Button

IT HAD BEEN A DAY OF action. Our 'unofficial drugs squads' (more on these shortly) had organised about 20 arrest warrants, which meant a day of raids.

Bart and I were supervising the raids in the north of the county when Nick rang me to say he'd run into a dead body and it was, for the moment at least, being treated as murder. At this time, I'd been part of the CID for 18 months and most of the early suspicious deaths I'd encountered had been drug related. As Bart and I had organised the warrants, we travelled down to the scene.

The suspected murder was on a third-floor balcony in a brand-new block of flats just by Woking train station, which was mostly filled with young urban types who had paid over £200k for a shoebox. Ten per cent of the flats had been given to the local authority, as per new building regulations, and this flat was one of those.

It was modern, with stripped wood floors, chrome switches and so on, but with a few interesting touches, including pizza boxes, burned and holed-through furniture, forgotten burned-down fags and a sprinkling of used needles, beer cans, bits of foil tissue, bare, baseless mattresses on stained carpets, yellow duvets and a sink full of what I will loosely describe as 'washing up' (it was beyond hope, and looked as if it were alive and possibly about to attack). A new and fascinating ecosystem had sprung up inside the fridge, the only working electrical device in the flat. There was also a new-ish 42-inch plasma TV, with a large crack running down one side of the screen. In our experience, even the worst flat usually had a nice flat-screen TV.

'Give drug addicts something nice and they will fuck it up,' Nick said, voicing the thoughts of most cops. 'These gaffs cost more than any of our poxy terraces and semis on modern estates on the edge of town. They'd had it for free and look at it.'

It seemed as though no one had been here for at least a couple of weeks. The team had picked over and poked their way through each room, finding nothing of interest until they reached the balcony.

Nick had opened the door and was treated to a bland view of a largely lifeless-looking Woking. A rolled-up carpet lay end-to-end across the balcony. He bent down to take a closer look and then grabbed hold of his nose before ducking back inside.

'Er, Bill, I think you're going to want to take a look at this,' he said.

'Goodness me,' Bill said with his usual understatement. 'I bet he's been there for a month at least.'

A mop of black hair protruded from one end, a pair of boots out of the other.

The victim had most probably overdosed, although 'hot-shotting' was also a strong possibility, hence the abandoned flat. This occurs when one junkie annoys one of his friends so much he's given a special gift of a triple-strong dose of heroin and *voilà*, he will never annoy anyone again.

His 'friends' had rolled him up and then put him out of the way, where the smell would take longer to be noticed by the downstairs neighbours. Of course, apart from hot-shotting, this death might have been the result of dodgy gear (in which case we'd need to issue an alert) or he might simply have had a knife poking out of his chest. We'd only know for sure once he'd been unrolled.

That wouldn't be easy. The putrefaction was extraordinary. The carpet had held him together like an egg mayonnaise wrap and he was now about the same consistency; officers had hastily smeared the inside of their little plastic masks with Vicks, but it gave no relief from the smell.

'We need to preserve the scene,' Bill said, 'so we can't carry him out of the flat.'

Nick nodded thoughtfully, at a loss as to how to do this.

Bill then looked up, a eureka moment. 'What we need,' he said, 'is a cherry-picker.'

One of the things you have to get used to as a detective is being audacious in your selection of resources. An hour later, the team was assembled, a cherry-picker in position. A large, curious crowd had by this time gathered below, watching the detectives at work.

'Steady, lads,' Bill said.

Bart and I watched from inside the cordoned-off area below as Bill, Nick and two other techs eased the body, still in the carpet, onto the picker. As it descended, the picker shook and the body slid across the metal floor to the edge.

'Oh God, please no,' I said.

The crowd had grown; journalists were now among them. The cherry-picker operator seemed unaware of the problem and we were powerless to stop it. All we could do was watch.

With every jerk, the body inched towards the edge.

'If that body falls anywhere within sight of that crowd, we're going to make the front pages of the nationals, never mind the *Guildford Advertiser*,' Bart said.

Bart started to grin. So did I. Sniggering followed and it snowballed from there. Soon we had our hands over our mouths, trying not to laugh at the thought of that five-week-old body rolling off the picker and the reaction from the crowd when it kersplattered in front of them.

Thankfully, the poor man stayed on the cherry-picker, just.

'Boys kept that together well,' Nick said afterwards in his typically dour northern tone.

Our laughter hadn't gone unnoticed by the local press, however; but it had been misinterpreted. The reports stated that 'detectives were overcome with emotion'.

Ain't that the truth.

We were callous, I know. A young man had died and this was indeed a tragedy (a long and difficult autopsy concluded that an overdose was the cause), but it was thanks to the proliferation of drugs throughout the county that my colleagues and I became fairly immune to the horror of the lonely death of an addict. The only way to avoid early onset insanity was to laugh.

A few days later I was standing in front of a corpse of a young man that had exploded with gas and maggots and was stuck to the armchair he had shot up on, the TV still playing in front of him. As his insides had filled with gas, they'd pushed his head back, mouth and eyes open. The liquids had travelled down, causing his lower limbs to swell so much that his trousers split; fluid seeped from every orifice. This one did not 'keep together'. When we moved him from the chair to bag him, his insides literally fell out.

Once the body was away and the day was done, it was down to the pub, our other office, for 'debriefing'. Along with laughter, alcohol played a major part in our lives. It was our release, the 'off-button', whether we wanted to commiserate or celebrate.

At the time I joined, every major police station had a subsidised bar where Stella Artois was a pound a pint. This made drinking games, rounds and the concoction of bizarre and deadly cocktails extremely affordable. If you'd been promoted, just become a father, turned 30, 40, 50 or – God help you – 60, then you were expected to drink a 'top shelfer' – a shot from every top-shelf bottle in a pint glass, to be downed in front of your cheering section.

Most people would pop in to varying levels during the week, but there was a hardcore who were there every night. A plaque above our bar read: '*DCI Dave Smith* [not his real name] *Stood Here: 1992–1996*'.

That night after the body on the balcony, I watched as a detective urinated in a pint glass and staggered over to the window. The custody yard was on the ground floor below. It was where prisoners could have a smoke and stretch their legs. The detective took careful aim and let the contents fall on a prisoner's head.

The target was Jim Maxwell, the man most responsible for filling the town with smack, the smack that put the dead body on the balcony. Sadly, Maxwell knew how to play the system and he wasn't ever in a prison cell for long.

There was always something happening in the police bar. One night I was on duty and waiting for the lift. When the doors pinged open, they revealed a drunken DCI and superintendent fresh from the bar, with their hands around each other's necks, engaged in a bizarre version of a cage fight. I had to summon help to get them separated.

On another night, a WPC came in and yelled at us to keep the noise down. A PC (the same one who'd emptied the glass of urine over the prisoner) was dancing on the pool table with his trousers around his ankles. He gave her the finger and shouted 'Fuck off!'

This sort of behaviour was not that exceptional. Most of us were young guys in our 20s with lots of income, few expenses and minor God complexes. We all thought nothing of drinking five pints in our pound-a-pint pub before getting free and immediate club entry by abusing our warrant cards. We were young enough and fit enough to party all night and work all day.

Alcohol is still a huge problem in the police and has proved to be the downfall of many a policeman. One PC with serious drinking 'issues' went on a TV show with his wife, also a PC, to discuss their problems. Someone had left sparkling wine along with the canapés in the green room. He got drunk, yelled at his wife, pushing and shoving her, before the production team intervened and called the police. He was a big fellow and managed to assault six police officers before he was nicked.

When most people start a new job, they have to undergo various inductions, covering things like equal opportunities, manual handling, first aid and so on. An induction topic that is unique (as far as I know) to the CID is 'How to drink sensibly', where you are taught how to manage drinking in rounds, as well as useful things such as safe timings for drinking then driving the next day.[9]

The subsidised bars have since gone but, worryingly enough, recruits are still given this lecture. As a friend of mine recently asked, 'How many of those officers who drank and released their tension in a controlled environment are now doing this in public bars or, worse, at home on their own?'

I only once met an officer who'd never been drunk but knew many who drank all the time – several of whom were disciplined or arrested after a night out on the town.

---

[9] 'Twelve hours between bottle and throttle.'

A friend who'd just joined the Met as a sergeant couldn't make a team night out, but the team went out anyway and got hammered. By the end of the evening, a WPC had given a PC a blowjob in a public bar, while another three officers had had a *ménage à trois* in the loos. My friend was extremely relieved he hadn't gone out with them. Social events are classed as extensions of the workplace and, as their sergeant, he would have been royally up the creek before he'd even finished his first week.

There were, of course, many times when social drinks were just that and served a useful purpose, allowing us to sound off about the day and the Job in an informal atmosphere. It's just that putting police officers together in a pack in front of a cheap bar comes with a significant risk.

Police officers are trained to be aggressive (in some situations) and fearless (in that we have to run towards danger). We also have many more major stressors than the average person and tend to go weeks at a time with little release. When you add alcohol, a drug that removes inhibitions and often leads to aggression and exhibitionism, well, anything can happen.

Police officers operate at the extreme end of society. We are society's warrior class, duty bound and proud to do the jobs that no one else wants to or can do. As a result, we see so many things that the normal human mind is not conditioned to see that they become the everyday (dead, putrid addicts being a case in point).

Those police officers who use hobbies instead of booze to let off steam often take them to extremes. Those into motorbikes ride faster, harder and further. I used to ride superbikes with another detective and would think nothing of going on 100-mile-plus rides, sometimes reaching 140 mph on public roads. Those who play rugby, hockey and football are more focused, deliberate, aggressive and professional than your average weekend player.

When police officers do start drinking, it takes a lot to stop them. One officer from my nick was drinking in the police bar before being chucked out at closing. He then broke into a pub, where he carried on through the night before being arrested the following morning for burglary. He claimed he was an alcoholic, sought treatment to avoid a disciplinary hearing and remained in the job. He still drinks.

As I've already mentioned, apart from acting as a stress release, alcohol also acts as an 'off-button'. After spending several seven-day weeks on a job, dealing with witnesses, following leads, chasing sources, sorting evidence, reading up on the legislation, the strategy, along with the sheer importance of what you're trying to achieve (it doesn't get much more important than taking someone's liberty away from them), your mind doesn't switch off.

One very well-spoken, university-educated DC who was on the promotional trail would sit at home alone and polish off a bottle of wine to sleep at night. You'd never know it if you met her. She's been promoted a few times since and still drinks (but has reined it in somewhat).

One factor for me, personally, is my visual photographic memory, which served me well on the job – I could replay a scene as seen through my eyes from start to end from almost any day of the year from any year.

Off the job, it developed into a real pain. Sometimes I would see something as innocuous as a bunk bed and it would trigger a terrible memory I'd packed away nice and deep, in this case the hanging body of a depressed mother of four who gave up hope in her children's bedroom.

My own son fell critically ill when he was still a baby. When I saw him in the hospital, connected to drips and tubes, I saw a baby lying on the stainless steel draining board of a mortuary sink. This cot death post-mortem had happened nine years earlier, but suddenly I couldn't shake it from my mind. Now, whenever I see a stainless steel draining board, I see the dead baby, lying as if asleep, scarred by the post-mortem, in a clinical environment designed to deconstruct human bodies.

If I'm waiting in a train station and I look down at the tracks, I see a decapitated head, eyes open, looking back at me. A young man who was depressed and had drunk too much calmly stretched out in front of a train that was depositing its passengers on the platform, placing his neck on the rail. When the train moved off, his head was slowly removed from his body, ending up about 15 metres away.

It was indescribably sad and horrific, so when an officer joked, 'That's not the way to get ahead in life!' we laughed with relief. We're cops – we can't stand there and cry. We have to clean it up, investigate and restore normality for the commuters fuming at the man who'd selfishly topped himself on their railway line. We never did find out what the trigger had been. I still remember exactly which point on which rail this happened.

The welcome relief that came through laughing with friends had evaporated by the time the shift was over and we returned either alone to our flats to stare at the box (doing this reminded me of the junkie in front of the TV and I had to get up again) or to our families to face the impossible question of how our day had been. Not something you want to share with loved ones.

There are so many other things that trigger vivid thoughts like this. I know these events sound extreme but thousands of other police officers see and experience similar sights all the time. Perhaps the lowest level of this is getting into bed after 24 hours on duty, knowing that you still have prisoners to deal with in the morning. The details of the job will go round and round in your head. There will be little sleep.

The bottle is always there, a cheap and quick solution. Unfortunately, it's also a tolerance-based and dependence-forming drug. The more you drink, the more tolerant and dependent you become. The most common alcoholics in the UK aren't binge-drinking clubbers or tramps, they're middle-class professionals who think nothing of having at least half a bottle of wine every night with dinner. For the police, it's a quick way to take the knot out of the back of your neck, to calm and numb your mind, to switch off the video replay, replacing it with white noise.

4

Problem Families

I WAS IN THE O'DONNELL HOUSE again. Spencer's mum Maxine had hung herself from her two youngest kids' bunk beds with the belt from her dressing gown. Her seven-year-old daughter Molly had found her and had then told the neighbour, who hit the nines.

I knew Spencer well. He was 16 and an all-round bad lad – serial mugger, thief, drug user – with a record longer than many lifelong felons.

Maxine was wearing a vest and knickers, a short suicide note tucked into the elastic, along with a half-empty blister pack of Valium. The note was short, almost illegible, and full of spelling mistakes.

The gist of it was: 'I'm sorry. I can't do this any more. Take good care of the kids.'

The room stank of alcohol and death. A probie (probationer constable) was standing outside, shaking.

* * *

When I'd started life as a PC, I was panic-stricken at the thought of stepping out into the city streets. I walked nervously, hoping I didn't stand out as a probie and that nobody would ask me something I didn't know the answer to.

I found life much easier as a learner detective. Although at first working with seasoned officers had been intimidating, I had quickly slotted in. I never dreaded the day's work and tried to stay ahead of the game by ringing custody as soon as I left the house, checking whether we had anyone in the bin. I'd catch up with paperwork on rest days, stay late whenever asked and snuck onto interesting jobs after hours.

Life was exciting. Uniformed officers of senior rank were asking me, a mere 23 year old, what to do. Most of the time, my first point of contact would be that honourable and now dying British institution, the foot-patrolling PC. I'd either sigh in despair or with relief, depending on whom I saw when I rolled up to a crime scene.

What I wanted to see was the experienced omni-competent officer who not only knew most people in the town, from businessmen to burglars, for it was in his interests to do so, but had also seen enough crimes to know what to do, whom to detain, what to ask and what to tell me when I rolled up.

Men and women like this are almost extinct. About 75 per cent of today's patrol officers are still in their probationary period (so yes, policemen are getting younger) and it's very rare to see a patrol officer with more than seven years on the beat. A probie often finds (to sudden alarm) that they're under the care of another probie who arrived just a few months earlier.

In Surrey, we have particular problems with gangs of gypsies and paratroopers getting drunk and destructive in the town centres every Friday night. Recently graduated PCs have a much harder time trying to talk a platoon of trained killers or a mob of bare-knuckle fighters out of ripping one another's heads off in a nightclub, with 'Murder on the Dancefloor' playing at full volume in the background.

A seasoned beat officer will already know who the protagonists are and will tell them he'll be round to pick up the survivors when they're bruised, bloody and hungover the following day – a sobering thought.

On the job training has to be part of becoming a police officer, but, without experienced beat officers to lead the way in these delicate operations, naive probies end up having a much tougher 'training' than necessary. The same thing is happening with detectives. In one month in 2011, 21 very experienced Surrey officers were served with compulsory retirement, all part of a money-saving exercise. At the same time, many civilian investigators (former experienced detectives) were put through the same process. We lost men and women with priceless experience going back decades to the IRA pub bombings. They'd saved the force immeasurable amounts of money in recent years by using their local knowledge to clear up investigations much faster than newer teams of officers who did not know local families, histories, locations and the repeated psychological patterns of certain kinds of offenders. One of these civilian investigators might say something like, 'That sounds like the murder where the killer hid the knife in the air-conditioning unit at the back of Iceland,' and sure enough that's where it would be found, *after* a team had already been through the area looking for it.

They weren't replaced. I ended up with a stroppy member of the public on the phone late one night who'd reported a stolen garden gnome. She was demanding to know how long before a squad turned up to fingerprint the area and take plaster casts of the suspect's footprints.

'How many detectives do you think are on duty at the moment?'

'I don't know. Fifty?'

'Let me see, I'll just do a headcount. There's me and – um – yes, Tim here and the other two are investigating a violent burglary. So that's four. For the county.'

All it took was one major incident (a riot, GBH, serial gnome-knapper, etc.) and we were done for the night.

A lot of detectives can't handle the intensity of the job and leave after a year (or two) for a cushy post elsewhere, sometimes in a CID support role or an office job at headquarters office spot, which is understandable and fair enough. If that's what you want, then go for it. But this did mean we were always short.

* * *

I checked Maxine's body for any signs of foul play and then took a look around the flat. No need to form a squad for this one: most definitely a suicide. I called it in and waited for a senior officer to come and confirm the obvious.

I returned to the lounge, where seven-year-old Molly and three-year-old Becky were sitting on the sofa. They were beautiful kids, untainted by their notorious older brother and sister (Layla, 17, who was killing herself slowly by consuming a truly outstanding amount of heroin). Maxine had been really trying with them.

Thanks to their older siblings, however, Molly had often answered the door to cops, something she made clear when she spoke to me.

'Mr Detective,' Molly said, 'is Mummy dead?'

Oh God.

'Just stay there for now, sweetheart. Would you like some orange juice?'

She nodded. I went to the kitchen and found some squash. God, I wanted a smoke.

I'd recently dealt with Spencer, along with his 15-year-old partner-in-crime, Curtis Davis. They'd robbed an 84-year-old great-grandmother on a sunny morning in Esher. They'd knocked her to the floor before taking £50 from her purse, after emptying the contents on the pavement.

The old lady did her best to summon what remained of her Blitz spirit when I spoke to her, but she was really shaken. This would have a lasting effect – beyond the severe bruising all down her right side, from shoulder to knee.

She was able to provide excellent descriptions, however. A couple of very switched-on uniform lads in the area crime car found the two boys in a supermarket car park drinking blue label vodka and smoking their way through a quarter ounce of skunk, bought with the victim's shopping money.

'In the cells. You're nicked,' I told them when they arrived at the station.

'Fer what? We ain't done nuffink,' Curtis said.

Spencer just stared back at me through a fog of hash and vodka. His family life was miserable and he told us as much once he'd sobered up and we had him in the interview room. Dad run away, mum an alcoholic, big sister a junkie, no school would have him. Spencer cried his eyes out and coughed the crime, not that he deserved our sympathy or that Tim and I gave him any other option.

Curtis also coughed – until his mother arrived.

'He were with me at the time!' she shrieked before I was able to tell her that he'd already confessed.

'I don't care,' she said. 'You fitted him for it, he were with me!'

We warned her about perverting the course of justice (PCJ) but she still insisted on giving the statement. Despite our efforts, the Crown Prosecution Service (CPS) didn't charge her. You should go to jail for PCJ. The course of justice relies on the honesty of witnesses and is sacrosanct. The law is meant to reflect this when witnesses misbehave. In this case, the message received by Curtis's mum via the CPS is that PCJ is not something we care about.

Thankfully, the judge was as outraged as we were at the mugging and popped Spencer and Curtis away for three years apiece. Spencer was still inside when his mother decided to end her life.

DCI Paul Feast arrived to endorse my judgement of non-suspicious death and immediately got into an almighty row on the phone with the operations room inspector, who was piqued that I'd called it a suicide before a senior investigating officer (SIO) had arrived at the scene.

Paul told the ops inspector to stop being 'a blithering fucking idiot', which I thought was appropriate, considering Maxine was still hanging in the bedroom and it was about time we got her down and her kids into care.

The pissed off ops inspector then did everything he could to stall us, which meant instead of transferring the two little girls into the care of Social Services, I had to take them by the hand and walk them out of the house before driving them back to our office.

The cop in all of us wanted to do something, anything, to fix their lives and we burned with frustration at our helplessness and made bitter predictions for these poor kids' futures. All these thoughts stayed internal, however, as cops don't talk about their feelings.

Having said that, when we became involved with cases involving young children, all too often the WPCs would be instructed to look after them while the immediate situation was taken care of and somewhere was found for them to go. Almost always this was a 22 year old, single, unmarried and highly trained WPC whose sole interests outside the job were Chardonnay, nail bars, clubbing, holidays and hair dos and 25-year-old male gym fanatics.

So, guess who was up, sitting cross-legged on the floor with the kids watching Pingu and playing imaginary tea parties, five minutes later? That's right, the over-30, male detectives. Why? Because they're dads. Whenever a kiddy was in the office, whether a child of a suspect or a colleague, the hardened male detectives would all start singing 'Twinkle Twinkle' and performing all the actions besides.

In this case, these kids, sitting quietly in shock, didn't even yet realise the enormity of what had just happened. Social Services arrived in the small hours. Molly and her sister were carted off, fast asleep; in the morning they would wake up in a strange house and life would never be the same again. Spencer (who was let out for the funeral) and the girls were placed in care in separate counties. Layla simply vanished.

* * *

Not long after Maxine's death I found myself listening to a recording of a 999 call.

'999 Operator. Which service do you require?'

'Give us the fucking money.'

'No! No!'

'We'll blow your fucking brains out!'

Along with some of his mates, Justin Davis (Curtis's brother) had ambushed a car full of immigrant workers as it left the factory where they worked. One of the victims had left her mobile phone on to 999. It was terrifying. I've had a gun pointed at me during training and that was unnerving enough.

There followed a great deal of screaming, threats and beating for the next seven minutes before Justin's crew escaped with their booty: £16.

We were able to place Justin at the scene because the young idiot had touched the victims' car, so we had his prints, not to mention a couple of witnesses who would now never forget his face.

We spent the following night jacking up a firearms job and at 0530 the next morning we toddled around to Justin's house with 16 armed bastards from the Tactical Firearms Unit (TFU).

I was in the command vehicle, worrying about what might go

wrong when 'COMPROMISE! COMPROMISE!' came over the air from the entry team. Just as they were approaching the house, Curtis (freshly released from prison) opened the front door, cup of tea in one hand, fag in the other, having just got back from a night spent gurning at girls at a warehouse party, to find several large men in black with machine guns. His natural scrote reaction was to flee. He ran back into the house, triggering off a spontaneous dynamic entry – the riskiest kind there is.

The TFU guys screamed at Justin to exit his bedroom, which he did, and then he was arrested in a none-too-gentle manner.

'I didn't do nuffink,' he told us.

'Justin, we have a voice recording of you during the robbery, a print of yours is on the victims' car and two witnesses have described you, right down to the tattoo on your left wrist.'

'It weren't me.'

I charged him with every firearms and robbery offence I could think of.

Despite the overwhelming evidence, and despite the harrowing testimony from traumatised witnesses who deserved a medal for identifying the accused, the judge refused to remand Justin, leaving him with another six months to create havoc for the citizens of Surrey before we finally got him to trial.

We had him on forensics and eyewitness ID. We thought about voice-matching the 999 call, but there was a lot of distortion: there was so much screaming and the phone wasn't near enough to Justin.[10] Justin still denied it, and his loyal mum gave a statement saying he was at home all night despite the warnings (again) about perverting the course and despite the court's later decision not to prosecute her for this.

Justin was convicted on all counts and still the judge did not remand but said she would allow him home for Christmas 'before I have to do a terrible thing to this young man'.

---

[10] Voice matching is also prohibitively expensive at £5–10k. It isn't done by computers but by a handful of accredited experts in the UK who have finely attuned hearing.

In January, we were back in the courtroom.

The victims became more and more pleased as each sentence for each charge was read out separately, but we knew she was going to make a concurrent ruling. We should have warned them, but police officers sometimes forget how little the public know about everyday events in the justice system. As a result, victims often feel let down. As we shall see, victims are too often put on trial themselves and the process can become unexpectedly vicious.

The sentences added up to 22 years but, served concurrently, this meant six years, which in itself translates to four served inside at best.

Curtis later admitted the offences in his probation report, blaming social depravity and naming his accomplices, to which the CPS said, 'All very nice, but we've only his say-so and it's too late.' It was. Curtis's accomplices walked away free men.

The judge gave us commendations but was slapped in the press for this sentencing. We would have swapped our commendations for another year in prison for Curtis.

Two months later, Nick and I got a sniff of a gun in a house in Stanwell, so called the TFU. We were waiting for them at Staines nick when they rolled out in a four-car convoy, windows open, guns overtly displayed, all wearing clear plastic goggles.

Nick and I shook our heads in amazement. 'I know Stanwell's not the best part of Surrey,' Nick said, 'but where do these guys think they are? Helmand?'

Two hours later we had a Brocock blank firing gun in our mitts, along with converted ammunition: the same gun used in Curtis's robbery.

Curtis didn't tell us where the gun was in his probation report. In the meantime, it had been rented out over and over again to Surrey's finest criminals.

The man living in the house where the gun was found offered to turn informant, telling us about some local drug dealers who'd been boasting about their success and lack of police interest.

'Something for your secret drugs squad, methinks,' Nick said.

5

Schizophrenia with a Salary

EACH DETECTIVE TENDS TO BE DRAWN into specialising in certain areas and I ended up being interested in drugs. Along with sex (prostitution, unwanted children, the poverty of single motherhood) and alcohol (which turned Surrey town centres into no-go areas and filled our cells and hospitals every weekend), drugs cause most damage to society. It also seems that no matter how much of any of these three things people get hold of, it's never enough.

Bart felt the same way and together we gradually evolved into the local drugs squad – actually, Bart and I were Surrey's *only* drugs squad. And even then we didn't officially exist as such.

The first rule of Surrey Police is: nobody talks about drugs squads.

If a police force has a drugs squad, then that means they will (hopefully) arrest drug dealers and record all of their many drug-dealing offences. By recording drug crime, the crime figures say that drug dealing is on the rise, or at the very least that there is a 'drugs problem'.

If there is no dedicated drugs squad, then little or no recorded drugs-supply crimes occur. Chief constables then get to say they have no drugs problem, even though the traffic police are constantly pulling over 'unemployed' 18 year olds driving M3 BMWs with 20-inch chrome rims. A weekly income-support cheque wouldn't even fill the tank.

County forces do not generally have a dedicated drugs team. The Met, on the other hand, do. When I asked a prolific dealer why he offended on my patch when he lived in London, he said, 'Met's too hot, innit? You lot are soft as shit.'

Our superintendent asked Bart and me to perform quick-hits and work up the chain from one job to another, identifying networks and suppliers. We were still CID detectives but slightly removed with the title 'drugs investigators'.

We were relentless, and if there was even a hint the evidence pointed towards an offence, I'd charge it and find some really obscure offences to get the crime cleared up – or to send a message or disrupt a criminal operation.

One drug dealer had pissed me off something awful by consistently avoiding arrest with the help of dumb luck – popping out a minute before the enforcer splintered his door, selling out of gear moments before he was searched; on one occasion, forgetting where he'd hidden his stash before he was picked up on the street for acting suspiciously (looking under rocks and unscrewing lamp-post bases).

One day I pulled his car. We were not allowed to search it just like that, unless we had grounds due to the Misuse of Drugs Act. If we didn't, we could still carry out a vehicle inspection for safety, however, allowing us to search the car. Sometimes we'd find gear, but if we didn't we always found a road traffic offence and summonsed the scrote just to mess them about. In this case, as I 'examined his brake pedal for wear', I found a nine-bar (nine ounces or a quarter-kilo) of cannabis under the driver's seat.

Similarly, if I pulled over someone I knew to be a prolific burglar and they had a screwdriver in the car, then I'd arrest them for going equipped. Even if the CPS refused the charge, I would have at least kept a scrote off the streets for the night.

I may have been overzealous, but it's the law. I wouldn't have done it to Mr and Mrs Average – although every member of the public undergoes the ministry of attitude test. Don't forget (I know we make it hard sometimes), we are human. Some of us are even quite nice.

I'd already done some test-purchasing – meeting drug dealers, either scoring in the street or entering a crack house. Although this was continually terrifying – junkies and dealers are rightly paranoid and some have a Gestapo-like ruthlessness when it comes to questioning new clients – I actually came to enjoy the excitement.

The easy way in was to find a 'Muppet', the most desperate, weak-willed junkie. Then I'd be very nice, telling them I really needed their help and that it would be much appreciated, that I had plenty of cash and a decent car.

I'd then send them off to buy drugs for me. They'd get gear and take a bit out of the parcel for themselves as a reward, which is, technically, supply. Yes, the police – on occasion – facilitate the supply of drugs.

Usually, these desperate fellows were unable to keep their mouths shut and a 'friend' of theirs would see a good thing, take it off them and transport me a step up the ladder until I was sitting with the supplier, talking about taking part in hijacks and buying serious weights.

Doing it this way was expensive. For every two Test Purchasers (TP), an investigation team made up of a detective sergeant, several detective constables, including an exhibits officer and disclosure officer (DC), three or four PCs running errands, surveillance teams (which could range from eight to thirty officers) and TP handlers; authorisations for actions from arrests to visiting a crack den also had to be obtained from a detective inspector, detective chief inspector and superintendent, all of whom had to be regularly briefed. A three-month deployment would cost about £50,000. It was expensive work, but it had an effect.[11]

Climbing the criminal ladder has gone in the counties now. All that counts are the figures. Her Majesty's statisticians at the Home Office want to see 34 drug arrests each year and no more. This could be done in a couple of days by picking up ten to fifteen street-level scumbags at a time.

Bart and I could get to four or five proper dealers in just a few

---

[11] If you think this sounds costly, consider the fact that Surrey Police managed to spend £1 million on a screensaver for their 'Drive Safe' campaign. A superintendent was given a £1m budget of joint police, fire, ambulance and local government funds. She produced a brand, leaflets and posters, a screensaver and another leaflet that basically offered a ten-minute roadside lecture on the dangers of speeding.

weeks, but all Surrey wanted were the numbers. As soon as we reached 34 arrests, we were told to back off from drugs.

Bart and I ignored this and continued to use lots of different techniques to carry on with our now personal project to clean our streets of hard drugs. Sometimes we curried up a warrant based on two small bits of intel and crashed the door, hoping for the best. Other times we'd use surveillance to identify the optimum strike time, with a heavy team standing by. A fellow tech called Piers and I once set up an OP (Observation Point) in the bedroom of a certain boy band member (this was before he hit it big and bought his family a nice house away from the local crack dealers).

We studied the house, then waited until a delivery of drugs had been made and the house was nice and busy before triggering the team. We ended up with 136 wraps of crack. This was also the first time a crack house closure order was used in Surrey; in fact, anywhere outside of London.

Then there were the times we would surround a house and pop the door only for first and second slip lying in wait at the back of the house to catch the gear that came flying out of the window. Although this was all good fun, I wanted more, much more. I wanted to get higher up the ladder and nick the really nasty people. To do this, I would have to go undercover.

* * *

There were three ways to get on the undercover course. There were those who asked – the wannabes who were considered high risk (a bit like the guys who begged to be put on the firearms course, eagerly hopping from one foot to another . . . slightly worrying) – those senior officers who had to supervise undercover (UC) officers and so needed to know what they went through, and those who were approached and asked if they'd like to have a go.

I received a tap on the shoulder in the dinner queue at HQ from a handler. 'Any chance of a quick word?'

'Sure, what's up?'

'You thought about doing undercover work, son? You've got the look for it.'

'Well, I suppose.'

He explained in loose terms what they did and repeated that I had a good look for the job.

'Still interested?'

'Sure.'

'OK, I'll be in touch. See you.'

And that, apart from the 24-page application form (designed just to piss you off, which went through the shredder as soon as Special Ops took you on), was that. Once I was eventually accepted, I disappeared on a 'driving course' in another county. Only the divisional commander knew what I was really up to. A friend of mine, Ian (from the Preamble), was on the same impossible and completely surreal course.

We – there were 16 of us – started Monday at 8 a.m. The chief constable came in first to give us a speech. 'Thank you for signing up. As you know, most of you won't make it, but I wanted to thank you personally for the effort. As you are about to discover, this is one of the hardest and most dangerous aspects of policing. Good luck.'

Then the training staff walked in. They looked like East End gangsters. They were suited and booted and wearing Rolex watches. We were all in our suits too, as instructed.

During the first lecture, we watched surveillance videos of deals gone wrong (the officers had been wearing covert cameras). They started with an officer in a betting shop in Clapton's murder mile in East London having a knife pulled on him. Then there was one of an officer being attacked with a large knife. Then another one being beaten up after the dealers had taken him to a pub and openly burned the crack on the table to prove it was real. Once the deal was done, they were charged by another user, who tried to steal the drugs and cash. The final video was of an American officer being shot in a hotel room – a 'drug deal gone wrong', as the phrase goes.

'Right,' one of the trainers said, 'time for a coffee. If you still want to do this, then we'll see you back here, dressed in your street clothes, in half an hour.'

Three people didn't return. The rest of us, dressed in our 'street clobber', our novice attempt at being undercover, were picked over by the experts.

'What have you got your wedding ring on for? Junkies don't own jewellery; they steal and sell it.'

'Who irons their jeans these days? A cop, that's who.'

'There's not a single stain on any of you, anywhere.'

Every day for the first week, lectures started an hour earlier and finished an hour later.

We worked through various role-playing scenarios. When we were sent to buy heroin or crack from certain houses, we were met by some very unpleasant and extremely convincing individuals (they were all Level One UC officers, i.e. living as full-time criminals to gain intelligence).

We were also sent to score from 'actors' on the street – one unlucky trainee was sent to King's Cross and in the seven minutes he spent struggling to find the role player had a knife pulled on him three times by three different drug dealers. We stopped going to London after that. On another occasion an actual dealer so closely resembled the description of a role player, a live buy was made and, embarrassingly, we had to let him walk with a caution for possession, as we had acted illegally and with no live authorities.

One evening at 8 p.m. we arrived back in the classroom to find two crates of cold beer waiting for us.

'This next lecture is one we have to give for health and safety reasons. It's not important and we'd really prefer not to give it, especially as you guys have been going for 13 hours straight. So, have a couple of beers and kick back.'

After we'd had a few beers, another one of the trainers came in and said, 'Sorry, people. We've got to change tonight's lecture. It's now going to be something incredibly important you'll be tested on tomorrow.'

Bastard.

The following day we were taken to a firing range. Although we didn't need to be firearms trained, we did need to know how to make a gun safe, in case we ever came across one. Just as we reached the range, the instructor said, 'There's been a change of plan. Any reason any of you can't deploy to Godalming right now?'

'Er, no,' was the general answer.

'Good. It's 1300. I want you back here in three hours. Any one of you who cannot find and be offered a job that pays over 15k per year during that time, then you're off the course.'

I drove to Godalming, a small but prosperous suburban town, and walked into a pub. A few minutes later I was talking to Martin, the pub's owner, about taking over the nightshift. He hated nights. I had once worked in a bar in Brighton and on some doors of the town's nightclubs, so knew my way around. It was a gastropub and he offered me a Brie and bacon sandwich before we shook on the deal. Job done, back I went.

One of the other guys had an HGV licence and found work as a lorry driver for a firm on the edge of town. Three didn't manage to get employed by anyone and went home.

Only four of us finished the course. One was a senior officer who would never be deployed, then there was Ian, whom I'd end up working with, and one other guy who was only deployed a couple of times because he wasn't that good in a 'real' situation with serious criminals.

'Congratulations on passing one of the police's more unusual and difficult courses,' the instructor said. 'Now off you go and don't call us, we'll call you.'

A few weeks later, I got a tap on the shoulder while strolling along the corridor.

It was the instructor.

'Can you do a six-monther? In Camberley?'

'Six months away? Impossible.'

'But could you work in Camberley? Any reason you shouldn't go there?'

'Camberley's fine. But six months, forget it.'

'Who's your guv'nor?'

I told him.

He returned a few minutes later. 'All sorted. Get your gear and take six months.'

'How on earth did you do that?'

'I told him I needed you for three weeks – by that time, you'll be in too deep for him to pull you out again.'

Yes, UC officers do things a bit differently.

We always worked undercover jobs away from our home patch – for obvious reasons: nobody wanted to bump into the Mr Big they'd been buying smack off for the last six weeks while freshly scrubbed and escorting a ladyfriend on a night out.

I was paired with Steve, an extremely resourceful, experienced and brave UC officer. Steve, who was Welsh, looked the part; he had two teeth left in his head and was simply amazing once he started playing a role. We were given a Peugot 405 with brand-new tyres, freshly taxed and MOT'd.

'That'll never do,' Steve said.

So we drove to a remote car park where we burned rubber until the tyres were worn right down, and then threw away the tax disc, filled the car with McDonald's food and wrappers, then smoked 20 fags, dropping ash everywhere.

'Now, that's more like it,' Steve said.

The operation would take four months and involved us looking the part. I was playing the role of a heroin addict, so I put in a cheap earring, grew a beard and didn't wash myself, or my clothes, for weeks at a time.

My girlfriend of the time wasn't happy – at all – but we'd been going out together for a while and I promised that while it might feel like it at the moment, it wouldn't be forever. She tried to persuade me to clean up a little every now and then, but I wasn't having it. Looking the part was my best protection.

I was ambushed by my mum, however. When I popped over for a visit, I went as far as to climb into a bath, not to get clean, just to sit there and enjoy the feeling of hot water after two weeks of zero bathing. When I got out, Mum had washed and ironed my undercover clobber.

Steve got an even harder time at home. His missus found his covert phone and called me, demanding to know what the fuck we were doing and if he was 'over the side' (having an affair), which he wasn't.

First day on the job we spotted a likely target, waiting outside a known drugs house. He was a horrible-looking man – tall, shaved head, gangly, covered in bad tats. He had a tattoo on his neck in large italics that read: 'Phil'.

Steve walked up to him and said, 'You must be Phil.'

'Right. You boys waiting for what I'm waiting for?'

We scored two bags of heroin and we were away. Easy.

Our 'legend' (cover story) was that we were a pair of drug-addicted robbers who were trying to persuade 'T', a Yardie robber, gun and drug runner, to join our operation hijacking lorries full of electrical goods.

We spoke to Phil and made lots of references to our boss and other associates, so the door was always open to introduce other UCs and TPs if and when necessary. Soon Phil was so relaxed in our company that he served us up (weighed and bagged the drugs) in front of his four-year-old daughter.

I loved living the life. I became so trusted that I worked as doorman for a crack house, letting the punters in and out, making sure all the activity was being recorded on the easily discoverable 'lump' – the Sony NT2 transmitter the size of a Dictaphone hidden under my crotch – another occupational hazard.[12] This house was run by Wiggy and Reta. While Wiggy smoked his brains out on a crack pipe, Reta yelled at customers who owed them money for 'white' (crack) or 'brown' (heroin). It all went on the tape.

Working undercover was exciting but also extremely stressful. Not only did you have to wear a lump, you also had to watch what you said. If it sounded like you were leading someone to commit a crime they might not have otherwise committed, then you could kiss any prosecution goodbye.

Apart from that there was the worry of what might happen if Mr Criminal finds out you're not who you say you are. The worst danger was if they thought you were a rival dealer and decided to sort it using violence. If they found out you're Job, then that would just provoke them into running away instead of hurting you because our gang was bigger than theirs.

These operations were extremely expensive and so it was down to the UC officer not to blow a significant proportion of the county's crime-fighting fund.

---

[12] The police now use much smaller ones.

THE MIND OF THE UNDERCOVER OFFICER

Working undercover means you have to operate using multiple personalities. As a normal copper, you already have a few to be getting on with. You are:

  the professional copper your colleagues see
  the harder, more unforgiving copper the suspects see
  the caring copper victims see
  your normal self, the one your family sees, which was hard for me
    because all my family were police

As for working undercover, you adjust some of these and add a few more. It all depends what role you are playing. Traits include:

Acting and thinking like a criminal while being aware all the time that you are a cop. This is difficult when everyone around you is flagrantly disregarding the law, and you have to appear as if you are too, but you're constantly being videoed, photographed, watched and recorded.

Living with paranoia. Do they know you are wired? I walked into one house and saw the suspect watching my right hand in my pocket as I pressed the record button. In reality, he probably thought we were there to rob him and was looking for a weapon, but all I could think was 'Fuck, he knows, and any minute we're going to be searched.' Try keeping your cool in a room full of drug dealers with that going through your head.

You can overplay and misjudge. For example, one target we worked on was a horrible shitbag on record – robbery, burglary, violent assault, and so on. First time we met him, we turned up the hardness. An old lady was trying to cross the road in front of us but couldn't move quickly enough, so had to keep stepping back onto the kerb. Our target went over and escorted her across the road, then came back and called us cunts for not helping, too. This guy actually was very funny; he was charismatic and had a code of honour of sorts. At the end of the job, we didn't want to lock him up – a dangerous way to feel.

You know that the ops team and handlers are looking at you for impropriety (you're always only one word away from becoming a stated case, an example in law of how not to behave during an investigation), loss of focus and so on, so you develop another persona for them. If you've been on an ops team before, you also know the massive amount of work going on behind the scenes, with exhibits, surveillance, phones, authorities, intel and reports. This leads to massive pressure.

Undercover work depends on forming and maintaining relationships as you would normally but with a malfunctioning set of people. In addition, relationships are usually formed in a natural way and for good reasons, like business, friendship or romance. We were forcing the relationships and for all the wrong reasons – to stitch these people up. This can play havoc with your mind.

We climbed the criminal ladder in the usual manner, flashing some cash and talking about hijacks, and we were soon speaking to T's minions, who asked us for samples of the sort of goods we could get hold of.

'Any chance of 42-inch plasmas?'

'No probs, bruv.'

T's people paid us for the samples in crack and heroin. We always gave him a good price.

One night we were doing a hand-to-hand (buying drugs on the street) when a marked car saw us and gave chase. We jumped into our car, roared off and were chased around a local estate before we got away.

We bought from all sorts of lowlifes: Asif, Edwin, James, Gordon, Kevin, Norman and a girl called Lynn whom the Ops Team had tried to latch onto twice before, but she'd refused to play with the UC officers. She sold to me because, as she explained, 'You've got nice eyes.' Lynn, who was the mother of two very young children, was killed the day before the Ops Team were due to arrest her. She was high on heroin when she crashed her car into another vehicle.

Steve and I became so well known that we were put on Hampshire

Constabulary's criminal hit list. We also kept getting pulled when we were out on the road because of our missing tax disc.

There was no way we could be cops, right?

To supply T with the goods, Steve and I paid a sanctioned visit to the police storeroom to see what we could find in the stolen property section. Once a suitable plasma had been found, we'd deliver it to T with a lump inside.

When the storeroom ran out of high-end electronic goods, I started calling the ops team. A tech called Stu (who, as far as T was concerned, was my source in the warehouse) would check Argos had it in stock before giving me the OK and I'd tell T we could get whatever it was he was asking for this week.

After a few runs, we thought we'd earned T's trust, although he made some half-hearted mumblings about how we were so good at supplying what he wanted that we simply had to be undercover feds. Oh, how we laughed.

Eventually, T said he wanted to join our hijack operation and asked to meet us in the small hours in a Camberley car park. Steve and I went without back-up and sat waiting for an hour for T to turn up. When he did, it was in two cars and with four friends. They drove up at speed and before you could say 'busted' they had our car trapped.

I wound down the window. 'What's goin' on?' I asked.

'Get out,' T said, with a jerk of his thumb.

'Five against two,' Steve whispered. 'That'll teach us for coming out to play without back-up.'

With no other choice, we climbed out of our respective sides and were shoved, protesting, in separate directions. T had brought one of his enforcers, an unhinged Somalian, all muscle and no brain, who pinned me face down on his car's bonnet while T walked back and forth, questioning us each out of earshot of the other, checking our story.

Talk about pressure.

T did this for half an hour but was unable to find anything wrong with our legend. We lived the life too well to slip up in that way.

'Let him up.'

The Somalian stood back and I straightened up.

'For fuck's sake, T, there's no need—'

'Smoke it.' T was holding out a rock of crack, a pipe and a lighter. 'Prove you're for real.'

I had no intention of smoking anything. 'What the fuck? No way.'

'Smoke it, you cunt!'

'Look, I can't, mate,' I said. 'I'm sick. It'll make me puke.'

This was actually true; I'd had a bad case of flu and had been throwing up, so I flicked my tongue at the back of my throat until I retched and projectile vomited, splattering the Somalian's shoes.

T threw the rock at me in disgust and they drove off without another word.

* * *

At the following morning's debrief with the operational team, it was decided that it was time to say farewell to T; we weren't going back. Steve, myself and the whole team were gutted. We'd blown a small fortune in man-hours. It was all experience, however, and an officer from the Test Purchase course made immediate use of it by presenting this real-life incident as an example.

Lots of hands went up when the instructor described our confrontation with T. They wanted to know how we dealt with not taking drugs as a 'test'. Getting out of taking gear was something we prepared for while waiting around – something we did a lot while on this job. We would also test each other's cover stories by asking each other 101 questions, so we were well rehearsed.

'We've had TPs and UC officers threatened with car jacks, knives and strip-searched, but they've always talked their way out without revealing themselves,' the instructor told them.

Most dealers don't want their customers hanging around. Once they've got rid of the gear and have the cash, they want you gone. Many drug users, especially heroin addicts, are private. You'd say something like, 'Nah, man, I want to take my gear on my own. If I boot up here, it'll ruin my high, I'll be all para [paranoid].'

Besides, once the high hits, heroin users are very hard to get rid of, so it's just not worth it for the dealers. Similarly, people high on crack are very annoying to have around while you're trying to do business, so demands that we took gear in their presence were rare. When they were made, it was fairly easy to persuade them that we wanted to 'enjoy' our high elsewhere.

When we were in the story, we believed in it totally and, for me personally, I became that character, much like an actor; the fact that I was a cop didn't come into my mind. I knew there were rules, so I stuck to them, but they were easy to work into my performance as part of my character's code (I wouldn't take drugs, commit a crime, say something that would lead someone else to commit a crime, etc.).

Some officers would go above and beyond the call of duty. We were once trying to get into a gang that dealt in Ecstasy and coke. Their distribution point was a car wash – 'Get a wax and polish with every ounce'. The boss was a paranoid and violent monster and we couldn't get near him to buy. Our research showed that he owned a tattoo shop. One officer volunteered to go and get a tattoo.

'Needs to be a big one,' he said. 'So I've got time to talk.'

He went into a grimy basement full of muscled and leather-clad heavies and got a tat of Man United on his shoulder.[13] It took them four hours to do and by the end of it he had a drug deal. With all this secrecy, the same officer unintentionally convinced his wife he was having an affair. She stabbed him right in the tats (he recovered). I had to call her up to explain that he was telling the truth.

We also used theatre to convince the criminals. We'd get arrested by uniform cops who'd been 'tipped off', so even the arresting officers didn't know we were undercover as they pushed us into their car, right in front of criminal witnesses who would spread the word amongst our targets that we'd been pinched. We'd be taken into custody and booked in, and then, at some point, our file would be handed over and we'd be freed.

We were still in the middle of debriefing T's job when my covert phone rang.

Steve shrugged. 'You might as well answer,' he said.

It was T.

---

[13] Not really, but I can't tell you what it was or where he got it, as it would ID him.

'Sorry, man. Had to be sure. Let's meet and I'll serve you up [supply you some drugs]. And I definitely want in on those hijack jobs, big style.'

At our next meeting, held in a greasy spoon, T nudged me and nodded over his shoulder towards the door. A uniformed PC had just strolled in for a bacon butty.

'Eat now, talk after,' he said.

I nodded and looked at the PC. Oh Christ, I recognised him. He wasn't based in my nick, but we'd been at training school together. T's back was to him.

I hoped to hell he wouldn't recognise me. My disguise was convincing – beard, earring and filthy coat – but the PC, trained to never forget a face, spotted me and then tried to place me. A flash of recognition lit his face; this was quickly followed by puzzlement, as he tried to imagine what had caused me to transform from hopeful copper to hopeless dosser.

I found his eyes, stared hard for a second and shook my head slowly as T crouched over his egg, beans and chips. Realisation dawned, the PC bought his butty and left, leaving T and me to finish our business.

Steve and I exchanged increasingly large amounts of gear before the warrant was finally called. So that we weren't revealed, we were kept off the plot when the heavy-duty brigade stormed T's home.

I woke up and switched on the radio to hear: 'Today, 20 properties across Surrey were raided by 200 police officers after a months-long undercover operation identified and gathered evidence on the county's major drugs players.'

I smiled. This was what the job was about. You took risks, played hard and, with a bit of luck, the rewards were there. We'd taken some dangerous people off the streets. Surrey was actually safer that morning than it had been the day before and Steve and I had played a significant part in that.

I had little time to reflect – there was somewhere else I needed to be that day. I was training as a firearms officer and needed to renew my certificate. This involved travelling to a range and hitting a certain number of targets with suitable accuracy.

Just before I left for the range, my phone rang. I was needed straightaway to attend an ID parade in Woking to identify one of the gang. Only I knew who he was, so we had no choice if we wanted to keep him in jail.

I called the firearms officer and asked if I could go tomorrow.

'We can't just change this around,' he said. 'This is firearms training, after all. You either do the test and pass or don't come and fail.'

'But I really can't come.'

'Why not?'

'I can't tell you.'

'Then you're off firearms training.'

I hung up. Keeping quiet about undercover work was necessary, but a real pain.

Afterwards, the ops commander came and found us. He was smiling, so I assumed all was well.

'What happened?' I asked.

'When we hit T, he ran for it. George floored him, right enough. Cracked a few ribs. He was in the ambulance screaming police brutality.'

George was a police rugby prop about the build and weight of a bear. Ouch.

Although Met Intelligence said that T carried a gun, no weapons were found at his home; however, a .22 calibre gold-plated revolver – originally burgled from a private home in Scotland – was recovered from another address. It contained five rounds. One had been recently discharged.

T went down for five, the rest of his crew between three and five.

At the trial, the judge read some of our recordings. 'These chaps really have the lingo, don't they?' he said to our barrister.

He then added, in a more formal manner, 'These men are to be commended.' A commendation is simply an A4 sheet of paper with the judge's words of praise on it.

We then went for tea and toast with Surrey's Chief Constable Dennis O'Connor, who asked, 'How can you guys do this kind of work?'

The question was fair enough. The answer was that we were obsessed with the idea of being the most effective cops we could be.

Going undercover was the way to get to the most dangerous criminals and the sacrifices, so far, had been worth it.

Having said that, after celebrating our success, I went home to my girlfriend and walked straight into a 'we need to talk' conversation.

I had to accept it. I was still planning to carry on in this line of work and, including the test purchasing jobs, I'd spent the past eight months of our relationship buying heroin, wearing wires and being searched and held against my will. I looked filthy, wore an untrimmed beard and earrings, and stank. I was constantly stressed, the margin of error being tiny.

But the rewards had been high. We would go on to prop up the drugs stats for the entire county two years in a row, thanks to the number of dealers we caught in the act.

I decided the sacrifice had been worth it and put girlfriends on hold. I threw myself into my work. My plans for a chaste and single life didn't last long, however. That's love for you.

I fell for, chased and then won a girl whom I then caught having an affair. I got drunk, phoned her up, had a row, marching through the house in anger as I did so – then everything went black.

I forced open my eyes. There was a cop standing above me, screaming into his radio. What was he saying? In between yelling, he kept saying over and over, 'You all right, mate?' I was lying on the floor, half on my patio, half still in the lounge, broken glass all around me. Something felt sticky. I touched my head; it was soaked with blood.

'Don't worry, mate,' the PC said. 'The ambulance is on its way. Can you remember who did this to you?'

'Yeah,' I said, slowly coming round. 'The suspect's eight inches tall and made of green glass.'

'You've got concussion,' the PC said.

I pointed at the empty bottle of Jameson's just inside the door.

I'd tripped over a rug and gone head first through my patio window. A neighbour had pressed the nines. I ended up with fifty-six stitches and a six-inch scar across my forehead.

When I got back to work, I simply pushed myself deeper into the job.

6

Grass, Snitch and Squealer

THE AFTERMATH OF A HOUSE PARTY on a warm spring night: bottles, beer cans, overflowing ashtrays, fag burns, stained carpets, cheap, torn furniture, cups half filled with uncertain liquids and a dead body in the bedroom.

This wasn't an overdose or a case of vomit-induced suffocation. Judging from the state of his body, several drugged and drunken youths had kicked and beaten this young man to death. One thug had jumped up and down on the victim's head so hard that he'd forced brain matter out of his ears and across the carpet.

This murder wasn't a planned 'hit', punishment or grudge killing: it just happened. Sometimes there's a meanness in this world that can't be explained away. Stupid and cruel bastards do stupid and cruel things, especially when they're drunk and high on hard drugs.

The address was known to us, as were many of the people at the party. Most of us in the office had a good idea who the youth was who'd done the jumping, as well as some of the others involved, so a vanload of uniformed officers scooped up everyone they could find, which included the sister of Jumping Jack Flash, a well-known criminal.

I'd recently been potting (jailing) multi-kilo dealers, recovering guns and hundreds of thousands of pounds worth of drugs with Bart. We worked on a simple premise: flip each target, turning them into an informant to set up the next target. We had got so used to flipping criminals into employees of Her Majesty's taxpayers that I applied it to this gruesome murder.

I was waiting in the police yard when the van with the sister rolled up. 'Hello, fellas,' I said to the officers. 'Time for tea and a sandwich.'

One of the PCs, who looked like a probie, started to say something like, 'But we're supposed to book her in,' before his older and wiser partner answered, 'Two sugars in mine, Kev. I'll be in the smoking area,' then walked away without another word.

I stared at the probie until the penny finally fell through the slot and he made for the canteen, no doubt muttering to himself that nobody told him about this sort of thing in training school.

I joined the woman in the custody cage in the back of a marked van, well out of sight of anyone else, looked her in the eye and made a bet with myself that I would turn her in ten minutes.

Every good copper does this, to a degree. If you've stop-searched a scrote and found nothing, you'll have a chat and maybe pick up a snippet or two. She was potentially in the shit and wanted to save herself.

So, I spelled out her situation in graphic detail (this works especially well if the target hasn't done time before): threaten her kids with care, talk about life sentences, or anything else I could think of. Then I switched and spelled out the benefits of being helpful. In this case, it was a concentrated effort in breaking her down and building her back up in another mould. It's a mix of leverage, threat, treat and interview.

Detectives have relied upon informants since Henry Fielding founded the Bow Street Runners in 1749. Known to us now as Covert Human Intelligence Sources (CHIS), criminals still refer to them as grasses, snitches and squealers.

It used to be that any good tech relied on his own informants and ran them as he saw fit – a method that led to a great many problems. Bent detectives played off informants against one another, misused the intelligence and sometimes shared in the reward money. Things have recently been tightened up with the creation of a Dedicated Source Unit (DSU), but other problems with sources occur with frightening regularity.

One thing to be kept in mind when dealing with sources is that they cannot be trusted. Coming to the police is a high-risk strategy and the reasons for doing so are likely to include more than one of the following:

Financial gain

Self-preservation

Eliminating competition by informing on rivals

Feeding disinformation to the police

Thrill factor

Public spirit

Mental illness (people in this category are sometimes also referred to as a 'Special Population Group', which covers a variety of temporary and permanent mental illnesses)

Currying favour, with a view to learning about ongoing police operations and/or protecting their own criminal business

Assisting police corruption

Once a source handler thinks they've established their source's motivation, they then have to risk assess the source and value of the information, covering:

Compromise: will the source's position, actions or information compromise their safety, their handlers' safety or any police operations?

Physical risk: what are the factors that could result in physical harm to anyone as a result of using this source?

Psychological: could we cause psychological harm to the source primarily and/or any other person by using them?

Police and community: will we cause risk to the larger community, both civil and law enforcement, by using this source or, just as importantly, by not using this source?

Economic: will payments to the source, the cost of operations and the value of seizures justify their use?

Moral: is it morally acceptable to use this source in the authorised manner or is it morally acceptable to *not* use this source's information (e.g. to protect other operations by letting other criminality go unchecked)?

Legal: are we acting in a legally authorised manner by using this source and are we fulfilling all of our other legal duties by using – or not, as the case may be – this source?

All these factors can change as a job develops, so the source needs constant re-evaluation.

There are several ways in which sources are recruited. The most well-known opportunity arises when someone is arrested and they spy a way out of their predicament or the interviewing DC/DS decides to make an advance.

The source outlines what they can do for the police and then, if we're agreeable, they have to decide whether they're willing to sign on with the DSU.

The source will then be furnished with a cover story including a name and a reason why someone from DSU will call. They're sent on their way after being provided with another cover story for their arrest. (It should have nothing to do with the crime we brought them in for, as this would seem a little suspicious. 'The Old Bill nicked me with an ounce of coke and let me go,' for example, will not satisfy that person's drug supplier.)

The investigation into the original offence continues as normal and the DSU then decides when, if at all, they get in touch with the source. Sometimes the DSU executes a 'Bump'. This is the technical term for walking up to a newly recruited source on the street and interviewing and assessing them as they walk.

Alternatively, 'The Walk-In' occurs when a potential source walks into the nick or approaches an officer directly. This is surprisingly common, but you have to be extremely careful with regard to their motivation. For example, the brother of a known ram-raider and dealer arrived at the station, asked for me and offered to become a CHIS. Once I'd interviewed him, it became clear that he'd offered his services because his brother was suspicious of a new customer and thought he might be a cop. His hope was that his brother would become an informant and would then be able to find out if this was true or not.

'The Witness' is usually an innocent member of the public, for example the housewife who witnesses a murder whilst doing the washing up. In the case of something like a gangland murder, they may be given witness protection, which is dealt with by a top secret unit.

Sources in this category may also include someone who has witnessed ongoing criminality by a loved one and has decided that the only way to help them is to approach the police.

'The Recruit' is the sort of informer we treat as prey. Within a loosely organised gang of drug dealers (contrary to what you might read in the press, criminals, who are naturally opportunistic and disloyal, are rarely organised into clearly defined gangs), detectives, with the help of specialised source handlers, will identify the people whom we think we can recruit to the police cause. Surprisingly, some recruits turn out to be very astute and professional. Although the Association of Chief Police Officers (ACPO) may say otherwise, this method is as old as informing itself.

In one colonial policing jurisdiction (this story came to me second hand, but I've no reason to doubt this particular source), the wife of a top criminal was photographed in flagrante delicto with another male.

She was then approached in a supermarket and handed an envelope with some glossy 8x10s, along with a business card upon which was printed a phone number.

Five minutes later she met the handlers in a nearby coffee shop and signed up. Informing was a better option than returning to her husband.

This would not happen in the UK (at least if it has, then it certainly shouldn't have), but other types of leverage are employed – such as time off for crimes committed, or safe passage to a new part of the UK and a clean start – where nobody knows their new name.

In the case of my murder witness in the back of the car, she not only told us where we could find our chief suspect with enough blood-spatter evidence to send him down for life, but she also knew every aspect of the local drug scene and worked with us on that, too. Fantastic.

Once you've bumped your source and got an agreement, a handler and co-handler meet with the controller (a detective inspector). Between them they work out the limits of exploitation, risk assessment and the law. This is then presented to the authorising officer, normally a superintendent, or in the case of juvenile or participating informants (in that the source will have to break the law as part of their cover story) an assistant chief constable.

Then, subject to the controller's instructions, the handlers meet with the source. Each of these meetings is tightly controlled and set up with cover stories, counter surveillance and contingency plans.

I've used hotel rooms to conduct debriefs and vehicles with one-way windows, wired for sound and vision. I have been involved in operations that required running the source through a complex route, with surveillance and choke points built in.

At these meetings, transactions take place. The source tells you what they know and you task them to find out what you want to know. The source might be provided with a mobile phone and/or paid. Some high-level informants make a very good living. Payments can run into tens of thousands of pounds. A participating informant might be allowed to take part in offences to further their credibility with the criminals and their worth to the police.

After this meeting, the source goes to work, while the handlers write up the latest information and enter it onto the Police Informant Management System (PIMS), sanitising it to prevent the source from being identified before the information is shared among those units and officers who will benefit from it. Then the cycle starts again.

County forces employ a central DSU, which will run about ten to twenty sources per year. The Met and Greater Manchester Police (GMP) are slightly different in that some of their boroughs are the same size, if not bigger, than an entire county force. There's an estimated fifty DSUs in the Met, a further forty-one nationally and five in the GMP.

This makes a total of ninety-six units running ten to twenty sources, so nationally there are between 960 and 1,920 active criminal informants. But this is all guesswork. Dozens of sources are recruited on the bounce and used in one-time-only deals.

Still trust the mate you're about to do that robbery with?

And I haven't factored in the National Crime Agency or the security services.

Can it go wrong and, more to the point, does it go wrong? Largely, the system works, but every now and again glaring errors occur and they are, frankly, terrifying.

In 1999, career criminal Kenneth Regan was about to receive a 24-year sentence for heroin smuggling and the attempted murder of a police officer. He offered to become a police source and, as he proved to be so incredibly well connected, he was freed just three years later.

Regan kickstarted some of the biggest police operations in history, including Operation Extend, an investigation into a £2 billion drugs-smuggling ring, as well as several gangland assassinations. He was pure gold – or so it seemed.

In February 2003, millionaire businessman Amarjit Chohan (45), wife Nancy (24), Nancy's mother Charanjit Kaur (51) and sons Devinder (18 months) and Ravinder (8 weeks) all vanished from their home in West London.

DCI Norman McKinlay and his 33-strong team from the Serious Crime Directorate were eventually convinced by the persistent detective work of Onkar Verma, Nancy's brother, that the family had been kidnapped but failed to turn up any leads until 24 March, when they discovered papers signed by Chohan handing over control of his courier company, CIBA, to Kenneth Regan.

Then a canoeist found Chohan's body floating near Bournemouth pier. A post-mortem revealed he had been bound, gagged and drugged. The police hoped the rest of the family were still alive and mounted a desperate search, but the body of his wife was recovered in the same area in July. Charanjit Kaur's body was found in a bay off the Isle of Wight in November 2003. The bodies of the two boys have yet to be found.

When Chohan's body was retrieved from the sea, scientists found a piece of paper inside one of his socks. It was a letter addressed to Kenneth Regan and dated 12 February 2003 – the day before his disappearance.

Regan had kidnapped the family from their home, murdered them and then buried them on a Devon estate. Along with two accomplices, he later dug up the bodies and dumped them at sea.

He'd murdered the Chohan family just four months after his

release. His motive? To take over Chohan's international freight company and use it to import heroin from the Continent.

The eight-month trial was the longest murder trial in the history of the Metropolitan Police. The judge spent a record five weeks summing up the case for the jury. The trial alone cost £10m. The police investigation involved 1,000 officers and detectives travelled to the USA, Spain, India, Belgium and France.

Judge Sir Stephen Mitchell imposed a 'whole life' tariff, telling Regan this meant he had 'no prospect of release'.

Considering the scale of this crime, little is known about this case, partly because Regan exposed the weakness of using Covert Human Intelligence Sources. When they're good, like Regan was, they lead to convictions that the police would find impossible to achieve otherwise. When they go bad, they can cost lives. There was no way Regan's contribution to the police service could ever outweigh his horrific, psychopathic crimes.

It was argued that if Regan had been properly supervised after his release from prison, then the Chohan family would still be alive. Instead, he was allowed to roam free, with too little contact from his handler.

As detectives, we always have to remember we are dealing with the 'human factor' and that dealing with Covert Human Intelligence Sources is a dangerous game.

> Covert – because of the intrusive supervision, it focuses on the more serious criminality. More serious = more risk
>
> Human – human error looms large when working with or as a CHIS
>
> Intelligence – a murky world of rumour, truth, half-truth, misinformation, back-stabbing and intuition. It's bound to go wrong somewhere.
>
> Sources – an informant. Informants are widely recognised as a risky option. They're often regarded as being lower down on the moral ladder than the criminal the police are after because they themselves are criminals 'selling out their own'.

Remember the sister? And her promise of help? She was handed over to the DSU and for a while things seemed to work quite well. For operational reasons, it was decided that a co-handler should come in from outside the DSU to work with her on some high-level drug-dealing suspects.

Two years later, the Met's anti-corruption squad received some intel on the handler and put a surveillance team on him.

It didn't take them long to discover that the handler:

> was co-habiting with the sister – BIG no-no!
> had cocaine wraps of supply quantity in a bedside cabinet, which forensics linked to him (his fingerprints were on the inside of the wraps, positioned in such a way that it was clear he had packaged the cocaine)
> tested positive for cocaine consumption

They also learned that the informant's associates were surprisingly well informed with regard to police drug investigations. When he next showed up at the CID office, the handler was arrested for malfeasance and conspiracy to supply Class-A drugs.

This never made the press, nor did the offending officer end up in prison. It was simply too embarrassing.

Like Regan, the handler and the informant should have been rigorously examined, managed and scrutinised by ACPO ranked officers. Considering what he managed to get up to, he clearly wasn't. A public admission would have hurt those managers.

7

Bad Education

DURING MY JOURNEY INTO THE UNDERWORLD of drugs I made many unexpected and fascinating discoveries. For example, chemical analysis of crack cocaine recovered from our neighbourhood revealed that the same cook was producing the same mixture of crack for dealers in Nottingham, Manchester, Doncaster and Liverpool. We also learned that some dealers built up 'franchises' only to sell them for £25,000 (about five days' turnover). All they had to do was hand over a mobile phone with all their contacts.

While my experiences in the unofficial drugs squad and then as an UC officer felt like time well spent (allowing for the cost to my social life), we still struggled to persuade the Crown Prosecution Service to take our prisoners to trial, and then fought to convince the magistrates of our county courts that these people who suddenly looked so humble and had all these character references and mitigating circumstances (fantasy sob stories) were indeed deserving of prison. All too often drug dealers and drug-addicted burglars were able to persuade magistrates to give them bail (after which they went on the run).

To try and educate the courts of this approach, Bart and I arranged a special training day where we put all the CPS lawyers and magistrates we could persuade in the same room and explained to them exactly how 'the game' worked .We laid bare all the excuses that are used to get bail: unfortunate product of today's society; victim of abuse and neglect; girlfriend having a baby; living with my mother;

91

strong links in the community; haven't offended for six months.

'Every one is a lie,' we told them.

To you or me, this might seem obvious; but to the magistrates, it was a revelation. It was as if they thought people didn't lie to them, as if they believed people took the sanctity of the oath of truth seriously.

For balance, we also told them all about the scams drug dealers use to dupe innocents to work as drugs mules. We'd just started one story when a senior CPS prosecutor interrupted: 'Yes, I could see how that would happen to anyone. Something similar happened to me. We were on holiday when a couple got friendly with us and gave us a bag – they'd gone over their luggage allowance.'

'Jesus,' I said.

'What? What's the problem?'

'Where were you on holiday?'

'Turkey. Look, they were very nice—'

'I'm sure they were. Who met you at the airport?'

'The same couple. Well, the husband. Look, they were genuine; these people weren't drug dealers . . .'

'Met him in the car park, did you?'

'Er, yes.'

'What was he driving? A black Range Rover?' This always seemed to be the vehicle of choice for major dealers.

'Er, yes.'

'I can't believe this. It's very likely that you've smuggled heroin into the UK.'

The talks really worked. Fewer people got out on bail afterwards.

But it wasn't just the courts that needed educating; the police were even more clueless.

Bart and I planned to raid a dealer who kept her coke and heroin in plastic wraps inside a cigarette packet. We needed to surround the property to keep an eye out for anything being thrown out of windows or suspects trying to get away, but had had trouble finding enough officers at our nick, so I rang the training school and asked if we could borrow some probies.

'Just bring them back in one piece,' the instructor said.

The raid went smoothly and we decided that it would be a good experience for the probies to carry out the search. But they couldn't find the drugs.

Afterwards I picked up the cigarette packet with the wraps inside and asked, 'What about this?'

It was sitting on the coffee table. It wasn't as if they could miss it.

'Oh, we saw that,' said one of the probies. 'But we didn't know what it was, so left it.'

I called the training school and explained what had happened. The instructor told me that drug education wasn't on the syllabus. When I asked him why not, he um'd and ah'd for a bit before telling me, 'We've no one to teach them.'

'So we're releasing new recruits onto the streets of Surrey who have never even seen street drugs, who wouldn't know a crack pipe if someone poked them in the eye with one?'

'Um, well, when you put it like that . . .'

We persuaded the college to let us do a special talk.

When we arrived, the lecture hall was packed. A uniformed sergeant was in the audience and, assuming he was in charge, I went over to say hello.

'I'm going to evaluate this talk on the basis of our procedures book,' he said, tapping his clipboard with a pen.

I smiled: 'We're not going to show them anything they can find in that.'

He frowned. 'Well, I doubt if you'll be allowed to continue.'

We showed them real drugs and jaws hit the floor as we explained the reality of drug dealing and showed them pictures of a Porsche that one dealer had been able to buy after about six weeks, brand new and in cash (albeit using a huge stack of crumpled, drug-tainted £10 notes).

We also described all the drugs-smuggling/selling tricks in the book. For example, drug dealers don't carry when they're driving their Porsches or other top-of-the range cars. Instead, they use older vehicles that won't draw as much attention. When pulled over, the simplest way to get away from the cops is for them to start acting emotional, crying, saying that they've lost their job, their wife has left them and they were just driving around to clear their mind. Traffic cops do not like to listen to depressing sob stories. They can't say 'Move along, sir' fast enough.

We got a round of applause at the end. The sergeant came up to me with his clipboard, pen poised.

I nudged Bart and sighed. 'Here we go.'

He removed his evaluation page and ripped it in two. 'That was amazing,' he said. 'Can you come back next week?'

We were asked back and even gave talks to groups of senior officers who should have known better. Watching some of their faces as we showed them the drugs was like seeing their brains' dimmer switches being turned up, as if they were thinking, 'So that's what all that white powder was!' I wondered how they could have made it so far through their careers without knowing at least half of what we were telling them.

Trainees and senior officers alike told us that ours was the best and most useful class they'd been on. We expanded the talks to include guns. One day the police lecture theatre was double-booked, so we hired the hall in Guildford library.

We brought guns that we'd recovered from undercover work, including an Arnie-style street-sweeper with drum magazine and laser sight (although God knows why you'd need a laser sight with one of those). We also included an air pistol that a man had waved at firearms officers in 1999 in Dorking who, sadly, shot him dead. You couldn't tell the difference between it and the real, live-fire handgun we put beside it. Now, imagine it's 50 feet away from you.

We were in street clothes and as we carried the guns from the van to the hall my holdall, which was the size of a cricket bag, burst and a dozen handguns spilled out into the street in front of shoppers and septuagenarian Miss Marples heading to the library to return their Agathas and Archers.

After scrambling to get them back in the bag, we made an urgent phone call to the office: 'To any teams scrambling to the library, stand down, chaps, it's only us.'

We also started delivering these talks outside of the police. A nursing school found out they had a drug problem amongst the students and called the police for help.

For this reason, as well as the fact that those who managed to graduate would end up working with addicts (addicts spend a lot of time in hospitals, particularly A&E departments), it was decided it would be worth delivering our talk.

It went well. Afterwards, a trainee nurse who would score top marks in anatomy approached me. Her boyfriend was beating her up.

On top of that, he was selling drugs. As we swapped numbers, a friend of hers saw us.

'What do I do?'

'Say I asked you out for a drink.'

In the end, we caught her boyfriend with a nine-bar of cocaine.

Sadly, these talks were shut down after just two years as part of the eternal cutbacks of doom.

If we'd been allowed to continue, I would have expanded the course to include the fascinating topic of 'drugs economics', a subject that should be compulsory in every police training school.

The economics of class-A drugs and related crime are shockingly simple, but the facts continue to be ignored by senior officers and politicians: 90 per cent of crime is committed by 2 per cent of the population; 99 per cent of that 2 per cent are addicted to drugs. Dealing in drugs is easy money, and it's easy to get away with it. It is, as far as the crime figures are concerned, a victimless crime. Dealers have an easy ride: as we've already seen, hardly any forces have drugs squads any more. Proving intent to sell is very difficult and so the clear-up rate is low.

Addicts spend, conservatively, £100 a day, so have to find £30–40k a year to fund their habit. Most do this by theft and burglary. If the items they steal are brand new, they can sell them for about one-third of their market value. If they're used, then the going rate is about one-fifth. So the average addict has to steal at least £150k worth of goods every year. According to the Home Office, there are 306,000 registered drug addicts in the UK (that's the ones we know about).[14]

---

[14] The estimated total number of opiate and/or crack cocaine users in England in 2009–10 is 306,150. (National and Regional Estimates of the Prevalence of Opiate Use and/or Crack Cocaine Use, 2009/10)

That's a lot of zeros.

Going after burglars is expensive. My team will spend an hour on house-to-house inquiries and then another hour on the crime report before finding out if this burglary may be linked to others. The whole file will take four to five hours to complete, with £500 spent on forensic submissions. Then there's the community support officer, the phone calls and the victim-support team, who all pitch in a few hours at a cost of £500. We can spend £185,000 a year chasing just one drug-addicted burglar.[15] If that burglar stopped taking drugs, it could save over £300,000 per year in police hours and stolen property.

Compared to crack, heroin is a slow-release drug. The 'hit' – which puts most users into a stupor – lasts for several hours and so addicts only have to 'work' once or twice a day to find the cash they need for their next fix. Many heroin users rely on burglary, which takes time. You have to find a suitable property, wait until the right moment and then, once you have the goods, you have to find someone to sell them to, or find a dealer prepared to accept stolen goods in return for drugs.

Crack is far more addictive than heroin and the effects wear off after just a few minutes, so users need to earn cash quickly if they're to feed their addiction. Burglary takes too long. Mugging, on the other hand, takes a minute. I saw another 'dimmer-switch moment' when I explained this to a senior officer as I was trying to argue the case for raiding crack houses. Although they are expensive in terms of man-hours and have an element of risk to them, closing them and staying on top of them can dramatically reduce street robbery rates in the surrounding area. Despite the strong arguments in its favour, this idea was binned.

After the arrest of Jake Michaels (see Chapter 1), it was made even clearer to me that senior officers use drug investigations to play politics instead of reducing crime and improving living standards. Local newspapers ran reports about louts just like Michaels – thugs that make lives a misery. In response, the higher-ups decided that we

---

[15] And if we ever get them to Crown Court, a trial costs £10k per day. A single burglary trial typically runs for one to two days.

needed to send a zero-tolerance message to other drug dealers so we could show the papers that we were doing something to combat the problem.

A team of officers made up of two UC officers, a DS and several DCs, an exhibits officer, a disclosure officer and four PCs, along with divisional force surveillance units, had been running an unusually large intelligence-led operation. They'd been trying to reach the major players in a small area of Surrey that seemed to have a higher drug turnover than Bogota. Customers came to score there from all over the county. It was an expensive operation, costing about £60k, but the team had been making real inroads towards the top dealers, collecting some first-class intelligence along the way.

Suddenly, the higher-ups decided that this operation was ideal for them to use to demonstrate 'zero tolerance' and so ordered the team to stop, and they, along with every other available officer, were ordered in to scoop up all the criminals they could, addicts and minor dealers alike. All the bosses wanted were numbers to meet targets and newspaper photos of themselves standing next to big piles of drugs.

They actually preferred it if we brought home ten to fifteen street-level dealers instead of one Mr Big, as did the CPS. The little guys were easier to convict through shorter (cheaper) trials, the pathetic outcomes of which (short and suspended sentences worked out many weeks, if not months, later after plea bargaining) would never make it into the press.

To say the team were pissed off when we stomped over their delicately balanced operation is putting it mildly. As I've already mentioned, working undercover is extremely stressful. Apart from the fact that you have to wear a recording device, you have to watch what you say, as every word is recorded. If it sounds like you're leading someone to commit a crime they might not have otherwise committed, then you can kiss your prosecution goodbye. Now all their careful labours, all the personal risks they'd taken, had been for very little.

To add insult to injury, one senior officer joined us at a pre-raid briefing where we had all our gear laid out on the table. He picked up a radio and asked, 'What does this do?'

I explained and then he picked up the next piece of equipment. 'And this?'

On it went until he picked up a piece of tape that you peel off the seal on evidence bags before sticking them together.

'What does this do?'

We all looked at one another in disbelief before I explained.

'Oh, I see. Very clever. Well, carry on.'

On the night of the raid, the area was sealed off. The line to the local train station developed a 'fault' so no trains stopped. Traffic cops 'organised' an RTA, shutting off traffic. Twenty people were arrested.

Two hours later we sent some Test Purchasers to see if they could score. They returned with their pockets loaded. Six months' work, an operation that cost £60k: the result? We disrupted the supply of drugs for less than two hours.

Doing things like hunting Mr Bigs, or even Mr Mediums, or raiding crack houses is expensive, dangerous and suggests that we have, horror of horrors, a drugs problem. We're told to chase burglars instead, a near-hopeless task. It's simply dealing with the symptom, not the cause.

Take Gary and Derek Blythe, for example. Both were addicted to crack and were prolific burglars. Gary, who was also a long-term alcoholic, was 30 but looked about 50, like something out of *Night of the Living Dead*.

I thought there was still hope for his brother, 18-year-old Derek. One day I told him as much, after questioning him about a series of burglaries.

A short while later, Derek turned himself in at Staines nick and asked to see me, saying he wanted to get clean. I was off duty in Leatherhead but drove cross-county straight away, only to find Derek was hopped up on heroin.

'OK, we can start by arresting you,' I said. 'But we can only talk tomorrow, when you've sobered up and I'm on duty.'

The following day we drove around with Derek to all the burgled addresses we had on our database.

'All you have to do is nod if you see one of yours,' I told him.

He nodded 27 times. We then interviewed him in detail, asking him how he did each one, what was taken and lots of other details, in order to avoid the accusation we'd somehow coerced him or buttered him up into admitting to crimes he hadn't committed. Derek helped us to recover £35,000 in stolen goods.

'Right, if you cough to that lot in court, I'll do you a favour,' I said.

'Rehab?'

'We can but try. It won't be the Priory, though.'

In court, I argued against prison and recommended treatment. Judge Cropper looked at me for a long moment.

'You and I, Officer A,' he said slowly, 'have known each other for a long time.' He paused for emphasis. 'And this is highly unusual of you.'

You get to know judges, barristers and solicitors pretty quickly in the police game. I was well known in courts across the county for arguing for the longest possible sentence at every possible opportunity.

'In this case, your honour, I think Derek will benefit from treatment. He wants to come clean. He's come clean here before you today and helped recover an extraordinary amount of stolen property.'

'Which *he* stole, Officer A.'

'Yes, your honour.'

'Hmmm. Very well.'

The judge went for it and Derek was paired with a mentor who helped him get clean. Now *that* was good police work. Loads of crimes solved, property returned and a criminal treated fairly by the system and ready to go straight.

Sadly, this scenario was all too rare – and it didn't last.

Seven months later, I was standing in a recently burgled house. The owner, understandably freaked out by being burgled in the small hours, was also gutted that his brand new 42-inch plasma telly had been taken.

'Anything else missing?' I asked.

'Well, yeah. It's a bit strange, really. The duvet from the spare room.'

Damn. I looked up. 'Have you got a shed?'

'Yeah, why?'

The Blythe brothers. Their MO was always the same. They found a house with a shed, took an implement, which they'd use to force open the patio door (this way they avoided being arrested for going equipped) and they always took the TV wrapped up in a duvet, laptops in pillowcases or, if they could find one, a suitcase.

When I next saw Derek, I groaned in despair. He was back on the gear. A uniformed officer had arrested him and he'd asked to speak to me. We went through the exact same routine, except this time I didn't make such a spirited defence and Judge Cropper gave him 18 months.

Liam and Richard Smales were another pair of drug-addicted burgling brothers who plagued the good people of Surrey. We had custody pictures that charted Liam's rapid physical disintegration. The drugs ate away his spine, causing him to hunch over, his weight declining from ten to seven stone along the way. The last time he was in jail the prison dentist removed every single one of his teeth. He was 26 years old. He's still out there now, but I suspect he'll be dead fairly soon.

The Smales brothers were from a gypsy family and always had the same MO. They tended to look for the most vulnerable victims and therefore targeted the homes of the retired and elderly. The Smales brothers weren't interested in TVs or computers; they wanted cash and jewellery, usually family heirlooms, the sorts of things that old people keep at home. They usually found their way in through a ground-floor rear window. Although the cost to the innocent old people they robbed was enormous, the brothers weren't considered big enough fish to justify surveillance, so we just had to hope someone would catch them in the act. When they did, they'd simply bounce in and out of the courtroom and would carry on burgling while on bail. After all, we might have caught them committing a crime, but we hadn't cured their addiction to drugs. The habit demands feeding.

One of the best ways to solve crimes and catch burglars is to open a sting shop (usually disguised as a second-hand electronics store) and spread the word that this shop was buying anything anyone cared to sell, no questions asked.

Sting shops are very effective but considered resource-intensive and so we were never allowed to do them in Surrey, although they have been used in London with much success. Usually, within days of their opening, every last scrote in the locality swaggers through the doors with stolen goods, everything from silver-tipped walking sticks and stuffed animals to laptops and TVs. In one case, the shop developed such a reputation amongst the criminal community that a gang offered the shop owner a selection of guns.

So, setting aside the fact that drugs are rife in some prisons, our best hope when going after burglars was to lock them up and hopefully persuade them to clean up while inside. At least while in prison they weren't stealing hundreds of thousands of pounds in property from taxpaying, law-abiding citizens. And that's what police work is all about.

8

The Criminal Protection Service

A TRAFFIC OFFICER PULLED OVER A speeding car. When the driver's door opened, an extremely drunk MP tumbled out onto the pavement.

It went to court. The defence barrister – obviously instructed to do whatever was necessary to get his client off the charges to save his licence – was excessively aggressive. His main point of attack was that the officer had no right to stop the MP, who had not been driving erratically.

'Why did you stop him?'

'I thought he was speeding.'

'Did you have a radar gun?'

'No.'

'Any form of speed measuring aid?'

'No.'

'Then how could you know?'

'I've been doing this for 22 years, so I consider myself a good judge.'

The barrister threw his pencil across the courtroom.

'So, officer, can you tell the court how fast that was going?'

Without a second's hesitation and in a perfectly dry tone, the officer said, 'I don't know, mate, I've never driven a pencil.'

The MP was duly prosecuted for drink-driving.

Giving evidence is a performance – sometimes a very difficult one – and police officers, used to dealing with tough and tricky questioning, often come up with some outstanding responses to barristers' questions.

You quickly get to know the different barristers and can gauge how good/bad they are. I've got into the witness box in the past and shared a look and a slight smile with the barrister, knowing we've had a decent tangle before.

Detectives can spend an awful lot of time in court, waiting to give evidence. It can drive you a little stir crazy, as you know there's a whole host of criminals out there you should be chasing. All you can do is pace the corridors, drink machine-made coffee and swap stories – and come up with daft ideas to pass the time.

A senior police officer once said, 'The courts have become a playground for barristers.' And while this might be true, as they look for any loophole or technicality to get their client off a charge and waste police time at every opportunity, some detectives have on occasion turned the courtroom into their playground.

With the worst minor repeat offenders, shoplifters who were on their fourth or fifth appearance in court, we sometimes bet each other who could fit the most song titles by a certain artist into our evidence, so you could hear the following phrases:

'After we got him to *surrender* . . .'

'The defendant was *all shook up* after the arrest.'

'Well, you might think that, if you're of a *suspicious mind*.'

'I told him to keep quiet, that I wanted *a little less conversation* . . .'

A judge, having encountered us before, once arrived at his bench and sat down, looking us all in the eye as he did so. 'I trust, gentlemen, that there will be no tomfoolery this time?'

Courtroom tomfoolery can be taken too far.

London barrister Mark Saunders was shot dead by firearms officers at his Chelsea home in May 2008 following a five-hour armed stand-off. A jury ruled that Saunders, who was an alcoholic and armed with a 12-bore shotgun during the siege, had been killed lawfully.

It has been alleged that the firearms officer who may have fired the fatal shot inserted a variety of song titles into his testimony in November 2010. The *Guardian* newspaper got hold of a transcript and found a number of possible song titles in the officer's testimony: 'Enough Is Enough' by Donna Summer, 'Point of No Return' by Immortal Technique, 'In the Line of Fire' by Journey, 'Quiet Moments' by Chris de Burgh, 'Self Preservation' by the Lucksmiths and 'Fuck My Old Boots' by the Membranes.

For example:

'I switched the light on, he turned towards me and I thought: "*Fuck my old boots*, I've got a gun trained on me . . ."'

'As he brings the gun down, his finger could be on the trigger. Action will always beat reactions. We have to decide where that point is and, for me, as he was bringing it down, I thought, "No. *Enough is enough*."'

As Saunders' mother Rosemary said, 'If it's all such a game, was it a game on 6 May? If this man can approach the inquest with such an attitude, then it makes you wonder about how he approaches shooting his gun to kill a man.'

The Independent Police Complaints Commission (IPCC) cleared the officer, concluding that the song titles in the officer's evidence were 'everyday, colloquial words and phrases that had legitimate and relevant meaning to the inquest'. In March 2011, however, it was reported that the same officer was facing a misconduct hearing after he'd subsequently admitted boasting to a senior colleague that he had, in fact, inserted song titles into his evidence. The officer explained that this boast had been a tasteless joke, a 'flippant remark as an act of bravado', caused by the stress as a result of the inquest.

In another case, we stood in court accused of fitting a suspect up. The man, known as 'Blacks', a violent drug-dealing Yardie, was horrible. He carried a gun and his standard MO was to intimidate local drug dealers and set up shop in their house, where he ruled by fear.

We'd previously put him away for 18 months, but as soon as he was out he got straight on with business.

We just happened to be watching another dealer when Blacks turned up and we arrested him after he'd sold crack to one of our officers.

The case was rock tight – except for one thing: the paperwork. The young detective who was supposed to fill in the surveillance log hadn't done it properly, so had crossed out sections before overwriting.

When the barrister saw this, he claimed we'd altered the logbook so that it contained the incriminating evidence we needed in order that we could arrest and charge his client, who was, in fact, innocent. On top of this, the ID from the test purchase officer wasn't that great; there'd been some hesitancy on his part during the identity parade.

When a case like this starts to fall apart in court, my mouth goes dry and my heart starts to pound. All those months of hard work were suddenly hanging by a thread, thanks to a simple mistake in a surveillance log.

The defence barrister must have been a fan of Kenneth Branagh. He spoke as if he were Henry V, pacing the floor theatrically: 'I must remind you that you are under oath and that perjury is an extremely serious offence. Now, are there any circumstances in which you would lie in the courtroom?'

Of course we all said 'No' very firmly, explaining what great cops we were, with all our many years of good service and files full of commendations – that is, until the barrister got to John, aka 'Shady', who was two weeks away from retirement.

'Are there any circumstances in which you would lie in the courtroom?' the barrister asked John.

'Yeah, there is,' he replied.

The barrister nearly choked. He could hardly believe his luck.

'Really?' he asked. 'You would lie in court?'

'Well, yeah, in certain circumstances I would.'

My heart was pounding. What the hell was John doing?

'Under what circumstances, detective, would you lie in court?'

Shady paused for a moment. The entire court was still, focused. He cleared his throat.

'If I was standing where your client is, pal.'

The judge fined him £500 for contempt of court, but he did it with a smile.

Sadly, Blacks walked free, thanks to the identity issues.

In my experience, judges were often as frustrated by solicitors, barristers and bureaucracy as we were. Many were as mad as a box of frogs fed on skunk and amphetamines and were totally unpredictable. Once a judge arrived in court in a bad mood and, seeing a barrister without his wig, demanded that all the barristers line up before him for an inspection, military-parade style. They did it, too.

One sunny autumn afternoon, we picked up Jonny, a regular offender who'd tried to use a credit card at a cashpoint two minutes after it had been stolen in a burglary. We had him on the bank's CCTV camera, so matchsticked his door and found enough evidence to tie him to at least six other burglaries.

His story was that he had found the card in the park and, as his girlfriend was having a baby (so he said) and they were desperately short of cash, had tried to use it. When we proved this story to be nonsense (he said he found the card before the burglary had taken place), he said that in fact someone else had done the burglary and had then given him the card (out of the goodness of his heart, obviously).

Jonny created quite a scene at the court holding cells, screaming at his brief about what he would and would not plea to. Eventually, the flustered barrister was standing in front of His Honour Judge Fergus Mitchell.

'What is your client's plea?' the judge asked.

'My instructions are that he will accept handling stolen goods.'

Judge Mitchell had read the case file. The impossibility of this being a simple case of handling was clear. Jonny really was, in the great police tradition, bang to rights for burglary.

'Let's see if two weeks in prison will change his mind. Remand him.'

Two weeks later and Jonny had a new barrister.

'Are we any further forward, Mr Smith?' the judge asked the barrister.

'In terms of a plea, my client will accept handling.'

Judge Mitchell took off his glasses.

'I see. Might I suggest you review the file and' – at this point he rose to his feet and turned it up to eleven – 'if your client comes back with handling next week I' – now slapping his hands on the bench, in time with each word – 'WOULD – BE – MOST – DISSAPPOINTED!'

The following week, fearful His Honour would send him down for a year just for being a stupid idiot, Jonny pled to burglary and went to prison for six months.

There is one man whom I wish I could tell you more about. Unfortunately, because of the way the case worked out, I have to leave out some parts and be rather circumspect with the remainder.

He was jailed for a multimillion-pound VAT fraud, which he appealed. During the appeal, it emerged that Customs officers had used a participating informant but hadn't told the defence (as they're supposed to). This was enough to overturn the conviction – the power of paperwork once more.

Fearful of the Proceeds of Crime Act, which meant he could potentially end up handing his assets over to the government, the man, let's call him 'Bobby', signed his house and everything else he owned over to his wife.

When Bobby got out, he wanted them back. His wife, let's call her 'Theresa', told him to sod off. Shortly after this, Theresa fell down a set of concrete stairs.

She was badly injured but survived.

Then somebody stabbed her and locked her in her bedroom to bleed to death.

Again, Theresa was badly injured but survived.

When we found out about these attacks and wanted to prosecute her husband, Theresa was too scared to support us. So we ran our own prosecution and Theresa became a 'non-competent witness'. Life with this despicable man had left her with terrible physical scars, severe mental-health issues and an alcohol problem. We could hardly rely upon her in court.

Between us all we wrote up the paperwork better than Shakespeare. We even managed to get Bobby remanded. His first bail hearing was held at the Old Bailey. The defence argued that their client was not a violent man.

The judge asked for evidence from me, Bill and Tim. He accepted everything we said and remanded him.

At this point Bobby jumped the rail, screaming at Bill, 'I'm going to kill you, you cunt!'

That ended the 'not a violent man' argument.

Bobby tried applying for bail again. This time when it was refused he shouted at the judge, 'You fucking old cunt. I hope your wife dies of cancer!'

She had, three months earlier.

The judge leant over to the recorder and said, 'Make a note, will you please, that this man, when he is next in this court for anything – anything, you understand – is to be brought before me and only me.'

A third-party prosecution is very hard to run. It involves running a case without a witness – it's hard enough to get anywhere with a competent, compelling and cooperative witness. In the end, the CPS offered no evidence because even though all of us gave evidence that we had seen Theresa injured on numerous occasions she would not corroborate the injuries or say that he'd done it. Sadly, the prosecution collapsed and the case was withdrawn.

A few weeks later, Theresa was found dead at the bottom of a flight of stairs.

We brought Bobby in and he assaulted all of us, making appalling threats. There were no witnesses. The CPS decided not to prosecute.

Theresa had been drinking heavily, so she could quite easily have fallen, as the coroner concluded.

Customs eventually put Bobby away for a few years for another VAT scam, but it just wasn't enough.

These sorts of cases are heartbreakers; enough to drive experienced detectives over the edge with frustration and unspent anger. It was just as exasperating trying to persuade the Criminal Prosecution Service to take the case to court.

The CPS has the final say on what a suspected criminal should be charged with. The problem is that their decisions are not so much based on getting the best possible justice for the innocent citizen but rather on the size of their budget, government conviction rate targets and the time of day.

The CPS has a limited budget and their solicitors have to answer to superiors who have an eye on the conviction rate, which has to meet government targets, which in turn means they only like to take 'bang to rights' cases. The CPS denies this, but as Alan Gordon, the vice-chairman of the Police Federation said, 'It's a shambles. The CPS charges people only when it knows it can get an easy conviction.'

The CPS was publicly criticised for not prosecuting the model Kate Moss for allegedly taking cocaine. Following an eight-month investigation, the CPS decided that although video evidence provided 'an absolutely clear indication that Ms Moss was using controlled drugs and providing them to others', the 'precise nature' of the drug could not be established and therefore there was 'insufficient evidence' to prosecute.

The CPS also keep an eye on the clock. They only work Monday to Friday, 9–5, so all the cases we'd end up dealing with after 5 p.m. and over the weekend (when most crimes happen) would get backed up overnight, meaning they were always in a hurry. That is until CPS Direct (CPSD) arrived as a pilot scheme in 2003, before being rolled out in 2006. CPSD is an out-of-hours system that runs from 5 p.m. to 9 a.m. If you've arrested someone within these hours and want to charge them, you call a 0800 number, enter your two-digit force code and a random lawyer answers. You explain the case, fax the paperwork and they make a decision.

CPSD are renowned for charging jobs that a local wouldn't because they are not answerable to the local CPS office. The work is more demanding and unsocial, and decisions have to be made quickly, so the pay is considerably better, hence only the best get hired. This proved to be quite useful, as long as you knew how to abu— – sorry, use – the system correctly.

Once I sent through a potential armed robbery, which, I admit, was 'optimistic', but the lawyer said, 'Go for it! Charge away.'

'Are you sure?' I asked.

'Yeah,' he insisted. 'It's a bit of fun for me. I don't have to answer to your bosses and I can charge whatever I want.'

After that we used CPS Direct whenever we could, even waiting to ask for a legal opinion from 3.30 p.m. until 5 p.m., when we knew a 'weak' CPSD lawyer was on call. As soon as CPS left the building, we'd start dialling CPSD.

Although CPSD was generally much better than the local office, sometimes we'd end up with a lawyer practising in deepest Somerset, which could cause problems if we were trying to charge a tenuous gun-crime job. A lawyer such as this wouldn't necessarily have the experience of fighting inner-city legal cases and know that there are all sorts of reasons to pursue a case besides the obvious one (intelligence, other crimes, keeping a dangerous person off the streets, protecting potential witnesses, making it easier for witnesses to come forward, and so on).

As a result, I used to open up with, 'Hello, it's Officer A from Surrey here. Who am I talking with and where are you based? Just for my notes, you understand ... Rural-on-River?' I'd hang up and redial until I found a lawyer in Hackney or Liverpool or any other inner city.

I quickly built a relationship with the best of them. I kept a few email addresses for some of my favourites. One would charge anything and often recommended more serious charges than we'd asked for. This enabled us to re-crime, achieving better clearance results for serious crimes. At court, the charges would usually be dropped back to what we'd originally asked for, but we still had our clearance for the stats ('clearance' will be explained; there's a whole chapter on stats).

One lawyer liked to while away his long nightshifts with a bottle or two of Cabernet Sauvignon. Anything after 10 p.m. would result in a charge.

Another lawyer, openly disgusted at the new CPS system, would charge anything for us because in his own words, 'That's what we're all here for. And if the head of your local branch doesn't like it, he can whistle.'

I'd email these three (who were based in Manchester, Dagenham and Hackney) half an hour before dialling the number. Nine times out of ten, one of them would pick up.

Even with the creation of CPS Direct, prosecutions that required substantial and skilled arguments delivered by barristers to a jury were not embraced with a passion for justice nor with excitement at the prospect of a good courtroom battle. Instead, the CPS looked for the easiest option – plea-bargaining.

Every job I've ever worked on has involved plea-bargaining. Every last one.

I've seen charges reduced from attempted murder to assault, and GBHs reduced to ABHs. I once arrested a drug dealer with 4 kg of coke and an 8-round sawn-off pump-action shotgun with a modified pistol grip (the hit-man's favourite). He also had a .357 Magnum revolver with 150 rounds of ammo of assorted calibres.

'I didn't know they was guns,' he said. 'They was packaged in boxes and I thought it was drugs. How should I know?'

'That doesn't matter,' I told him. 'You're going down for seven years.'

It doesn't matter what the item is, only that you had guilty knowledge. So if you've been ripped off by a coke dealer and are arrested with four sacks of flour (which you thought was coke), you're charged as if it was cocaine. If you think you have stolen property hidden in a box and it turns out to be a gun, then you're charged on the gun because you knew you were in possession of something illegal.

(So even if Kate Moss was whacking flour up her nose, she should have been charged with offering to supply by her actions and demonstrated knowledge, or to use lawyers' Latin: *mens rea* plus *actus reus*.)

The guns were fine, but then he claimed that the 4 kg of coke was for personal use. The CPS agreed.

'You can't seriously accept this!' I said. 'If he took 1.5 gm of coke every 12 hours, he'd end up in hospital in a few weeks, most probably the psychiatric ward. He had two years' supply at that rate. And where did he get the 30 grand per kilo to buy it? He lives in a bedsit in Thames Ditton.'

I had to spend three hours appealing to a superintendent and the deputy chief prosecutor before they finally went for possession with intent. We won the case.

I've also seen people walk away from court after being caught with 2 kg of cannabis, claiming it was for personal use, and attempted murder reduced to actual bodily harm. I've watched as defence and prosecution barristers haggle over crimes: 'OK, how about we accept the aggravated burglary and you forget about the subsequent rape? You're never going to get a rape conviction. You could try if you want, but it's a long and expensive way to hear "he says, she says" only for the foreman of the jury to say, "We don't know.'" A handshake and it's done. Money saved, crime successfully prosecuted, everyone's happy except the victim.

This is why detectives often refer to the CPS as the 'Criminal Protection Service'.

Bill and I were in a corridor in the nick when Hilary, 'Hills', stormed past us. Tears were streaming down her face and she marched past us without a word.

I chased after her. 'Hills, what happened?' I asked.

'I've had enough of this fucking job!'

She'd arrested a rogue trader who'd conned and then spent the £50,000 life savings of a little old lady.

The victim was lovely, just like your favourite nan, but she'd clearly been worn down by what had happened.

'The CPS went to the superintendent behind my back and agreed on a plea, so that bastard gets a two-year suspended sentence.'

Hills told us she planned to shove her warrant card into one of the superintendent's orifices. Bill and I held her back in the corridor and, after an hour, we talked her out of it. Hills went on to become a detective sergeant.

The little old lady died not long after; the trauma of the loss was too much, as was the impossibility of the idea that she might get some of her money back.

Two regular offenders spent an evening pestering their neighbour, a 16-year-old girl called Sue, to come round their house 'to party'. When Sue refused, they armed themselves with samurai swords and, in front of witnesses, kicked her door down, yelling, 'We're going to kill you!' They slashed the walls with their swords as they climbed the stairs. They then dragged the 16 year old out of the house, across the street and into their own.

Two friends saw them carrying Sue into the house at the last minute and tried to rescue her. They hoofed the door down but were badly beaten during their rescue attempt – which turned out to be successful. Sue was left too terrified to go out afterwards.

I managed to get the two scrotes in bracelets and charged them with aggravated burglary, false imprisonment, kidnap and public order – and, to my delight, they confessed.

I passed the file on to a senior CPS lawyer. She took a quick look and said, 'Overcharging again, are we?'

'Not this time. It simply doesn't get better than this. They 'fessed up.'

The CPS reduced the charges to affray (without telling me because they knew I'd mount a very 'robust' challenge) and the men (who had long records, don't forget) were both given non-custodial sentences. They were free to go back home, just across the road from Sue.

To deal with this kind of outcome, as a police officer you have to cultivate a 'nothing to lose' attitude to life: even if you make the perfect arrest, spend weeks working late to build a case, developing finger calluses getting the paperwork just perfect, if the CPS doesn't think it's worth it, your hard work is reduced to nothing.

It is another reason why police humour can be so dark, why we muck about in serious situations, from the courtroom to the crime scene. It isn't funny to a lot of people and that's understandable, but it's there because we deal with horror and despair (often our own) on a daily basis.

I was supposed to be protecting the good citizens of Surrey from criminals, but much of the time it felt like I had to protect them from CPS decisions. When they destroy a case, you really do need to hit something – even if it is just the bottle. This can lead to some very dark humour indeed.

* * *

Talking of barristers and bottles, one of the best senior officers I ever worked for was then Chief Superintendent Lynne Owens (now Chief Constable of Surrey).

Lynne won the amorous affections of an overconfident defence barrister during a murder trial. The prosecution barrister heard him boasting to his team how he was planning to seduce her, and so he told Lynne.

The next time she saw the defence barrister she said, 'If I win this case, then you buy me dinner. If you win this case, then I buy you dinner.'

As far as he was concerned, this was a win-win situation.

Well, although he was a top-notch barrister, we won. Lynne chose the county's most expensive restaurant.

On the night, the barrister rolled up, draped in old school Savile Row, double-breasted pin stripe, eyes full of hope. He stopped in the doorway and a look of shock crossed his face.

Lynne, who was standing in the middle of the restaurant, welcomed him. 'Oh, you did realise I meant the loser buys dinner for *the entire team*, didn't you?' Us cops all raised our champagne glasses – we occupied every table.

He took it in good humour and stumped up for the five-figure bill. He was paid enough, after all.

Of course, some police officers push 'humour' and tomfoolery beyond any sensible limit.

Two officers were about to leave Scotland Yard after a day of counter-terror training. They were waiting for the lift, which was coming down from the top floor. Assistant Commissioner Cressida Dick was inside but out of uniform and so they didn't recognise her.

'Going down, lads?' she asked.

'Not without a kiss and a cuddle first, luv!' one of them snapped back before the pair fell about into hysterics. Cressida was not amused. [16]

---

[16] They got their jobs back on appeal.

9

A Day of Rest

22 OCTOBER 2002 WAS SUPPOSED TO be my rest day but, as was often the case, I'd come in with Bill at 7 a.m. to catch up on paperwork. We were raiding a drug dealer at 6 a.m. the following morning and were expecting it to tie us up for the rest of the week, so this was our last chance to get through the reams of files, folders and forms that had accumulated over the past few days.

We were almost finished, alone in the office eating bacon butties at 2 p.m., when the phone rang. Bill picked it up. A uniformed sergeant identified himself.

'I've just been called to a property,' he said. 'The door was wide open, the occupant was missing and um – well – I've found some paperwork and I've no idea what to do with it.'

'Paperwork?'

'Yeah. It's job related, I think. You really should come and take a look.'

'What do you reckon, Dangerous[17]?' Bill said, grabbing his keys. 'Shouldn't take long, eh?'

Twenty minutes later, we entered a small council flat. It was a mess, full of the detritus of drugs: spoons used to cook heroin, balls of foil, joint roaches, crack pipes and lager cans. We passed through into the bedroom, where – in stark contrast to its surroundings – sat a black canvas holdall. It was packed full of papers.

I picked up a file. It contained court transcripts.

---

[17] I had a habit of getting into scrapes, so I became 'Dangerous'.

'The door was kicked open,' the sergeant said. 'I've no idea how long it's been that way. Anyone could have come in afterwards.'

'Fucking hell, Bill, take a look at this.'

I passed the file over and pulled out another one. This one stopped me cold: it said, 'Bloggs X'.

'Good grief, you know what this is, don't you?'

'You've done it again, Dangerous,' Bill said. 'What have we just walked into?'

'Bloggs' is the prefix given to those people who end up in the witness-protection programme. This file contained the identity, both real and assumed, of one such witness, the court transcripts of the case for which he'd given evidence, to whom and exactly what about.

This witness had been caught selling guns to a criminal with a reputation for extreme violence on a street in Islington, North London. From the files, it seemed as though the witness had flipped straight away and told the cops about everyone he'd been working with, including the IRA. A lot of people went away for a great many years as a result.

Bill and I went house-to-house. A man in his dressing gown, smoking a cigarette, appeared behind the first door we knocked on. 'Yeah,' he said. 'I saw two blokes come by this morning. Massive, they were. Hard types. Didn't like the look of them at all. Proper criminals, if I ever saw any.'

So, two thugs had kicked in a door belonging to a man who'd given Queen's evidence against some of the most violent criminals in the country and had presumably removed him from the premises, leaving behind a bagful of documents that identified him.

'Better call the National Crime Squad,' Bill said. 'If he's not already, he's probably going to end up tied to a chair in an empty warehouse and will finish the day with a bullet to the back of the head.'

We found the witness's mobile number and telephoned Assistant Chief Constable Frank Clarke for an emergency trace. Clarke agreed and, as this was an emergency, gave us authorisation over the phone.

'I can't believe this has happened,' he said. 'Please, get this person back safely.'

In some ways, the scariest thing about the job at this stage was the paperwork that had been left sitting on the bed, as if it were no longer needed.

It should have been impossible to get hold of Bloggs paperwork. It meant someone on the National Crime Squad (NCS) was bent or had made an extremely grave error.

When his handlers turned up a few minutes later, we explained what we'd found.

They looked at each other. These guys were from one of the most secret intelligence units in the UK. They'd showed us their IDs, which weren't in their real names.

'So you've read it, then?' one of them asked.

'Well, yeah,' I said, 'but we'd love to know what the hell's going on here.'

'It was us that went through his door this morning.'

'So you left the papers there?'

'No, we were just looking for our Bloggs. We didn't look in the bag. We had no idea he had the papers or how on earth he got them.'

They told us the story so far.

They confirmed that the witness had been caught selling three US 9mm MAC-10 submachine-guns. Known as 'Big Macs', these can fire 1,200 rounds a minute. They'd also found silencers, ammunition and detonators. The witness turned informer and named 45-year-old Anthony Mitchell as the source of the guns.

Mitchell was later linked to the seizure of 130 guns from crime scenes that had been used for murders, shootings against police officers and in gang wars. One of Mitchell's associates was found to have 2.7 kg of plastic explosives, two shotguns and a submachine-gun at his home.

Almost all the hundreds of guns Mitchell supplied from his workshop in an industrial estate in Hove, East Sussex, came to him deactivated. In other words, they had been disabled so that they could not be fired – they were 'ornaments' for enthusiasts.

Mitchell, a former Special Constable for Sussex Police with a penchant for Harley-Davidsons, was also part of a group of 12 who travelled the world pretending to be British police officers so that they could enter shooting competitions.

This organisation, which was styled on the SAS, was known as the 'Black Shods'. They dressed in black boiler suits and webbing, and used fake police identification cards to enter competitions in the United States, Germany, the Netherlands and Belgium. They had even won a few trophies.

As a trained engineer, Mitchell had developed a technique to reactivate firearms that were supposed to be permanently out of action. He did not have a criminal record, so he'd been able to set himself up as a legitimate supplier of licensed firearms to gun clubs and collectors. He obtained a ready supply of deactivated guns from shops and mail-order firms. His secret work brought in the real money, however. His speciality was the MAC-10, which he reactivated by fitting a new barrel and breechblock.

Fifty MAC-10s were found at his workshop. Police tests identified more than a hundred MAC-10s – seized in Liverpool, Manchester, Glasgow, London and south-east England – as being supplied by Mitchell. As well as MAC-10s, which cost £1,100 each, including a silencer and 120 rounds, there were revolvers and pistols, costing between £400 and £500.

One of the weapons had been used in a street murder in Brixton, South London, in April 1997. Another was fired by a youth at police officers in Moss Side, Manchester.

We were interrupted when the results of Bloggs X's phone triangulation came back.

'And?' the NCS guy said. 'Where is he?'

'Islington, North London.'

'Jesus Christ, he's only gone back to his old stomping ground.'

One of them took out a mobile phone and dialled a number.

'Who are you calling?' I asked.

'X's ex-wife. He shopped her brother. He always said he still loved her. Maybe he's gone back to ask for her forgiveness. All the Bloggs lose it at some point. That's why we came knocking this morning. He called us in a highly agitated state, saying he couldn't stand living this way any longer, that he had to see her.'

'We'd thought the people he'd shopped had tracked him down.'

'Looks like he's turned himself over to them instead.'

'Why did you stick him in such a horrible flat? I'd lose it in there.'

'Policy,' he said. 'We put them back to the state they were in at the time we plucked them out of their former lives. X was living in a shitty council flat when he was nicked, although of course he was making a tidy sum from dealing in guns.'

'From the amount of drug-taking, it looked as though he'd been off the rails for a while.'

'Yeah, well, not the last time we checked, he wasn't.'

His colleague finally got through. He put his phone on speaker.

'Is he there?'

'Yeah, the little shit is here, all right.'

Thank God.

'He came back here begging me for forgiveness. I told him to go fuck himself and called everyone I know to let them know he's here.'

The other NCS guy exchanged a glance with Bill. 'We're gonna need to call SO19 and get them round there an hour ago,' he said.

'Where is he now?'

'He's lost the plot. He's curled up and crying on my living-room floor.'

What followed was a blur of phone calls, fast driving and the shutting down of a large block of North London as the NCS guys fought to get to their Bloggs in time. Thanks largely to the mighty resources of the Met Police, they extracted him safely and he was carted off to another shitty council flat in another part of the UK with another new identity. His miserable and lonely life would continue – until the next breakdown came.

It was midnight by the time Bill and I were finally able to stand down. 'Some rest day, eh, Dangerous?' Bill said as we left the Crime Factory.

Sure enough, the next day we were up at 5 a.m. for our 6 a.m. raid. Crime never sleeps and neither do cops . . . not much anyway.

10

A Different Kind of Hero

ONCE AGAIN, IT WAS SUPPOSED TO be a rest day, but I was working in Guildford on a hare-and-hounds surveillance training exercise. I was with a team on the streets, trying to keep track of a 'suspect' when my phone went.

'Hello, son. Can you talk?'

Dad – Jack – who'd retired a few years earlier as DS, was 59 but indestructible. He'd been the archetypical '70s and '80s copper: he drank Scotch, was good with his fists, a razor-sharp investigator and interviewer – Jack Regan personified, with the same relentless energy, but at the same time he was more of a gent in that he was also scholarly, a qualified teacher who spoke Latin.

Dad and Mum had separated and married three times during their relationship (I gave Mum away at the last one in Ireland), but finally it seemed as though they'd settled – a rare thing in cop relationships. After Dad's retirement, they'd moved to Cornwall.

'Hi, Dad. Yeah, no problem. I'm on foot obs, but I can talk.'

'Well, it's like this. You know that cough and chest I had that the doc thought might be asthma?'

'Yeah, what's up?'

'Well, there's no easy way to say this. Son, I've got lung cancer and I'm dying.'

I stopped walking, suddenly light-headed. What do you say to that? I quickly found the DS leading the course, explained I had to go and drove down to Cornwall. After that my sisters and I went down every week.

* * *

Not long after this I was out on foot observations with Simon in some woods on the hunt for a sex attacker.

On a Friday a few weeks earlier, at around 12.30 in the afternoon, Louise – an 18 year old with blonde, shoulder-length hair – was walking through the woods, which were near her college.

She heard someone running up fast behind her and, before she could scream, a man grabbed her, snarling: '*COME HERE.*'

Louise, who was a petite five foot five inches tall, had done a self-defence course. She dropped all her bodyweight to the floor, out of his grasp, and emptied her lungs with the biggest scream of her life.

Startled, the man ran off, but not before Louise got a good look at him. Bruised and shocked, she stumbled out of the woods onto the road and into the arms of passers-by, who called the cops.

Louise's account was taken down and a crime report generated, which was then allocated to a DC at Esher. Louise later provided an e-fit image of her attacker.

He was:

> white
> 5 ft 11 in.
> in his late 20s
> of proportionate build, with short, cropped dark hair
> wearing black trousers and a black T-shirt with a white-and-
>   green logo on the left breast

Four weeks later, at 11.45 on a Friday morning, Sigita, a 17-year-old Czech au pair, was walking in the same area but closer to the railway station. She had light-brown to blonde shoulder-length hair and was five feet four inches tall.

She saw a man walking quickly towards her. As the two drew level, he spun around, grabbed her by the collar and thrust his hand up her skirt. He tried to pull her into nearby bushes, saying, 'Come on, come on.' Sigita screamed and struggled out of his grip and ran off towards the station still screaming. The family she was au pairing for called the police and the job was allocated to a different DC.

Sigita's description of the attacker was:

> white
> 5 ft 8 in. to 6 ft
> aged 25 to 30
> of proportionate build, with short, cropped light hair
> wearing dark clothing; his shirt had a logo on the left breast and
> a collar

The following Friday, 29-year-old Nicola was walking in the same woods, cutting through from her house to the main road at 12.17. She had blonde, shoulder-length hair and was five feet six inches tall. She heard running footsteps behind her and a man grabbed her, throwing her to the floor. She screamed and fought back as he tore at her clothes. In the struggle, she rolled over onto her back and came face-to-face with her attacker. Nicola refused to surrender and kicked out hard, causing the attacker to lose his grip and flee. Nicola went home, called the police and gave them a description.

He was:

> white
> 5 ft 7 in. to 5 ft 10 in.
> of proportionate build, with short, dark hair
> in his mid-20s, with stubble
> wearing dark clothing; a polo shirt with a red logo on the left
> breast

A crime report was generated and it came to me. I logged onto the CISS (Crime Information System and Storage, also called the CIS) and searched for any linked jobs and the other two came up. It was obvious this was the same guy, so I went to see Bill.

'What worries me is that the time between attacks has shrunk, while the violence has escalated,' I said.

It wouldn't be long, Bill and I thought, before this extremely deranged man raped and/or killed a woman in these woods.

The timing of the attacks and the description of his clothing suggested it was a local worker on his lunch break. As I'd identified the series, Bill agreed to allocate the other two jobs to me and we started looking at them all in detail.

In the first case (Louise), there wasn't much, just the initial statement. When I checked to find out why, I found that the DC in charge had been pulled out of the office by the dreaded Department of Professional Standards (an Orwellian police body that deals with officers' wrongdoings), who were investigating him for parking an unmarked police car at the railway station and taking the train to and from work. Nothing wrong with that per se – unless you're claiming the petrol expenses at 40 pence per mile and using a Surrey warrant card to get free passage on the train.

Nothing had been done with the second job either, mainly because no one had sorted out an interpreter to take a statement in Czech and translate it into English, then write out a report in both Czech and English.

I collated what little I had on all three attacks, arranged for the seized clothing to go off to the lab, so the boffins could check for DNA, and performed a CCTV trawl across the area. Nothing came up.

I put the case to Bill that we needed to move fast. This guy was a proper psycho, I thought, a man who would undoubtedly strike again, and judging by the increasing use of violence would cause an innocent young woman significant harm.

'I agree. Jack the RIPA's up and let's see if we can get a surveillance team to take it.'

I hacked through the 18-page Regulation of Investigatory Powers Act 2000 surveillance application form. It helps the powers that be decide if a job is PLAN:

Proportionate
Legal
Appropriate
Necessary

It also sets out what equipment you'll use, how, why, where and when. It contains an operational order and risk assessment (a separate 15–20 page document) and then it goes off to be sanctioned by a superintendent or above before being cleared at Central Authorities Bureau, who then become a total fucking pain about collateral intrusion and case law. It's reviewed every three months, using the same form-filling process, and when the job is over you have to fill in the Cancellation of Directed Surveillance, another ten-pager setting out what happened, whether there were any compromises and so on.

It was turned down. The job, they said, was too hit-and-miss and covered too wide an area to be put under surveillance properly. So, our last resort was to patrol the area in plain clothes and hope for the best. Four of us took the slots: myself and Simon were on one side of the woods, the other two the other side. I briefed the team and circulated the descriptions, as well as the e-fit picture, amongst the local uniformed police.

The following Friday we were on the plot. I wasn't really expecting to get a result. It's said that if you catch the 'proverbial burglar' coming out of a window once in a career, then you've done well. So catching a potential rapist, in the act, with four of us covering an area three miles square, would be a miracle.

The other two hung around at the top end of the woods, near the railway station, and Simon and I walked past the scene of each of the attacks, heading deep into the woods. It was a typical August day; a fine drizzle slowly soaked us through.

Forty-five minutes later we popped out of the woods and into a lay-by on the main road. Just in front of us was a white Ford high line transit van with the logo of a classified listings company on the side. The driver was a white male.

'Let's have a look at this bloke,' I said. 'Breaks it up a bit, eh?'

As we approached the van, he started the engine, so I pulled down the flap on my coat that revealed my police badge and signalled the driver to stay put, which he did. We approached the driver's door and asked him to step out, which he did.

It was 11.42 in the morning.

He was:
 white
 late 20s
 5 ft 9 in.
 of proportionate build, with short, dark, cropped hair
 wearing white trainers, black combat trousers and a polo shirt
  with a logo on the left breast

Just to be sure, I unfolded the e-fit picture. It might as well have been a portrait of this guy.

I asked his name.

'Marc Christophe,' he replied.

'You usually around here on Friday lunchtimes?'

'Yes, I finish early Friday afternoons, so I have my lunch here, hope I don't get any more deliveries and then head home.'

I arrested him on suspicion of indecent assault and false imprisonment.

This went out over the air and the DCI rang me.

'Is it him, though?' he asked. 'How positive are you?'

'Guv'nor, if this isn't the same guy and he's not ID'd, I will bare my behind in the CID office.'

'OK, OK. Good work. Keep me updated.'

We booked Christophe into custody and seized his clothing. Another DS, Tim and me interviewed him without a solicitor, as he waived his right to legal representation.

Again, he made several significant statements about times, descriptions and locations but denied the offences. We arrested him for more offences and, at this point, he lawyered-up. We interviewed him twice more and from this point on he only answered, 'No comment.'

Dad was desperately ill and I was due to drive down to Cornwall the next day. That night Tim and I organised an emergency live ID parade in Brixton. Nowadays, it's always done via video over a computer network, but, as this was an emergency, we did it the old-fashioned way, through one-way glass.

Tim and I also stitched together as much of a court file as we could, in readiness to try to remand him should the ID parade go our way. At around half-eleven, I got home and packed a bag. Early the next morning I left for Cornwall. I was halfway there when I saw the DCI had left a message on my phone.

'Excellent work. All three victims picked your man out. We'll speak more about this later, but well done – and even better, we're all spared the horror of an arse-baring!'

When I arrived in Cornwall, I played this message to Dad, who smiled and gave a thumbs-up. Minutes later he had a seizure from the tumours that had now spread to his brain. The doctor was called and Dad was sedated. Once we'd calmed him down, I rang Tim.

'Bad news,' he said. 'Muncy drove one of the witnesses to the ID parade.'

This was a big no-no because Muncy had been present at the arrest and therefore could not be said to be independent of the investigation. This was in breach of PACE (Police and Criminal Evidence Act, Code D) and would cause us problems at trial.

Nonetheless, Christophe was charged with six offences of assault, abduction for the purposes of sex and indecent assault.

The defence picked up on our mistake. Then they called me about another issue. 'We don't think it was Christophe,' the barrister said.

'Right,' I said, trying not to add, 'You do surprise me.' Instead, I asked, 'Do you have someone else in mind?'

'We think your attacker was Tony King [aka Tony Bromwich, aka The Costa Killer, aka The Holloway Strangler].'

Forty-year-old King had made headlines after murdering two young women in Spain. Since his arrest, he'd been investigated for a number of attacks and rapes committed in the UK, including some in West London. King was also, for a while, one of the chief suspects in Operation Ruby, the investigation into the murder of Milly Dowler.

This, to me, seemed ridiculous, but to satisfy the defence I needed to 'eliminate him from our inquiries'. I spent several days carrying out numerous checks with officers running the Operation Washfield investigation into King, Operation Ruby and with analysts from the Serious Crime Analysis Section (SCAS) at Bramshill in Hampshire (their job is to identify the potential emergence of serial killers and serial rapists at the earliest stage of their offending).

When I spoke to one of the senior investigating officers on Operation Ruby, I said, 'This is a total waste of both of our precious police time, isn't it?'

'You know that and I know that,' he replied, 'but if we don't do it, then they'll hang you with it in court.'

When I came back to the barrister with the news that King hadn't travelled to the UK on those dates, he suggested that he could have come through the Channel Tunnel and therefore would have bypassed any airports. So off I went to Eurostar.

Eventually, I established that unless King had used a disguise, a false passport and had left a doppelgänger back home in Spain, he could not have been in the UK on the dates of the attacks.

So began that long, lonely and difficult part of police work for which there are no commendations: paperwork.

I know everyone bashes police bureaucracy. But really, it's no good moaning about it. We're stuck with it and, if we're going to put bad guys in prison, we've got to do it properly.

One of the first questions Bill asked me when I joined the CID was: 'What's your paperwork like, son?'

'Why?'

'If you can fill in an MG6 at 3 a.m. in the morning after a day spent in a surveillance car, with two minutes of action for the arrest, followed by processing and a few hours of interviews, then and only then will you be a tech, my son.'

The poet Yeats wrote: 'Why should we honour only those that die upon the field of battle? A man may show as reckless a courage in entering into the abyss of himself.'

This is what detectives across the country find themselves doing in the small hours, as they battle with the Manual of Guidance, a 300-page brick of a book designed to help you build a file that will see Johnny Criminal sent down for the maximum stretch – theoretically.

I was once at a family get-together where the new police generation competed with the old generation in terms of who had/has it harder. I settled the argument over paperwork by bringing down a file from my briefcase/suitcase and laying it out along a 14-seat dining-room table. It wasn't long enough, or wide enough.

The younger cops looked at the retired officers' expressions of disbelief and so we explained each and every form and process. My old man shook his head and asked, 'If this is your case prep, how the fuck do you get anything else done?'

That's a very good question.

And as one of the world's finest modern writers David Foster Wallace wrote in his unfinished masterpiece *The Pale King*: 'Routine, repetition, tedium, monotony, ephemeracy, inconsequence, abstraction, disorder, boredom, angst, ennui – these are the true hero's enemies, and make no mistake, they are fearsome indeed. For they are real.'

Wallace was writing about the heroic levels of boredom and tedium that many people have to endure, for little reward, no acknowledgement and a hell of a lot of abuse from those who don't understand the vital nature of this necessary work.

'Gentlemen,' he wrote, 'welcome to the world of reality – there is no audience. No one to applaud, to admire. No one to see you. Do you understand? Here is the truth – actual heroism receives no ovation, entertains no one. No one queues up to see it. No one is interested.'

Perhaps proving his point, Wallace killed himself before *The Pale King* – the central theme of which was tedium – was finished.

One of our unwritten rules was that no one went home if someone had a last-minute late-night job. For example, Tim nicked a burglar on a matched fingerprint and linking him to stolen property relating to about ten other burglaries. While two of us went to the scene, the remaining three started building the file. For some reason, Bill enjoyed doing the remand form (MG7). I'd take MG5 and MG6 (see below). Filling out all these forms required a similar (if not better) level of knowledge of the law as any barrister and took all night.

It started like this:

Front sheet: suspect's details, including name, address, date of birth
Report to prosecutor

MG4: the charges

MG5: case summary: the story of exactly what happened and evidence (this was almost exactly the same as the report to the prosecutor, so we had to write the same thing out twice)

MG6: a confidential information form that went to the prosecutor, describing witnesses, vulnerable victims, etc. (the defence don't get to see this one)

MG6c: a complete list of any unused material, such as an incident log, crime report, medical notebooks, booking-in sheets, a Post-It note with a phone number on it, etc., just in case the defence or prosecution felt like using any of it in evidence later on

There are 52 MG forms. It takes about three to four hours to put together a good remand file, with three detectives working overnight to build up a case file (if you're lucky and have all the information you need nearby).

A recent addition is the updated and infamous MG3 and 3a. The MG3 is actually a duplicate of the whole court file that goes into another report to the prosecutor so they can decide whether to charge or not. They usually send us back an MG3a, which is their report on why they won't prosecute.

Doing this kind of paperwork takes a lot of practice. One misplaced tick, sentence or empty space and the defence will seize upon it, urging the dismissal of the case or a retrial, or anything they can think of to save their client. Then an expensive investigation and an even more expensive trial (remember, it costs about £10k a day for one Crown Court) will have been for nothing.

It took three weeks for me to put together the paperwork for our sex attacker and four of us to carry it to the van.

Theresa May – the police's pin-up girl – has recently said that she's cut police bureaucracy and paperwork. She hasn't because it's impossible. For a start, cutting paperwork would mean we need more paperwork to eliminate the paperwork she wants to get rid of and replace that paperwork with some other paperwork. And this would lead to further confusion amongst those police officers who have just got to grips with the present system.

It's also impossible for another reason: the paperwork that now exists and is used in any way to prepare people for trial simply cannot be cut.

What would you do if you were in jail and you learned that some of the paperwork used to convict you is about to be abolished? Why, appeal, of course!

No one can afford to abolish any part of the current paperwork simply because we've used it as a tool to prosecute and imprison people. We, therefore, have to go through the current process, remembering that we have to prove guilt beyond reasonable doubt. The defence has to prove that on the balance of probabilities their client is not guilty. This is fair enough, but it does mean that someone's freedom often depends on a few strokes of the biro.

In drama-laden police memoirs, you often find your fair share of moaning about paperwork – also in fictional police stories, TV shows and so on. It's understandable, of course. It doesn't exactly make for exciting reading. You'd never come across a passage like this, for example:

> The officer mopped away the sweat and, pausing for a moment, he rubbed his calloused finger before returning to the MG6, remembering that any information that undermined the prosecution case, or assisted the defence in their bail application, would go on forms MG6C and E. This would require him to look up notes 34 and 35 (Smith v DPP, ex parte LEE) on MG6 in section 3 of the Manual Guidance form. 'Now, where was I?' he muttered, chewing the biro anxiously, thinking this form-filling was a little excessive for a push and shove between two eighteen year olds in a nightclub queue outside Bensons on the High Street.

Dealing with paperwork is a tedious battle that detectives fight every day. Whether we win or lose depends upon whether forms are filled in correctly and effectively. Sometimes, though, no matter how good your paperwork is, something unexpected can destroy your case in just a moment.

11

Dangerous Goes to Miami

BETWEEN PREPPING CHRISTOPHE'S PAPERWORK AND HIS trial, I went on a five-day holiday to Miami, which I had planned well in advance.

Our family had hosted a Colombian student called Lina in the UK for about three years while she was studying English. By the time she left, she'd become part of the family. She'd since become one of Colombia's top models and had moved to Miami.

I was single at this time. Lina had a boyfriend, but her friends were all similarly gorgeous, so I'd *really* been looking forward to this rare break from work.

It was my first night in town and Lina and I had been to dinner at Nobu in South Beach, a trendy sushi bar drawn straight from the set of *Miami Vice*. We were heading for Coconut Grove, one of the oldest and most expensive parts of Miami, for cocktails.

On the way, Lina started to look worried.

'What's wrong?' I asked.

'I think I took a wrong turn somewhere. This is a bad neighbourhood.'

I looked around and had to agree. The houses were ramshackle, the streets were dirty and the shops were lit by cheap neon. Men grouped on street corners were eying Lina's sports car with what looked to me like jealous hunger.

As we drove along a main road, I spotted a pair of headlights flashing erratically in the door mirror and I turned around. A car was speeding, swerving towards us. I could see it was going to hit us on our rear offside.

'Brace yourself!'

'*Que?*'

Lina screamed as our car spun 180 degrees before coming to a halt. I had a clear view of the other car and watched as it swerved off to the right, still speeding, onto a petrol station forecourt, where it hit a Hispanic male who'd been washing windscreens for loose change. He was thrown in the air, smashed into a parked van and landed on the concrete on his back. The car then struck a petrol pump at about 40 mph.

'You OK?'

Lina nodded.

'Call 911.'

Cops are trained to run towards danger, so I ran to the car that had hit us. The driver, an old man, was clutching his chest and moaning. He was making a noise, so he was OK, as far as I was concerned. There was a woman in the passenger seat – his wife. She had severe head injuries and no pulse. I took a closer look. The windscreen post had broken off and scythed through her head. She was gone.

There was a teenage girl in the back, their granddaughter. She was unconscious but breathing and had a pulse. I tipped her head back to keep the airway open, then ran over to the guy who'd been run over.

He was unconscious but breathing. His right leg had been amputated at the knee and was hanging on ligaments. His left leg was half-severed at the thigh. I could see he had a pulse, as blood was spraying everywhere out of his right leg.

Several other people had appeared, including several gang members with suspicious bulges in their jackets.

'Help me out here!' I said, taking off my belt, and one of the gang bangers came over and held the leg as I wound the belt around the guy's right thigh, turning it into a tourniquet. I drove my right elbow into the left side of the man's pelvis, drew the belt tight with my left and held it there. The bleeding slowed and practically stopped.

Ten minutes later the cops and fire brigade turned up, along with news crews. Incredibly, not only did the Hispanic guy survive but the doctors reattached his leg and he walked again about a year later. The driver, who'd had a heart attack, lived, as did his teenage granddaughter. His wife died at the scene.

Lina went to hospital with whiplash and then home. Her boyfriend, Jorge, picked me up in his Porsche and took me back to the hotel to change before taking me out for a very, very stiff drink. Jorge took good care of me, helping me to 'debrief' – chat about the accident and then about anything and everything – and gradually I decompressed.

The next day, the cops and fire crews found me and invited me to a beach barbecue, then took me out for a spot of deep-sea fishing on one of their boats. The beach cops then took me for a ride-along. There weren't many differences in our policing problems (terrible bosses, hopeless policies and a too-plentiful supply of drugs for which there was a large public appetite), but they sure didn't take any shit. Like almost every other police force in the world, they couldn't believe UK cops did it all unarmed.

'Well, some cops do carry guns in the UK now,' I said. 'I'm firearms trained.'

So I got an invite onto their SWAT tactical range for a shoot-off. We spent a day firing SIG Sauer P220 pistols and MP5 carbines, all fully automatic. I did well enough, but I couldn't really compete with these guys, who practised every week.

While I was out with the team, they found a meth lab and I got to call in their pro-active team for the raid. They were exactly like the Strike Team in *The Shield* and were supported by a SWAT team. This, for a UK cop, was very cool: I got to do all the fun parts with no responsibility or form-filling.

I was given a commendation from the City of Miami for an altruistic act and then it was time to go home, where another commendation was waiting for me (along with the rest of the team) for the investigation into the sex attacks. Unfortunately, this was about to take a very unpleasant turn.

* * *

We took Christophe to Kingston Crown Court in January the following year. Our prosecutor thought we had a good chance, but we were met with an unpleasant surprise just before the trial, when Witness Care informed us they'd failed to keep in contact with

Sigita, who'd moved home. We were one witness and one set of charges down before the trial had even started.

Then Witness Liaison left Nicola just outside the courtroom while Louise was giving evidence. Nicola looked through the door's window and saw Christophe, who'd bleached his hair.

'Is that him?' she asked. 'He looks totally different now.'

This was overheard by members of Christophe's family, and his brief was able to spin this in with a Turnbull direction, a legal term used in cases which rely heavily on witness identification.

The judge then had to inform the jury that although the witness might have been certain at the time she'd provided a statement and again when she had been on the witness stand, she might still be mistaken in her beliefs – basically, that eyewitness testimony is sometimes unreliable.

The jury came back not guilty on every count.

Did he do it? A jury of our peers said not.

I felt sick when I looked at the huge files of paperwork, and even worse when I went to talk to Louise and Nicola, who were a lot more understanding than I would have been.

Tim and I bought our barrister, Brian, a nice bottle of red and in the lift down we saw the defence barrister, Oscar, and I thanked him for a good trial.

His reply will stay with me forever.

'That's lovely, officers, but I don't know why you're thanking me. That man must be one of the luckiest defendants I have ever had.'

Christophe, proven innocent, moved away from the area. There were no more reported attacks on young women in those woods.

Not long after this, a series of almost identical assaults occurred in another part of southern England. The perpetrator was never caught.

Even when you do everything right, something, somewhere is bound to go wrong. That's the way of the job. All you can do is do your part and hope everyone else does theirs. It's one of the most frightening and frustrating parts of police work.

12

Love and the Law

RELATIONSHIPS BETWEEN POLICE OFFICERS ARE ALWAYS intertwined with the job. There's no escaping it. I met my wife at a fatal RTA (road traffic accident). A drug dealer, high and drunk at the wheel, had flipped his open-top car, killing his mate in the passenger seat by scraping his skull across the tarmac until his head popped. Some of the first responders were in shock, cups of sweet tea trembling in their hands, while the older ones who'd seen much worse shook their heads and smiled at the youngsters ruefully. You never get used to seeing this sort of horror, but you do stop shaking after a while.

I was on one side of the huge cordon; Helen was on the other. To get to her, I bought everyone who was manning the cordon a cup of tea and a Twix and delivered them personally, until I finally reached Helen.

'You're going to have to do better than that if you're interested in me,' she said. So I cooked spaghetti bolognaise for the entire relief to have an excuse to hang around and chat. The team emailed DCI Steve Rodhouse to tell him how much they appreciated what I'd done.

'That's very nice of you,' he said. 'But what's really going on?'

'Sorry, guv?'

'So, which WPC is it, then?'

I smiled. OK, you got me.

'Well, I hope you realise you're going to have to cook for every night team until they've all been fed otherwise the others will be writing to me asking why one team gets spagbol and the other doesn't.'

So I had to share my romance with Helen with the Job literally from day one – and it never changed.

Helen and I fell in love. She was beautiful, smart, ambitious and, just as importantly, was in the Job, so we at least understood what the other was going through.

We'd moved in together within a couple of weeks and soon shared ownership of two Labradors (Benson after the cigarettes, and Regan after Jack Regan of *The Sweeney*). I'd wanted Benson and Hedges, or Regan and Carter, but Helen wouldn't allow it so we split it.

My family loved Helen as well and there was no greater testament than that of my father who, shortly before he passed away had a two-hour conversation with her. He told her he was so happy that she'd found me and that he could die in peace, knowing that she was going to take good care of me.

Dad's death, three weeks before Christmas, hit me really hard. Bill was great, he came to the funeral and told me to take as much time as I liked: 'I'll still put you through the timesheets.'

Ian (from the Preamble) was there, too. Around 300 people attended altogether, most of them Job or former Job. I'd told Sussex Police the date, but they'd published the wrong one in their magazine – another hundred officers pitched up the following week.

Not long before he died, Dad saw me get one more commendation from the chief constable. During the ceremony, I introduced him to Superintendent Richard Morris (who's now a commander in the Met), along with DCI Steve 'Tin Tin' Rodhouse (also now a commander in the Met).

Dad wasn't quite with it – tumours had appeared in his brain and he was prone to the occasional Prince-Philip-style gaff. Steve, who'd been fast-tracked, looked very young for his rank.

After hearing them speak for a minute or so about modern policing, Dad, one of the Job's toughest cops, who'd chinned more blaggers than the entire Sweeney, looked Steve in the eye and growled, 'Does your mum know you're out?'

They were embarrassed enough to pretend they hadn't heard it. Dad nodded approvingly, as if he'd been proven right.

Bill didn't call me until after the holidays. It was a really nice winter's day and I was having a beer with a couple of friends from the local cricket team when he called. 'Now might be a good time to come back,' he said. 'You could do some nights, it's really quiet at the moment.'

Bill had forgotten himself – he'd used the Q-word.

The first night I had a rare and violent case of attempted stranger rape. The second night, I was just settling down to play a game of Scrabble with Matt, a learner detective, when we got the call: a savage assault, blood all over the street.

We were on the scene by 11 p.m. I had asked for a weather report and although it was cold and clear, control told me the forecast was for rain and high winds in two to three hours.

The two PCs on the scene were almost in tears, traumatised by the state of the victim. A witness who'd seen the attack was understandably blubbing like a child.

As I walked towards them, I noted something odd; they'd placed a cordon about six feet from the body. The scene needed to be preserved, in as wide a circle as possible, in readiness for a fingertip search, if needed. Even at this cold, late hour, people were starting to gather and had a clear view of the horror, as the paramedics tried to work a miracle on the victim.

'Lads, I know you're in shock, but I need you to sort the cordon right away. We need to go big; we can always draw them in later. I'll call for some more people to relieve you.'

As the two traumatised officers did their best to extend the cordon until support arrived, I approached the victim. He lay on a pathway between two bushes about two metres from his front door, his feet towards me. He didn't have any shoes on. His face, from crown to cheek had been pounded to shapelessness. His right eye had been smashed out of him and stamped upon. Brain matter was in his hair.

'He's still got a pulse,' one of the paramedics said.

Good God.

I then called their duty inspector, who told me they didn't have the staff. 'I don't care! If this whole estate isn't sealed off, then you can explain to the chief constable why you scuppered a murder investigation during the golden hour.'

The golden hour, as any detective knows, is that precious time immediately after an incident when most information, evidence and statements can be taken – when the crime scene is at its richest. Fortunately, the sergeant managed to rustle up a vanload of enthusiastic probationers.

We had a prime witness, but he was so overcome with shock that he needed hospital treatment, but not before we'd got the story.

The killer had gone into the pub and demanded a smoke from the victim, whose name was James, in a way calculated to start a row. They'd never met before. The landlord threw the killer out and CCTV later showed that he had waited outside the pub, peeking over the windowsill to check when James was leaving. When he did, the killer chased and attacked him three times in the street until he caught James near his front door and took a brick to his head – hitting him about thirty times. Afterwards, he removed James's shoes, crossed the road, sat down on the kerb, drank a can of beer, lit a cigarette, took his shoes off and put the dying man's shoes on. Then he turned the victim over and hit him another 20 times in the face with the same brick.

Gale force winds and freezing rain were now predicted to arrive within the hour. I rang the on-call divisional DS and DI: both of their phones were switched off.

James lived for another three hours. I sent a probationer WPC in the ambulance to keep a continuity record of events. 'Don't leave out anything,' I told her. She took it literally, to the point of gowning up in the crash room at A&E. When I saw her notes, I couldn't believe the detail. She had the exact timings, e.g., *'0034hrs: Nurse Smith removes victim's watch, 0035hrs: shirt removed by same.'* She'd hardly had any service but did a brilliant job, especially considering the hideous nature of this murder.

By then, I had the killer's name: Robert Wicks, 20 years old, with previous convictions for violence. He'd also been diagnosed as psychotic, but Wicks preferred to self-medicate, using skunk amongst other illegal drugs, which is known to induce psychosis.

Once we had a name, Matt and I were able to find his home. We then called the TST (Tactical Support Team, which raids homes, firearms-style, but without guns) and asked them to be on standby to crash the door and make the arrest.

Forensics had meanwhile managed to get a good collection of evidence despite public contamination and closed the scene before the rain arrived. By the time Major Crimes finally got their arse in gear, all they had to do was ask the TST to go in and get him. The credit was all theirs.

'A thank you would have been nice,' Matt said afterwards. It had taken us just a few hours to 'crack the case'.

I shrugged. 'Does it matter? The murderer's behind bars, isn't he?' But I had to admit I was just as annoyed as Matt.

Robert Wicks, who had a long history of violence, psychosis and drug abuse, was indefinitely detained. An inquiry found that he had been 'unwisely given the benefit of the doubt' by the probation service and his medical carers once too often.[18]

The very next night we got a major arson and then an attempted murder followed by an abduction. Matt and I were – to use the CID term – 'Kentucky fucked'.

When Steve Rodhouse saw me, he jokingly asked, 'What have you done to my division's figures? And in one week as well! From now on, Dangerous, you're banned from working nights!'

I always seemed to find myself at the centre of a storm, whether at work or not.

I hadn't seen Helen for a few weeks and so one miraculous day, when our rotas matched and the citizens of Surrey managed to stay out of trouble for once, we went out for dinner to a posh restaurant. We'd just settled down when my attention was drawn to a fat Middle

---

[18] A few weeks later, his elder brother, Billy overdosed after being released from Wandsworth. He was found on a park bench, needle in arm. Their mum (an alcoholic who dabbled in heroin) drove her car into the Thames and killed herself, leaving two young daughters in care.

Eastern be-suited businessman sitting in the corner. He looked uncomfortable, and was flushed and sweating.

A minute later three men with shaven heads and tattoos covering every part of their arms marched in and started verbally abusing him. The restaurant was quite full, but it fell quiet as the men continued to curse the businessman.

'I'm going to have to say something,' Helen said.

Why now? Why us? I thought.

The angrier Helen gets, the more posh she sounds. 'Would you mind keeping it down?' she asked. 'I'm *trying* to have a meal with my fiancé.'

This got their attention.

One of the men looked over. 'We're sorry, luv, but this guy has stitched us up for sixty grand and we're very angry.'

They quietened down, but 20 minutes later there were 12 tattooed tradesmen all demanding their money – money this man clearly didn't have.

They were ordering and drinking lots of beers and they soon became very loud. Other diners, sensing their evening was going to end badly if they stayed, started to leave. The restaurant owner looked on helplessly.

'Oh, for fuck's sake.' I got up and followed the man whom I guessed to be the leader to the toilets.

'Can I have a word?'

'Wot?'

'Look, you're never going to get your money back from this guy, here and now.'

'Don't you worry about that. I've got it all taken care of.'

'Oh yeah?'

'Yeah. I got three pikeys outside who are going to sort him out.'

Great, just great.

I took a quick look outside and, sure enough, three bare-knuckle-boxing types were standing beside a red transit.

Doing nothing clearly wasn't an option. As a cop, you have to react to something like this, even if you are off-duty.

'Call the station,' I said to Helen, as I passed our table. I went back to the bloke, tapped him on the shoulder and looked him straight in the eye.

'Guess what I do for a living.'

'Wot?'

'Of all the people in all the world, who would have been the worst one you could have told you were about to "sort someone out"?'

'Wot?'

'I am a police officer.' I said. 'This,' I continued, gesturing around the restaurant, 'isn't going to happen. You are not going anywhere.'

We waited as Helen took the details of witnesses. The tradesmen all became very gentlemanly and offered to pay for our meal – which we declined – and a double-crewed van arrived 30 minutes later to cart the con man away.

'The perfect end to a wonderful evening,' Helen said.

But that wasn't the end.

Even though I'd just saved his life, the businessman decided it would be a good idea to allege that I'd been in cahoots with the gangsters.

Oh, how I laughed.

The problem was that the Professional Standards Department (PSD) took him seriously and had Helen and I up before a panel of office-based police officers who'd never once pounded the beat.

Police officers have as much love for the PSD as the public has for traffic wardens and the Inland Revenue, multiplied by about a thousand.

Helen only had three years' service, had never been near PSD before and was panicking. I, on the other hand, by now a slightly seasoned detective, was well used to dealing with the PSD and their personal questions about my cash flow, the sort of car I drove, whether I had any debts that had recently been paid off and so on.

'I've given three statements about this now,' I told the hugely overweight office-bound monster who interviewed me. 'I'm not corrupt, nor am I in cahoots with those thugs.'

'Yeah, you are.'

I shrugged, as they yabbered on about kidnap and extortion. The DS who interviewed me was totally removed from the reality of policing. His associate, a DI, had jumped ranks – he'd never been DS or DC.

I told them exactly what had happened, clearly and in great detail. They seemed to agree that my story was reasonable.

'Well, having heard your side of the story, that's a bit different, then. Let's just get this out of the way now with a formal interview.'

He then cautioned me and said, 'In as much detail as you can, tell me what happened.'

'I'll tell you exactly the same thing I did before you turned the tape on and cautioned me,' I said.

Getting me to make a full statement off-tape was a big no-no. They had used non-PACE[19] interview techniques to try and force me into some kind of confession. This, from the Professional Standards Department!

They were not happy about my catching them out, but the tape had them.

'That'll teach us to go out on our day off,' I said to Helen afterwards, when they'd finally slunk back to their office.

We should have known then that things weren't going to get any better between our relationship and the Job.

---

[19] The Police and Criminal Evidence Act 1984 and the PACE codes of practice provide the core framework of police powers and safeguards around stop-and-search, arrest, detention, investigation, identification and interviewing detainees. Break it and PSD is supposed to investigate.

13

One Wedding and
Half-a-Dozen Shooters

'MUM, WHAT *ARE* YOU DOING?'

Mum was helping Helen and I move into our new home in Woking. We were in the lounge, surrounded by boxes, but Mum had stopped unpacking and had positioned herself behind the boxes so she could get a clear view into the street.

'There's a heroin dealer across the road,' she said. 'I'm just keeping a surveillance log.'

'Great neighbourhood we've chosen,' I told Helen, staring across the road at a man in his 20s in an army coat doing hand-to-hands in an alleyway, ducking back into his house every now and again.

Mum tried to organise a bust before we'd finished unpacking, but the locals said they were too busy to come. Being cops and former cops we could sympathise, but as taxpaying members of the public it was a bad example of the public experience of modern policing. You just assume that the cops can come at a moment's notice, and they will – but only if it's urgent enough or quiet enough. There are far more crimes than cops.

Helen and I were about to get married, but my workload meant that Helen had shouldered most of the organisation. As a response officer, she tended to work more regular hours than I did, but I really needed to start weighing in with the wedding.

'I'll sort the cars, suits and venue today,' I promised as I set off for work on my way to meet Bart.

Bart and I started the day with a trip to an ID parade with an UC officer hidden in the boot of our car, for his own protection. He'd been buying thousands of pills and half-kilos of coke from a heavy crew and so we had to be very careful getting him in and out of Woking nick. When we let him out of the boot, he was wearing a scarf around the lower part of his face and a pulled-down baseball cap (this was just before the transfer from live parade through one-way glass to the modern VIPER computer parade).

That done, we went to the briefing location for our latest test-purchase job. As we drew up to the abandoned MOD centre, we saw military vehicles and dozens of guys in black assault kits.

'What the fuck is all this, Bart?' I said.

'Buggered if I know.'

We both assumed there must be something extremely big going down in Surrey until we spied Ross Kemp.

'Ultimate Farce,' Bart said.

'Only the police would base a covert drugs purchasing operation in the same place as a full TV crew, with constantly rolling cameras filming about a hundred actors.'

The job had been running for two months. The TPs were well established. They'd been buying crack and heroin off a little network and each day we were netting more suspects.

Bart was the case officer and I was supporting. We had about another thirty active intelligence packages (each pack represented one person) linked to this job, but every now and again we'd have a slow day during which we tried to organise a warrant using other packages from other unrelated operations.

Once we'd negotiated our way past Ross Kemp and his gang, we met Stuart, the TP handler from Specialist Operations. 'I'm going to give the undercover lads the day off to catch up on recordings and notebooks. That OK with you?' he said.

Everyone on this job had been putting in 12-hour days; Bart and I (along with James, Nick and two other new team members, Brett and Sharon, in other OPs (Observation Points)) usually spent six hours roasting slowly in the observation van before going through another six hours of debriefs and other job-related fun and games.

'Definitely,' Bart replied. 'I need to catch up on the unused and exhibit schedules.'

So we zipped off to the office, and while Bart unsheathed his biros and plunged into the paperwork, I sloped off for an hour of wedding-related phone calls, sorting the cars, suits and venue, as promised.

I rang Helen to give her the good news.

'Thanks for that. I was starting to worry.'

'No worries. Look, we've had an early stand-down on this job, so how about dinner tonight?'

'I'd love to, but I was trying to talk a man down from a roof when he jumped. I'll have to see how I go with the coroner.'

'OK. Let me know, and if not I'll cook.'

I was halfway home when my phone went. It was ex-city boy banker James, now a DS. He was a good guy, but he tried a little too hard to be both manager and one of the lads.

'Can you come back? NCS are sending something our way.'

NCS don't deal with petty crime and, as we were the covert drugs team, it was probably a fair guess that this was going to involve kilos and a lot of time away from home. I drove back into the nick. It was around 4 p.m. and the car park was emptying, as the early shift finished.

Tucked away in a shady area at the back was a 2004 Golf with all the doors and boot open. James was waiting there with three other techs from the main office.

'What's up, chief?' I asked.

James nodded at the boot and I saw three breezeblock-sized packages, wrapped in brown tape and sealed in cling film. Each block had a raised 'Cartier' logo on it.

Three kilos of cocaine.

The last kilo we'd bought cost about £28k, give or take, at wholesale. Wash this lot up into crack and it'll give around 30,000 £10 bags. Cut it and it could be worth £600,000 on the street. Nice.

NCS had called the strike, but they didn't want their surveillance officers exposed in court papers because leads relating to this job were taking them right to the top dealers and the criminals all shared the same defence firm. That's where we came in.

As I've previously mentioned, we were the only team of our kind at this time in Surrey and we'd been set up as a bit of an experiment. When NCS had called and asked for the local drugs squad, they were bemused to find that the civilian dispatcher had no idea who to put them through to.

Our target was a man in a flat who – after meeting a Colombian called Mauricio Albarracin, wanted in the USA – was suddenly loaded with cash and drugs. Several kilo-level dealers had been coming and going from his flat, which was assumed to be packed floor to ceiling with Colombia's finest marching powder.

NCS had called up a uniform unit to put in an innocent cause stop-check and 'discover' the gear, as one of these big-hitters, a man called Marc Stovell, left the house.

Stovell decided to take the car chase option and so the NCS surveillance vehicles broke convoy and rammed him front and rear. The three kilos were in the boot, along with £6,750 in the glove compartment.

'Can you take the papers on this one, mate?' James said. 'Bart is up to his eyes and the other techs haven't dealt with drugs on this sort of scale before. We need to organise a team to raid the flat, too.'

I nodded and asked, 'What about SMT?'[20]

He smiled. 'Well, it's after 1600 and they're not here. Oh dear, my mobile signal has gone. Let's do this and ask forgiveness later.'

I smiled and went on a tour of the offices, looking for some of my favourite and most robust raiding party officers.

Fifteen minutes later, we had a team of four uniformed guys and six detectives. Another DS and DC had changed into uniform and got hold of a patrol car to cover the eventuality of a fail-to-stop. We rolled out of our nick to a pre-arranged rendezvous point, where we met Nick, the NCS DI.

It was a blazing hot day and, out of sight of the general public, we all started to sort out body armour, PPE (Personal Protective Equipment: asp, gas, cuffs and armour) and in my case the universal

---

[20] Senior Management Team: they would have said this job was too big for us and would have passed it on to the SCIT (Serious Crime Investigation Team).

key (i.e., the battering ram, which meant I also got to wear armour on both arms). We were in rivers of sweat by the time Bart pitched up, a squeal of tyres, a smile and a warrant in hand.

Nick filled us in: 'Two-bedroom flat with one occupant – as far as we know – the man who supplied Stovell the gear.'

The Cougar set in Nick's car suddenly started to broadcast: '*Stand by, stand by, stand by. Subject 2 is out of the premises and into white Renault van, index ******. Vehicle is off, off, off towards Kingston Road and from view.*'

'*8–2 to OP. I have eyeball. Vehicle is towards the cross at speed three-zero mph. Back-up in place.*'

'*8–4. Back-up in place, two vehicles back and no choke point. Uniform, can you make ground to stop?*'

The now uniformed DS and DC screeched off to catch up with the convoy that would arrest whoever it was that had come out of the flat, while we made our way towards the address.

James was just ahead of me as we approached the locked communal door of the flats. I transferred the enforcer from my left shoulder to my hands, ready to swing.

As soon as we got to the door, I yelled, 'ENTRY!' James stepped to the side, placed his foot on the bottom of the door to load the lock and I swung at the handle. Glass and wood exploded and the door shot open.

Normally, the entry officer would stand aside and let the rest of the team go in, but I knew there would be another door, so I led the way. I ran up the stairs, barely feeling the weight of the 20-kilo enforcer, thanks to the adrenalin, my mind already on the other side of the door as we reached the top of the stairs and thundered along the corridor. I thought about guns. These were serious dealers who tended to take out extreme protection against rival gangs and those men crazy enough to make a living from robbing drug dealers. We hadn't had the time to research this properly, so were in the hands of the NCS intelligence.

I swung the enforcer and the door imploded first time. I stood to the side as the others piled in, screaming, 'POLICE, POLICE, POLICE!' in an effort not to be mistaken for a rival dealer and assaulted, stabbed or shot.

As I dropped the enforcer, I saw a figure dart into a room at the end of the flat's hallway.

'FUCKING GET HIM!' I yelled, as the suspect slammed the door.

Two guys kicked it open again and jumped on the suspect, crashing over the bed and onto the floor on the other side. As they fought to get the cuffs on, one of them said, 'He's a woman!'

The suspect, Deborah, was taken into the lounge. The guy the others picked up outside was the suspect, Stuart, who was also Deborah's brother.

'What we got, then, team?' James called out. 'Any damage?'

We were in an upmarket two-bedroom flat, with separate lounge, bathroom and kitchen – blond woods and cream carpets.

'That communal door was about a grand,' Bart replied. 'And Dangerous has fucking matchsticked that front door!'

I turned to look and, sure enough, the door was split into two halves, lengthwise, and the separated half was in several pieces on the floor.

'Who's got the camera?' I asked. A photo of the smashed door would go up on a corkboard in the office, where it would sit next to photos of many others. Our unofficial league table of smashed doors made a point of identifying those who were still in the 'in-one club', i.e. only one strike was needed. If an officer took more than one hit, he or she was branded sloppy and weak.

We stripped off our body armour and broke out the 'go box', with all the exhibit bags and books.

Not a bad afternoon's work so far, but now we needed to tie Stuart and Deborah in with hard evidence. Time to don the gloves and root around. We spotted several empty cocaine wraps and rolled up banknotes straight away.

I went into Stuart's bedroom, checked under the bed and pulled out a wheeled, black canvas flight bag. In it I found a black-tape-wrapped, breezeblock-size package. A puff of white powder escaped from a loose edge. That's ten to fifteen years right there.

'James! Come and take a look.'

'Whaddya got? Oh wow!' he smiled.

'And check this out.' Also in the bag was Stuart's passport, with some addresses of hotels and casinos in Puerto Buenos, Marbella (the upmarket part of the Costa del Crime), and a grey plastic air-courier bag.

James and I cut along the non-sealed edge to preserve any evidence and found an identical bag inside. We cut this open in the same way.

'Holy fuck!'

'Fucking fuck fuckity fuck fuck!'

Inside was a matt-black Glock 19 self-loading pistol, with two magazines and a speed loader. Also in the bag was a box of 50 full metal jacket 9mm rounds.

They were wrapped in the same clear heat-sealed plastic as the blocks in Stovell's car.

'Just think, if another person had been in the flat and that pistol had been loaded and in their hands . . .' I said.

'And here we are, unarmed and wearing armour designed to stop knives, not bullets,' James added. He patted me on the shoulder and stood up.

'Good job,' he said quietly, 'Good fucking job.'

We then split the team. Half went off to Stovell's house, where they found mobile phones, SIM cards and a money order transfer to an account in Marbella for 180,000 euros.

'Tidy job, lads,' Nick said. 'It's all tying up nicely.'

We also found a package wrapped in tape with the logo of a local storage company on it. Inside this package was half a kilo of what looked like very good weed. At the storage company depot, we found records linking a box to Stuart that had more cash inside.

This, in turn, was connected to a job SCIT were working on at the time, featuring a 46-year-old man called Ray Harmes, who owned the Happy Landing Pub in Stanwell. He was later arrested after plotting to fly coke in 40 kilo batches from South Africa to the UK hidden in the nose of a jumbo jet.

By the time we got everyone back to the nick and stashed the evidence in property, it was midnight. And Bart and I still had an ongoing undercover operation in full swing, not to mention all the other jobs on our docket.

As this job had arrived out of the blue, and we had three warrants set for the next day, James had a bit of a headache finding enough officers to cover this plus all the other jobs we were running, but he managed, a sign of his professionalism and a demonstration of yet another unsung skill in police stories – management. This involves persuading police officers to come in on their day off to cover a boring task while the officer they're covering for does something more exciting, as well as calling in or begging for favours from anyone who'll listen.

Bart and I took our prisoners to the custody sergeant to get them checked in. I've always admired those custody sergeants who can remain professional in the face of two annoying bastards like us who bring them three bundles of joy in the small hours, telling them we need to get them bedded down for the night as soon as possible, so we can all get some shuteye and prepare for interviews the following morning.

Custody sergeants require a calm approach that goes beyond Zen. They get abused by everyone: the officer in charge, the duty inspector, defence briefs, detention officers, lay visitors, visiting forces whose cells are already full, etc., not to mention those occupants who like to sing the Prison Song, 'Let Me Fucking Out!', for hours at a time.

I walked through my front door at 2.45 a.m. As I eased myself into bed, Helen murmured, 'I hope you haven't forgotten about ring shopping tomorrow.'

Shit. Tomorrow was supposed to be my rest day. Now I had three in the bin for serious offences. I'll tell her in the morning, I thought, as I set the alarm and closed my eyes.

Four hours later I was up, showered and a brew in hand when Helen wandered down in a sleepy state.

'Don't tell me,' she groaned. 'Job on.'

'I'm really sorry, love. It's a biggy. Promise I'll make it up to you.'

'What, with the dinner that you didn't cook last night as well? I was knackered when I got in at eight and had no food, or any idea where you were. Can I remind you we have a wedding to arrange, my parents arriving tomorrow and planning dinner at your mum's on Friday!'

'I'll try harder, I promise,' I told her as she re-climbed the stairs.

Helen was right. Months of twelve-hour-plus days, six days a week was bound to annoy any partner and I wasn't pulling my weight at home. I did mean to try harder, I really did.

The problem I had then was that the job was just too good.

That morning the coke came back between 87 and 89 per cent pure. It is impossible to have 100 per cent pure cocaine due to the chemical manufacturing processes; this is about as good as it ever gets.

Both Stovell and Stuart gave us 'no comment' interviews. It didn't matter. They were done.

James couldn't resist emphasising this fact.

'Stuart, when you were arrested and cautioned, you said, "This is all a big mistake, I was only trying to earn a few quid." Was it a mistake getting caught?'

'No comment.'

'Or just a mistake in that you're going to prison for a very long time?'

Stuart started to cry.

We charged and remanded both of them for possession of class-A drugs with intent to supply and Stuart, additionally, for possession with intent of a class-B drug and possession of a firearm and ammunition.

Stovell and Stuart pled guilty and got ten and fourteen years respectively, taking into account an early guilty plea and previous 'good character' with 'no convictions' (i.e. they hadn't been caught before).

Of course we'd been gifted this terrific job; however, we allowed the NCS team to stay anonymous at a crucial time. This meant they were able to get one rung further up the ladder and a couple of weeks later two men, Daniel Reynolds and Alan Harris, were arrested in Hounslow having just taken delivery of 55 kilos of cocaine packaged in Italian shoe boxes that had been ripped onto a plane in Spain and ripped off at Heathrow. They got 26 and 19 years respectively.

Another man who was part of the same network brought a boat into Brighton loaded with cocaine, heroin and guns worth a total of

£2 million. He received thirty-four years, reduced to thirty-two on appeal, after two captured accomplices turned Queen's evidence (they were sentenced to eight years instead of twenty-four).

From our end, using the evidence we found on Stuart and Stovell, I uncovered some extensive money-laundering activities and, after making inquiries with the Seguridad and Spanish casinos, we ended up with some valuable pinches.

One female cash courier was put on a plane to Mexico by a surveillance team and scooped by the Federales at the other end with £500,000 in euros.

Another lead took us to a man called Kerry Reed, who was found guilty of laundering millions of pounds for Stuart's network, amongst many others. He was convicted for three years in 2009. Lest you should think money laundering is not profitable, Reed bought seven Range Rovers, four Porsches, two Ferraris and two Lamborghinis between 2004 and 2007. He spent £1,008,147 (that we knew about) between April 2004 and May 2007 on jewellery, designer clothes and socialising alone. When he was arrested, he said he was unemployed.

Another little crew was also identified and later snatched trying to sell ten kilos of cocaine to Middle Market Drugs Team UC officers in the Met.

Stuart did not learn his lesson. Some time later he came out of prison on day release and was arrested with a half-kilo of heroin. Chalk up another ten years, consecutive (this meant he'd have to serve this after he'd finished his first sentence).

The job also allowed us to forge links with NCS where the usual political bullshit chain was cut out, so we were able to deal directly with one another. We liked what they did and they liked what we did – the start of a beautiful friendship.

Immediately after the Stovell arrest, Bart and I had to perform another covert ID procedure with an UC officer. After this I had to choose wedding bouquets and table arrangements with Helen. Although I would have been happy with petals of any colour, I needed to show Helen I was in this with her.

We were just done with the ID parade when my phone rang. It was James.

'Hope you two haven't got any plans this week,' James boomed.

'Why, what happened?'

'Brett.'

James had asked me to send newbie tech Brett on a nothing job for him to practise on, the theory being that if he screwed up it really wouldn't matter too much. I had two ropey bits of intel about an address that was marginally suspicious that Bart and I had somehow cooked into a warrant. It was perfect for Brett, so I had handed it over.

'What about him?'

'Brett's so-called "nothing" job has thrown out three kilos of powder, a shitload of weed and half a dozen shooters!'

'Guns?'

'Yeah, and lots of bullets, too!'

'I don't fucking believe this. It was only supposed to be a quick in and out.'

'Well, now you've got to shake it all about, Dangerous. We've got another warrant off the back of it and more leads than a dog walking school. I need you back here yesterday.'

I rang Helen, giving myself minus marks in the PDR category for Prioritisation.[21]

I knew I had to do something if Helen and I were going to live some kind of life alongside our careers rather than at their mercy.

Problem was, I was a born cop. I couldn't do anything else.

Then a solution presented itself, one that would change our lives – far more than we would ever have dared to imagine.

---

[21] Performance Development Review: every year you fill in one of these about how great you are and then your skipper and inspector either endorse it or not. It has far too many categories and is a total pain.

14

Leaving the Factory

HELEN AND I WALKED THROUGH THE gates of Australia House on the Strand, on the edge of London's West End. It was February 2006 and that day we were hoping to overcome our last hurdle: the interview.

A friend had first highlighted the benefits of working as a cop in Australia. He'd loved every moment and had eventually become a ministerial bodyguard.

'What's not to love?' he'd said. 'The weather, the lifestyle, the pay [he was mortgage-free on a detached property the size of Blenheim Palace, with land to the horizon]. Plus we're better trained than they are. It's like being the big kid at school when you get here.'

I loved the Job, but I also wanted a life outside of work. That meant putting the wild 24-hour shifts behind me. I was married now. Helen and I wanted to start a family and so we both needed to be around to see our kids grow up.

So when the Western Australia Police launched a campaign to recruit 400 English officers to boost their ranks in Perth, I remembered my friend's words. Helen and I went along to a presentation at Australia House.

It was all blue seas, white sand and smiling police officers of all nationalities. The citizens were well behaved, and there was little paperwork and low crime rates. Perth, home to 1.6 million people, known as 'the City of Light', was consistently in the *Economist*'s yearly top-ten list of the world's most-liveable cities.

It was the most remote big city on earth. It's actually closer to Singapore than to Sydney. But both cities are over 2,000 miles away. Behind the city stretches 1,700 miles of dead, red empty desert, all the way to Adelaide. In front, there's nothing but sea for 5,000 miles – until you hit Africa.

It doesn't sound that great . . . until you look at it up close. The weather is glorious – the kind that puts a spring in your step and makes it seem as though everything is going to be just fine. The city itself is large, spacious, broad, clean and modern. People will tell you that there's something about the light, and they're right – it's not too harsh but sharp enough: everything from the sea and the sky to the gardens seems to glow with happiness. As the writer Bill Bryson said of Perth: 'You will never see bluer city skies or purer sunlight bouncing off skyscrapers than here.'

To Helen and me, it looked like heaven.

Successful candidates would be given permanent residency from day one. All you had to do to qualify was to be forty-five or under and have a minimum of three continuous years on a UK force.

'Officers who have already made the move Down Under are thriving in their new roles,' the presentation – which was given by a man with a perfect bronze tan, perfect white teeth and perfect blond hair – went. He spoke in a deep but soft Aussie accent, designed to charm. 'The feedback we've been receiving from our colleagues in the Western Australia police force, as well as the public, is that the former "bobbies" are highly competent, professional and friendly.'

Houses and food were cheap, as was every kind of entertainment and sport; from cricket to waterskiing, they had it all, whatever you were into. There was no better place in the world to raise a family, they told us.

Even their motorways were called 'freeways'. They looked like they belonged in Beverly Hills, I thought, as we circled a choked and sodden M25 on a grey winter's afternoon on our way back to Woking, where the local heroin dealer was still working across the road and our over-inflated £150k mortgage repayments, car loans and ridiculous working hours awaited our urgent attention.

We calculated that we could sell our house and buy a four-bed house with pool for £250,000 in Perth. We'd be mortgage-free in just a few years. Distance was an issue: we'd be 9,000 miles away. However, we would travel back to the UK a couple of times a year, and Mum and anyone else could stay with us for as long as they liked.

We had to admit, standing the two options side by side, life in Woking or Perth, Woking lost by some distance.

But to get there we had to satisfy WAPOL (Western Australia Police) that we were good enough, hence the interview at Australia House. We'd passed the physical and psychological tests and now the interview. If we were successful, we'd be off to Perth, where we'd train for three months at the Oz version of *Police Academy*. Australian cops carry firearms, so there were some important differences.

It was five days before we were due to get married, so we were already excited when we rolled up to the front desk half an hour early.

We'd barely sat down when a tanned and be-suited Australian stepped into the corridor.

'Officer A?' he said.

'Yes,' I replied.

He smiled. 'I'm Senior Sergeant Ian North. We'll do you now, if that's OK. The bloke who was supposed to be before you is running late.'

I sat down on a chair in front of three men: Superintendent Alf Fordham, Senior Sergeant Jim Cendrowski and Senior Sergeant Travers. I suddenly felt very pale amongst so much golden skin. I wanted that sun.

It started off formally enough. I'd been given three questions before the interview to give me time to prepare some answers. The first was: 'Describe a situation where you have displayed tenacity in order to resolve the matter.'

I talked about the drugs-trafficking investigations I'd been involved with, described in these pages.

This was followed with: 'Give an example of when you have had to deal with unethical or inappropriate behaviour in the workplace.'

Where to begin? I thought. I gave them two examples of racist and unprofessional behaviour, action taken and the results.

Then came Question 3: 'You are the first officer assigned to an armed robbery at a video store. Describe what actions you would take, considering all possible implications.'

This was a straightforward step-by-step response, listing all the possible investigative and legal implications. As I started to answer, Superintendent Alf Fordham stopped the interview.

'I'm more than confident in your ability to tackle an armed robbery based on the detailed answers you've already supplied us. I would be interested to hear what questions, if any, you have for us.'

'I do have a few questions, as it goes. How will Australian police officers react to UK officers coming in to work on their patch? If the situation was reversed, I think there might be some resentment from some UK officers.'

'There will be no problem,' Fordham said. 'Western Australia is a multicultural place with people and police officers from many different backgrounds. We need more cops. They will just be happy to see a fresh face.'

'Look at my name,' Cendrowski said. 'It's not Australian and I fit in. You will, too.'

'OK,' I said. 'My wife and I are keen to start a family and under our current contract we're guaranteed a long-service leave. We're very keen to know whether this will be upheld at WAPOL.'

Our decision hung on the answer to this question.

'It will,' Fordham said. 'WAPOL takes good care of its employees. Rest assured, Western Australia is one of the best places in the world to raise a family.'

They told me that Helen and I would be stationed close by and 'family and work–life balance are of utmost importance to WAPOL', adding that all our years of service would be recognised and transferred.

Both sides satisfied, I left and it was Helen's turn.

A few minutes later, Sergeant North came and found me. 'Why don't you join us?' he asked.

Unusual, I thought, following him inside.

Inside, Fordham told us that we were more than competent.

'Would you like to know the answer here and now or wait until Monday?'

Helen and I exchanged a glance. 'Now, of course,' I said. 'Welcome to WAPOL!'

* * *

Once that day had passed, there was no going back; we were on a rollercoaster ride to Western Australia. We sold the house for a slight bargain, just to make sure it was all taken care of in time. Getting our beloved dogs, Benson and Regan, to Australia cost £5,000. The whole move came to about £20,000, but the sale of the house covered it and left us with enough to get started in Perth.

Tears fell as we checked in at Heathrow. Both of our families had come along to see us off and it was desperately difficult not to fall apart there and then. Doubts niggled as we hugged everyone goodbye. But I knew we'd made the right decision – the Western Australia Police had made everything happen so easily, assuring us time and again that a bright future was waiting for us.

15

Welcome to Hell

'WHY THE FUCK DIDN'T YA SHOOT the cunt?'

I lowered my Glock and looked at the young man lying in a twitching heap on the tarmac.

It was lunchtime on Christmas Eve and 39 degrees Centigrade. I'd been called to a disturbance in somebody's front garden and had found a drunk 20-year-old man waving a knife.

I'd spent half an hour trying to talk him into a calmer state (there was no way I was going to shoot him – think of the headlines: British Bobby Shoots Man Dead On Christmas Eve) when a patrol car arrived and two officers climbed out. They dug out their tasers and shot the young man five times without any warning.

Still stunned, I looked at the cop who was now pulling on the taser wire that had hooked on the young man's skin.

'Not so hard now, are ya, ya fucking moron?' he said to the twitching figure.

I'd quickly learned that in Australia you were much more likely to be shot dead by a cop than get eaten by a shark. Australia has a robust gun culture. In the UK, we thought about kitchen knives during domestic calls; here, it was hunting rifles.

My finger had brushed the trigger three times as the man had threatened to charge me. I simply didn't want to kill him or leave him with an injury he'd carry for the rest of his life. It just wasn't the British way. OK, fair enough, if the firearms unit had been called because there was a real danger to the public, but I was just a patrol officer. I didn't need to shoot the citizens of Perth dead in the street to do my job.

The cops seemed pissed off that I hadn't shot him. Now they had a live prisoner to deal with.

We'd only arrived three months earlier, but it already felt like forever. It had all started so well. We found a house, moved in, got settled and admired Perth.

We walked through Kings Park, a thousand-acre paradise on a bluff above the broad basin of the Swan River. Kings is all those things a city park should be: playground, sanctuary, strolling area, extraordinary botanical garden, vantage point, memorial – and huge. About a quarter of it is a managed nature reserve.

Thanks to the discovery of iron ore (when an entrepreneur landed his plane in bad weather outside the city and realised he was standing on a mountain of almost pure iron), quickly followed by just about every other mineral in existence (including gold), Perth was transformed from a sleepy wool producer into a mining millionaire's playground. It was once the world's biggest exporter of minerals. That's why Perth has so many skyscrapers.

The coastline of Western Australia north from Perth is astoundingly beautiful and almost entirely untouched by development for 2,600 miles, all the way to Darwin. Altogether, Western Australia has some 7,800 miles of coastline and only about three dozen coastal communities. There's space to breathe there. Life is good. The people are friendly, the city is beautiful and, as we walked to our induction, it was true, the light had put a bounce in our step that we never knew we had. We were full of enthusiasm and excitement, ready to serve the people of Perth.

Superintendent Michelle Fyfe (now Assistant Commissioner) gave the 'pep talk' and her pissed-off, backhanded welcome to Western Australia was somewhat different from the presentation at Australia House.

'Now you are here, we don't want to hear new ideas and about how you do things,' she told the assembled British police officers. 'You are here as frontline officers, so you need to get your heads down and integrate. We do things pretty well here and we don't want change.

This is a bums-on-seats thing here. There has already been conflict, with foreign officers thinking we are backwards or not quite up to speed.

'You need to get on with it. We know you're experienced officers and that is why you're here, which we're glad of, but you need to get used to the Western Australian way and we think we do it pretty well. Welcome and good luck.'

This was our first contact with WAPOL staff in Australia, on day one, week one, minute one. How could there have been any conflict?

After the 'welcome' speech, the UK police officers looked at one another and smiled, typically making sarcastic comments. 'Welcome to WAPOL, then!' one said. 'Nothing like motivational speeches,' said another, as we mused, 'How exactly does one get one's head down to integrate?'

After signing our contracts, we were then posted – without choice – to a variety of locations across the district. As Sergeant Goebbels[22] stated, we would have to trust in her judgement of postings 'and if you don't like it, it's tough'. Helen and I were posted 26 miles from our newly bought home and 8 miles from the nearest train station.

When we complained to an Australian officer, we were told with a laugh to forget it: 'You can try Johnny Goebbels [he pronounced it Gobbles], but he'll tell you the same. You knew you could get sent south, but you bought up here. Jeez, that *is* funny!'

'Um, no it's not,' I said, thinking this wasn't the famous Australian humour I'd been expecting. 'There were many postings close to the area we've moved to,' I said, 'and we were told—'

'You'll go where we post you and if you don't like it, stiff!'

I persisted but was told if I didn't shut up about it we'd be moved even further away.

We worked in a place called Murdoch, near Fremantle. Fremantle, a coastal suburb of Perth, is a trendy hangout, a place of latte and gelato and little shops selling things of an arty nature. The cool ocean breeze is called the Fremantle Doctor (because it makes you feel better).

Murdoch, however, was a dump of trashy bars and 7-Elevens

---

[22] I know, I would have changed my name too.

selling cheap alcohol. The breeze there, to use the local lingo, smelled like a 'dead dingo's arse'.

These sorts of 'don't think we're pleased to see you' sentiments had been repeated throughout our training course, which concluded with computer training.

'Right!' the instructor barked. 'We've already had problems with you lot. Any messing in this class – any email sending, any game playing – and I'll write the papers up myself and the superintendent will sign them. He's already agreed to that. And those papers mean you can get on a plane back to England because it's your jobs that those papers will finish. I don't care. Mess in here and I will send you home, got it?'

This should have been impossible. As permanent residents, Western Australia was supposed to be our home.

The one thing we all learned on the course was that the local cops hated us. Only 17 out of the 26 police officers on my course managed to stay in the job for more than a year. The others either left for other jobs in Australia or returned to the UK.

Helen and I were still determined to make Western Australia our home, though. 'It'll be better once we're actually in the job,' I said. Besides, I could never be anything else except a cop and going home wasn't exactly an option.

The problem was, policing in Western Oz was like policing in the 1970s in the UK, but more violent, racist and sexist, and the cops had free use of guns and tasers. Like *Life on Mars* but without the bonhomie.

Non-whites were stopped with the phrase, 'Oi, nigger, come 'ere!'

A significant minority of officers tasered anybody that pissed them off, which was usually anyone with a different skin colour. I saw two officers attack a pair of harmless sailors. They were a bit drunk but were completely inoffensive.

ZAP! 'Not so 'ard now, ya fuckers, eh? Ya want more?' ZAP![23]

---

[23] WAPOL made worldwide headlines in 2010 when footage of their officers tasering a prisoner in East Perth Watchhouse 13 times was posted on YouTube. Their 'prisoner' was an Aborigine man.

Solicitors weren't present in interviews. After I'd spent 20 minutes questioning a ram-raid suspect, a sergeant asked me, 'So, what did 'e tell ya?'

'Nothing.'

'But youse were in there for twenny minutes.'

'He no-commented.'

'Right.' He marched into the interview room and slammed the door. He came out five minutes later. "E'll fuckin' talk to youse now!'

I walked into the interview room. My suspect, whom I had left in perfect health, now had a broken nose, swollen ears and a fat lip. He promptly confessed to a series of ram-raids, spitting teeth as he talked.

As strange as this sounds, I found myself wishing for more paperwork. The scant number of forms and limited record keeping were a shock to behold. Information and records were missing, incorrectly filled in or weren't done at all.

Helen and I had been posted miles away from each other and Helen was put on day shift, while I was on night shift. Despite this (thanks to some fortuitous synchronisation), Helen fell pregnant. We'd always been very clear that this was our plan – right from the moment we made our application. When she was seven weeks, Helen went to see Senior Sergeant Anderson to tell him that fully operational duties would be a risk to her and the baby.

He congratulated her and then sent her to execute a warrant on a woman with convictions for drugs, theft and violence. Helen collected OC spray, a Glock self-loading pistol and 31 rounds of .40 cal ammunition, and drove off to arrest the woman. Luckily, it passed off quietly.

A few days later, while driving to work in the outside lane of a busy freeway, Helen suddenly projectile vomited all over the car window. This was followed by a nervous collapse.

'We're no better off than we were in the UK,' she told me through tears. 'We're seeing even less of each other here and now we're away from our families and without their support, and I feel like it's all my fault.'

I promised her it would get better.

It didn't.

I started applying for detective jobs. I received a letter telling me I wasn't eligible, even though I had more than enough experience and was the only applicant.

When I called up to find out why, the officer thought he'd put me on hold but hadn't.

'Hey, Steve. I've got a Brit on the phone, one of the ones who put in for detective. What's happening with that?'

'Oh, we'll send them out for a year or two to offices as probie investigators and see if they're up to the job.'

'What, like the hard-to-fill spots?'

The other man laughed. 'Yeah, something like that. And some of the squads, if they're up to it.'

I pressed him when he came back until he finally admitted, 'We don't think the skills of UK detectives are up to those of WAPOL.'

Then Helen was refused a non-operational post.

Shortly after this, I was called in for a 'chat' with Sergeant Wood, one of my supervisors.

'Anything wrong, boss?' I asked.

'Yep, there sure is, and we're going to talk about that as well as a few other things. Siddown.'

Three other officers hurriedly left the room as I did so.

'It's your fucking attitude. Moaning about your posting and going off like a fucking pork chop!'

'Don't talk to me like that. If this is your idea of a developmental chat, you need a visit to training.'

'See! There. You're a dick talking like that. I am a SERGEANT!'

'And? If you want to talk, let's talk, but you are not going to bark at me.'

'I talk, you LISTEN! You've come here moaning about your post and thinking you're special just 'cos your fucking wife is pregnant—'

'You can stop there! She is my wife! Not "fucking wife".'

'Oh, give up, mate! You're not special. You're pissed off with the organisation. So are we. I've got a grumpy wife because I'm still here and only should have been here for a year. There're others out there who've got real problems. Health, divorce, ra, ra, ra. And none of them want to work with you because you are going off like a pork chop. We didn't ask for a load of poms here, you know. All that is, is a doctor's quick fix. So you might be good at what you do, you might be experienced, but right now you are here and you will do your job. You know, moaning about the posting and RBT[24] stations, ra, ra, ra, isn't going to get you anywhere.'

'I'm not moaning about RBT stations. I questioned the sense of doing 200 in the same spot night after night. Anyone drink-driving is going to avoid it. Maybe it's a culture clash?'

'Culture clash nothing!'

We carried on like this for a while before I finally left, then went back to the car and tried to calm down.

We hadn't worked hard for years, building successful careers, to move 12,000 km across the world to deal with a situation or work for an organisation as plainly stupid as this one.

And then, just as Helen and I were about to give up, I was made an offer I couldn't refuse.

---

[24] Random Breath Test: they'd sit on the same lay-by for three nights in a row doing 'random tests'. All the locals figured it out after an hour and just went another way.

16

They Kill Cops, Don't They?

I READ AN ARTICLE IN THE WAPOL public newsletter about a superintendent, Paul Richards, who'd moved to Australia from the UK to head up the State Intelligence Department (SID), which would replace the outdated Bureau of Criminal Intelligence. I sent him an email, detailing my experience and explaining that this was something I was very interested in. We met the next day.

Paul was a stocky six-foot-tall Welshman in his early 40s, with the inscrutable smile of an assassin. 'This unit's mission,' he told me, 'is to take out the baddest guys in the country using intelligence, informants, undercover agents and the best electronic kit Australian tax dollars can buy. As you may have already noticed, there is no PACE, no RIPA in Australia, so we can do what we like, when we like. Our officers will be carefully handpicked and given top-level security ratings. SID is considered so sensitive that it will be exempt from the Freedom of Information Act.

'I've been tasked to undo everything and build a whole new system of undercover and source handling and, with the help of field officers, to start doing anything from taking down the motorcycle gangs that have been filling Western Australia with drugs to infiltrating the gangs who are supplying the inmates at Hakea [prison] with unlimited amounts of drugs of every type and strength.'

I already knew quite a bit about the 'bikie' gangs, as the local plod called them. I could never bring myself to call them 'bikies'; it made them sound harmless, when they were anything but.

Helen and I had arrived in Australia just as an inquest into one of the country's most notorious murders, which had taken place in Perth, finished.

Ora Banda (Spanish for Band of Gold) looks exactly like a town from the Wild West. It's flat, dry and dusty, with a few low buildings, the largest of which is currently the Ora Banda Hotel.

It sits at a remote point in the desert, 400 miles to the east of Perth. At its peak, at the start of the twentieth century, when gold was discovered, 2,000 miners and their families lived in the area. Today, it's a virtual ghost town, although every September it comes alive for Race Day, an annual horseracing event.

The Ora Banda Hotel was owned by former Perth Criminal Investigation Bureau Chief Don Hancock, who like many detectives around the world had long dreamed of retiring and running a pub in the country: in other words, he was after the quiet life.

This came to an end in October 2000, when four members of the Gypsy Jokers motorcycle gang arrived at the pub. The Jokers are one of Western Australia's largest biker gangs, with a heavily fortified clubhouse in Perth (surveillance cameras, concrete walls and reinforced doors). The bikers made lewd comments about the young barmaid, Alison, who was Hancock's daughter.

Witnesses later reported that Hancock said, 'This is my daughter behind the bar. Refrain from talking like that. If there's any sign of trouble, I'll close the pub.'

The bikers stopped. One of them said to Alison, 'Better that he cares than he doesn't,' while another walked up to Don Hancock and whispered into his ear, 'Don't you threaten us.'

Hancock kicked them out and the Gypsy Jokers returned to their campsite nearby.

Later that night the Jokers were drinking around their campfire when a gunshot cracked across the desert. The Jokers ran for cover and when they emerged they found one of their number, William Grierson, had been shot dead.

They were certain Hancock was responsible.

Hancock defied police instructions to stay at his hotel and instead went home, where he showered and got changed. He then refused to hand over his clothing. When he answered the door, he was eating an orange.[25] The investigation quickly stalled and Hancock went free.

The Gypsy Jokers vowed revenge. They repeatedly bombed Hancock's pub and home – concealing the explosives before one attack in the coffin of a teenage boy. Hancock – also known as the Silver Fox – returned from his isolated hotel to Perth, where a state-of-the-art security system was set up in his home.

The bikies found out he regularly went to the races with an old friend, retired bookie Lou Lewis. A source in the Western Australian Transport Department gave them the details of the bookie's car.

On 1 September 2001, the bikers searched the Belmont Park racecourse until they found the unlocked car and placed an ammonium nitrate bomb under the passenger seat.

As Hancock and Lewis arrived back at Hancock's home, one of the bikies rang Hancock. When the Silver Fox answered, the man said, 'Rest in peace, Billy.' The massive bomb detonated a second later, killing Hancock and Lewis in an explosion that was heard eight kilometres away. Hancock's torso landed in a neighbour's swimming pool.

The Australian Crime Commission states that there are 35 motorcycle gangs in Australia, with a total of 3,500 fully patched members and perhaps as many again who are associates. Australia has the largest ratios of bikers per capita in the world.

With a few precious exceptions, biker gangs in Australia have made themselves almost invincible to whatever crime commissions and authorities the government has set up to deal with them over the years.

Today, apart from drug manufacturing and dealing, biker gangs are involved in money laundering, tax fraud, firearms trafficking, protection, security and nightclubs.

Although generally speaking they don't break any kneecaps that belong to the general public, biker gangs infect legitimate businesses,

---

[25] Citric acid can help to contaminate gunshot residue.

everything from finance, transport, private security and construction to entertainment and natural resources.

Biker gangs wear their colours to show their criminal spots. It is a strategy designed to forge military-style loyalty between members while simultaneously intimidating outsiders.

The outlaw biker world remains in a constant state of tension, with smaller clubs at risk of violent takeover by the Hell's Angels, Coffin Cheaters, Bandidos, Rebels, Outlaws, Black Uhlans, Nomads, Finks and God's Garbage.

These larger gangs control Australia's drugs trade and one or more of them is always at war with another, usually over turf, as they try to gain control of the lucrative nightclub drug scene (covering nightclub ownership, club security, strippers and entertainment, as well as prostitution and legal brothels, all great for laundering drug money).

They fight to own security at popular venues so they can green-light the distribution of their drugs through sanctioned dealers. Control the front door and you control who gets in. Control who gets in and you control the distribution of drugs.

In recent years, bikers have been shot in ambushes at nightclubs and on the road, and firebombed in their clubhouses. On one memorable occasion, the Finks and the Hell's Angels became an unexpected addition to the bill when they went to war in front of a crowd of 1,600 people at a kickboxing event on the Gold Coast.

Biker headquarters are easily identified and heavily protected. On those rare occasions that the Australian Police have raided biker HQs, they've been forced to use bulldozers, ram trucks and explosives to get inside. I'd eventually get to see inside one of these palaces to bad taste myself.

Since the mid-'90s, outlaw bikers had fought a never-ending battle amongst themselves to control the country's slice of the massive amphetamine market. Although they usually left the public well out of it, their treatment of Hancock in 2001 made it clear that they would definitely kill cops if they thought it necessary.

In 2003, after an eight-week trial surrounded by heavy security, 36-year-old Graeme 'Slim' Slater was found not guilty of planting the car bomb that killed Hancock and Lewis.

The case rested on the evidence of Sid 'Snot' Reid, who broke the biker code of silence. Reid admitted planting the bomb that killed the two men, but claimed Slater was the mastermind. In exchange, 38-year-old Reid was given a reduced 15-year sentence and perks, including money, a Sony PlayStation and four annual visits from his girlfriend.

But a Perth Supreme Court jury, apparently judging that Reid – a drug user and thief – was not a credible witness, returned a not-guilty verdict and Slater walked free. The inquest into Don Hancock's murder, which concluded in the summer of 2006, just before Helen and I arrived in Perth, revealed little more about the case.

* * *

I wanted more than anything to be a part of the State Intelligence Department. Apart from the fact I would get a 40 per cent pay rise, this would be exciting and rewarding work, tracking new and dangerous targets. This was much more like it.

If we were going after drug dealers, then we would cross the paths of the biker gangs. They were in a different league from people like T, the drug dealer whom I'd hunted back in Surrey. These were outlaws who operated in plain view and relied on their strength in numbers and sheer commitment to the life of an outlaw for protection from the cops.

The only way to get to them, to find out when and where shipments were arriving and how they were being distributed, was through human intelligence sources.

Of course, anyone who was prepared to go up against these guys would have a whole host of reasons for doing so – the most likely of which would be that they'd pissed off the biker gangs in some way and needed our protection.

It wasn't long before one such character ended up before me.

17

Methland

Methamphetamine: *Batu, Biker's Coffee, Black Beauties, Blade, Chalk, Chicken Feed, Crank, Cristy, Crystal, Crystal Glass, Crystal Meth, Glass, Go-Fast, Hanyak, Hiropon, Hot Ice, Ice, Kaksonjae, L.A. Glass, L.A. Ice, Meth, Methlies Quick, Poor Man's Cocaine, Quartz, Shabu, Shards, Speed, Stove Top, Super Ice, Tina, Trash, Tweak, Uppers, Ventana, Vidrio, Yaba, Yellow Bam*

'COULD YOU COME HERE FOR A moment?' Paul asked me.

'Yes, boss?' He was studying the bit of paper I'd handed him a few minutes earlier.

'Why have you asked for a cigarette boat?'

'Why not? We've got everything else from Miami Vice.'

Paul screwed up the paper and threw it at me. 'Very funny. Now you've got all the toys, you can go and find us some drug dealers.'

Our 'office', a large warehouse in an industrial park close to the city centre, was better equipped than the Bat Cave – it even had a similar entrance, in that you got inside via a large roller-shutter door.

It had room for about twenty covert vehicles and eight large sea containers, which held all our brand-new equipment, including a fine selection of firearms and false identities.

We'd been given $500,000 to spend on guns, cars and covert equipment. Everything had to be obtained using fake identities and shell companies, a long and complicated process.

I'd added the $70,000 cigarette boat to our shopping list as a joke, but, by the time we were done, we really had more toys than Batman and Robin.

I became Paul's right-hand man along with another English guy called Jason, a scouser and ex-navy air wing who'd flown Special Forces about in Iraq. He was a very funny guy and a brilliant detective.

A few more members completed our team. Chris was an ex-Suffolk inspector, ex-SAS, a proud family man and an excellent manager.

Martin was a big guy, an ex-Herts traffic officer, who did not care a bit whom he pissed off. He was brash and outspoken and lots of people didn't like him because of this. I thought he was great.

Kev was ex-Met TSG and had been at the Broadwater Farm riots when PC Keith Blakelock was killed. He was also ex-navy and nothing could rattle him. He always knew exactly how to sort out any disorder and always had your back in a fight, physical or otherwise.

Steve was my age, an ex-Met vice detective and undercover. His cocky South London attitude was backed up by a clear self-assurance.

Andy Lumpkin was ex-Met and had worked with Kev on the TSG. He looked like a hippy, but you definitely wouldn't want to be on the receiving end of a 'Lumpy Lump' (his mighty right hook).

Finally, 'Butch' was a racist bully. He once asked me what would happen if he called someone a 'gay, black cunt' in the UK and I told him he'd probably get nicked. He then asked what would happen if two guys handcuffed a WPC and played tennis with her across a room. I said job loss and arrest. He replied, 'I used to be in Internal Affairs and when a job came in, we just thought it was real funny.'

Although, like most police forces, WAPOL had a long and chequered history of using informants, it was new to the modern world of covert operations. This was made clear when we discovered some practical problems with our location.

No one had thought of spacing out the locations of supposed covert units from one another, and for some reason we were all based in the same industrial estate – surveillance, us, various military and secret service units.

This became even more apparent during the next bank holiday. Only cops and government employees work bank holidays in

Australia, so it looked slightly suspicious when lots of young healthy-looking white males in high-performance vehicles were driving in, out and around the industrial estate all day long.

Also, a newspaper had its offices just at the entrance to the estate, which was hardly ideal. But somehow no one noticed – or, if they did, they didn't say anything.

I was tasked to run the Dedicated Source Unit. As I got to work building up an intelligence system using the UK's National Intelligence Model as a template, I asked a senior police officer who was in charge of WAPOL's informants.

Incredibly, it turned out to be a lowly clerk sergeant for the Assistant Commissioner, who emailed me a password-protected, uncoded Excel document that would have taken a sleepy cryptographer about two minutes to open.

This was an immediate worry. Most of the criminals we were after were bikers – true outlaws who enjoyed 'dealing with' finks. A typical slogan on a biker clubhouse was: 'If it's white, sniff it. If it's female or moves, fuck it. If it narks, kill it.' If this list fell into the wrong hands, then there'd be a bloodbath. And that's if it hadn't happened already.

WAPOL had recently been the subject of a corruption inquiry, something they hadn't mentioned during the presentation in Australia House.[26] There were 1,500 names on the list and so I ran risk assessments for every last one, clearing twenty-year-old names who were still listed as 'active' but hadn't been in contact for over five years.

The Australian officers didn't like it when I highlighted the poor security. Unfortunately, there was a great deal of 'this is my train set, so leave it alone' type of mentality and, during one heated discussion,

---

[26] I eventually got hold of the report. It said: 'the full range of corrupt or criminal conduct from stealing to assaults, perjury, drug dealing and the improper disclosure of confidential information have been examined. [The Western Australia police force] has been ineffective in monitoring those events and modifying its procedures to deal with that conduct and to prevent its repetition … The fact that there remain in WAPS a number of officers who participated in this conduct, and who not only refused to admit it but also uniformly denied it with vehemence, is a matter of concern.' I would soon grow to share this concern.

I pointed out that I'd spent a few years taking out multi-kilo-level drug dealers in the UK while the Perth cops still jumped for joy when they arrested a meth head with an ounce.

The reply came back as expected: 'Right, ya smartarse! Why don't you go and get us a bigger seizure then?'

All righty, then.

'OK, if we use the National Intelligence Model, I promise you'll be making multi-kilo seizures in no time.'

I was taking a gamble, but I simply had to press on with some real detective work. I got a grudging nod to my challenge and the local boys sat back, waiting for my inevitable fall.

* * *

As I was now a covert officer, I was supposed to have severed contact with non-covert colleagues. My cover story was that I'd left the police and was now working for a security company.

Most of the other guys in my unit didn't do this, however, and I was no exception. I made sure that a few other trusted officers knew what I was up to and what I was after. I put the word out that if they nicked anyone who offered to talk to save their own skin, then they were to call me.

On 10 June, I was at home and had just popped a post-dinner beer. Helen (by now heavily pregnant) was beside me on the sofa, feet up and ready for a film. My personal phone rang. It was one of the UK guys.

'All right, mate?' He was a northern lad. 'Listen, I'm at the nick and me and a crew mate have just nicked this pillock. He's got an eight ball of meth and a couple of ounces of weed that he says he was just delivering. He knows he's in the shit and is offering up info on a shipment of a pound of orange meth. Is this your game?'

'Definitely. Process and get him ready for remand as normal. I'll come down to the court in the morning to sort this out.'

Stu did as I asked. Unfortunately, his Aussie crew mate, who was not versed in the ways of covert ops, put a briefing note together and sent it to just about everyone in the district, Organised Crime, Gang Crime and our department, SID.

When I found out about this the next morning, I had the briefing note redacted and restricted in the SID intel system. This was yet another warning sign that the world of covert detection was very much in its infancy in Western Australia. Extra caution was needed.

Butch and I arrived at court the following morning. We needed a word with the prisoner to establish his worth and, as there was no official process for this, and as we technically couldn't explain why we were there or who we were, we had to talk our way past the civilian security guard and into a closed room with the prisoner.

Bravura usually does the trick and I was reassured when we saw the overweight guard yawn. Not a sharp tool. We marched without slowing, showing badges.

'Open the door, we need to talk to the prisoner.'

The POI (Person of Interest) was a young man, in his early 20s, a skinny wild-eyed, shaven-headed meth-head who already had the itch and was seeing shadows.

'Morning,' I said with my friendly copper smile. 'A friend of mine tells me you might be able to help us find some orange meth.'

Orange Meth is made from ephedrine sulfate, which has a similar chemistry to amphetamine and can be found in weight-loss tablets, amongst other easily obtained legal medicines, such as cures for colds and allergies. Other methods and chemicals produce different coloured versions of crystal meth – green, blue and brown, for example.

With enough time and the right ingredients and equipment, meth cooks can refine ephedrine into methamphetamine – crystal meth, aka ice, glass or Tina. Cooking is a hazardous process – many meth labs have exploded, thanks to the tendency of white phosphorus to auto-ignite, while many more cooks have gassed themselves to death on phosphine.

To many, the risks are worth the financial gains. Crystal meth is to amphetamine what crack is to cocaine: a lot of high for a very few dollars. Like crack, its God-like high is extraordinarily addictive and addicts keep coming back for more and more as their tolerance builds and as that elusive first high spirals out of reach – a phenomenon known as 'chasing the ghost'.

Users lose weight and develop 'meth-mouth', when teeth drop out, followed by psychosis and a whole host of medical problems, as artery walls collapse (occasionally leading to limb amputation), muscles die and the internal organs fail. Signs of addiction include formication (the sensation of flesh crawling), paranoia, hallucinations and delusions.

A United Nations survey revealed that New Zealand and Australia were second only to Thailand for methamphetamine use in 2001. Five years later, an investigation carried out by the Australian Crime Commission found that there were 102,600 regular meth users in Australia. A National Drug and Alcohol Research Centre study found that there were 36,900 regular methamphetamine users in New South Wales. Of these, three-quarters are dependent and are flooding the psychiatric units at public hospitals.

Its street names are many, but perhaps the most appropriate I heard was 'Biker's Coffee', because it's the bikers who control the growing, multimillion-dollar trade in Australia.

The cops had, until it was too late, underestimated how organised the bikers were when it came to drugs – the chance to make millions of dollars doing pretty much what you were doing already (intimidating people and partying with fellow bikers) does tend to focus the mind.

The kid, nicknamed 'Minty', looked back at us, frightened, jumpy, itching. 'What can you do for me?' he said weakly.

'It doesn't work like that,' I said. 'You tell me what you got and then we might talk about some topics that may interest you. You cannot bargain. If you are helpful, then I promise to do what I can to help you get what you want, nothing more.'

'I'll need protecting.'

'Understood. We can do that.'

The young man rubbed his close-cropped head. 'Fuck it,' he said.

And with that we became source and handler.

'I work for a guy called Harry who lives on Jonestown Road. He's the one who's dealing large weights.'

'Harry? What's his surname?'

'I don't know, some Eastern European name, no one can say it.'

'Where does he get his gear from?'

'I don't know.'

'You don't know? C'mon, you're giving us fuck all here.'

'I don't know! Some guy high up in the Rebels.'

'The biker gang?'

'Yeah, the biker gang, who the fuck else?'

'Harry lives on his own?'

'A couple of girls . . . whores.'

'What's he selling?'

'Meth. He's got shitloads and is expecting another pound or two of orange in the next week.'

The door banged open. Another private security guard – leaner, older and more switched on – stepped inside. 'What's going on here? You're not supposed to be here. Who are you?'

'It's OK,' I said. 'We're police and we're going.'

'What about me?' Minty asked.

'If it checks out, we'll be in touch.'

'What now?' Butch asked once we were back outside.

This was the first debrief that the newly formed DSU had conducted and I was determined to follow this through in correct NIM fashion.

'We'll go back to SID, research the information, see if there's a job and disseminate the intelligence product appropriately.'

At SID, I sat down with an analyst. Together we found that there was a Harry on Jonestown Road and that two females were living at the address. Minty had also told us the kind of car that Harry used and when we followed this up it turned out that the Organised Crime Squad (OCS) had already received info about a drug dealer using the same make of car and used this vague and uncorroborated piece of intel to get a job underway. The problem was their intel was about a different model of car, the car that they were following belonged to a female on the opposite side of the road to Harry, and the female in this car had nothing to do with the job. So they were following the wrong car, whilst the real target went about his business unchecked.

Butch and I went to see Richards and he gave us the go ahead to put a comprehensive intelligence package together.

I returned to see my source. He'd now gone through the court process and was in prison. Not a good place for an informant to be.

We went into more detail at this meeting and this time he added the name 'M' and some information about the East Coast.

'A big deal's going down in Sydney in two weeks' time,' he said. 'They're all involved.'

18

Dealing Drugs in the No-Tree Desert

I CRACKED ON WITH WIRING UP the main suspects. It was incredible. If we wanted a phone intercept, the judge signed anything we put in front of him. It took an hour. In the UK, it could take up to a month while we waited for the Home Secretary's approval.

Once Harry and M's phone lines were tapped, we uncovered more phone numbers, routes, names and weights. Surveillance was put on them. More intercepts revealed other players and we wired their phones, too.

I took the information up to OCS. Clearly my source had cast light on something because the next moment two other detective sergeants were brought in and I was asked to go through the intel again.

'We've got something on M,' one of them said. 'It's not much more than what you've already got, but he's a big-time dealer. We think he's in with the Hell's Angels, who're trying to find a way into the West Australian drugs market.'

The phone conversations revealed that M was due to fly to Sydney to meet a man named 'Les' to do a deal.

Les was the very senior Hell's Angels connection.

Some of the money had been sent ahead by courier. M was planning to take the rest on the plane.

The drugs were to be packaged into the chassis frame of Harry's Toyota Landcruiser and someone called Glenn would drive it back to Perth.

This is an excerpt from the intercept:

Les: 'You got the fucking dough, right?'

M: 'One-eight, yeah, I got it.'

Les: "Cos we can't keep on laying on big loads. I need that cash from the last deal, OK? If we don't get it, then things is gonna get fucked, know what I mean?'

M: 'I got you, brother. Now, don't you worry. My man's already on his way with the dough.'

'What does he mean, one-eight?' I wondered.

'A kilo of meth might be $180k,' Jason said.

'Maybe M owes Les $1.8 million on the last load?'

An OCS senior constable coughed out a laugh and said, 'Fuck, mate. If it is, it'll be the biggest drugs bust ever! It'll never happen.'

The deal was done in a motel. We didn't know the specific weights or funds, but we knew from the intercepts that it had happened.

Now we had to wait for them to get back to Western Australia. As soon as they were over the state line, we would pick them up.

Glenn started the long drive back to Perth, crossing 700 miles of the Nullarbor Desert. Nullarbor is Latin, more or less, for 'no trees'. It is a vast and arid land of flat limestone covered in red dust. There is no vegetation, no shade – this in an area four times the size of Belgium. The Nullarbor really is one of the most forbidding expanses on earth.

Australia could be just as grim as the UK. The difference being that Australia is spectacularly grim, whereas the UK is dully grim. Woking town centre on a wet Wednesday afternoon or the huge silence of the deadly Nullarbor: both vastly different, both vastly depressing.

Three days later the pair arrived in Eucla (pop. 86), a one-horse desert town, the gateway to Western Australia. The original town has long been buried by sand, although parts of it reappear every now and again, as the dunes shift with the wind.

The town is now home to the desert's only highway border checkpoint and as the courier Glenn drove the Landcruiser across into WA with M's brother, a drugs dog started to bark.

This was enough to spook the brother. He leapt out of the vehicle and ran for it before the cops even realised something was wrong. Amazingly, he managed to get away.

Glenn stayed put and was detained while the Organised Crime Squad sliced the chassis of the truck open with a disc cutter. Inside was a 1.5 metre long steel box packed with 13 kilos of meth, Ecstasy tablets and MDMA powder. It was one of the largest drugs seizures in the history of Western Australia.

M's brother was scooped a few days later and charged, while another team hit M's house. His home was like something out of MTV's *Cribs*, except it was done in the worst possible taste, with wall-to-wall red marble.

More than a kilo of Ecstasy tablets were in his safe, along with a pricelist for military-grade weapons and ordnance. There was also documentation relating to a house in a small fishing town outside Perth.

This house was hit, too. There the team found a safe containing self-loading pistols. One was fitted with a professional noise suppressor. There is only one use for a gun like this and it isn't for shooting roos.

Other raids took place around this time, including one on the headquarters of God's Garbage. Seeing inside this building was a real eye-opener. They had a large swimming pool, the bottom of which featured a mosaic of their logo. There was a huge bar running the length of the building and several large garages in which they stored and worked on motorbikes. Above the bar hung a huge spray-painted metal God's Garbage sign done in their colours.

During this raid, two cops from the Gang Crime Squad helped themselves to this metal sign as a souvenir. When I found out about it, I told the superintendent, who shrugged it off. So I told the press. As a result, the two cops were suspended, while other officers were suspended for failing to take action. An investigation was then launched.

The two brothers were charged and remanded, as was Glenn. Harry came in of his own accord. He was interviewed by OCS detectives and admitted complicity in the drugs run by allowing his vehicle to be used and involvement in at least two other similar drugs runs. He detailed these runs and they matched exactly what we had from the phone intercepts.

Harry was never charged, nor did he appear on my central register of informants, which I was responsible for at the time.

This still needs some explaining.

This operation was a unique success and, quite rightly, it was publicised publicly and internally. There was no mention of SID involvement, exactly as it should be.

Covert work is not an area for loud applause and the quieter my source was kept, the better. I plucked my source from prison, on bail, and tucked him away.

I had big plans for him.

Unfortunately, so did someone else.

19

'If It Narks, Kill It'

I WAS WALKING THE STREETS, GLOCK in my jacket, cursing at every step. I'd tried my source's hangouts and known addresses over and over during the previous 15 hours. Fuck! We were both dead men walking and all because of some senior cops' fucking egos.

A second article about the meth bust had appeared in the police magazine, and this time they had included the fact that the critical intelligence had come from an informant.

This publication was posted on the internet, was sent to the press and to every member of the police.

My reaction was not understated.

'For Christ's sake! We have just done the biggest job in the state's history and now we are telling the world it was source-led? Not only that, but we even narrowed down who the source was. *My* fucking source! And where is that source now? Nobody knows! *We* pulled strings to get him bailed. *We* put him back on the streets. *We're* responsible if he gets topped!'

'Erm, some more bad news, mate.' Jason had appeared beside me.

'What now?'

'You know we confiscated all of M's possessions?'

'Yeah?'

'Including his $250,000 yacht.'

'Yeah. And?'

'He's trying to have it firebombed. The job's been touted around town. Seems he feels that if he can't have it, then he isn't going to let the local cops use it for fishing trips. Word was that the Rebels were planning to do it, but we're moving it now.'

'Oh, great. So the Rebels are prepared to reach far beyond the prison wall, beyond police lines. Fucking fantastic.'

Well, if I found Minty first, he and I might just stay alive. If the Rebels found him first, Minty would simply 'disappear', but not before he'd told the Rebels everything they wanted to know – which would be all about me. Once they had my name, they'd soon find out about my heavily pregnant wife, the fact I was a Brit and that there was little love for me amongst many of my fellow police officers.

'I'm going armed at all times from this moment forth,' I said as I left the Bat Cave. The DI in charge couldn't disagree.

I'd already made up my mind we were going back to the UK as I started to walk the streets of Perth. I just didn't know how. We were committed. Helen couldn't fly; she was about to give birth. We'd have to sell the house, reapply for our old jobs – that's if they'd have us and—

'Watch it, mate!'

'Sorry.'

Lost in thought, I'd bumped into a biker at the door to a bar. My source's favourite hangouts were biker bars. Oh joy.

'Fuckin' idiot.'

We carried on into the bar and looked around before heading to the Gents. Drew, a young Australian officer new to SID, had joined me. He was a really nice lad, one of the few who accepted UK coppers.

For the first time in my life, I felt like events were out of my control. There were just too many random variables to be running sources here. Lack of awareness, training, idiocy and, possibly, corruption. What would Dad have done in this situation? I could hear his voice: 'Son, I don't care how, just cut your losses and get the fuck out of there.'

Yeah, but how?

The biker was still there when I came out. His leathers told me he was a member of the Gypsy Jokers, the gang that had blown Don Hancock halfway across Perth. He had a full set of coloured wings down each arm, earned after performing a certain sex act: brown wings for anal sex, for example – the other colours were red, yellow and green. Use your imagination.

As he was so into collecting badges, I wondered whether he wore the 'Filthy Few' emblem in the lining. This means they've killed for the club.

We pressed on into the night. I could see dealing going on in the nightclubs and bars. Doormen used to be there to keep the peace; now, they were there to get the punters high – for a price. They sold pills, supplied by the biker gangs for $35 a pop.

We were too late to stop the spread of drugs and, from what I'd seen of this city, probably the continent; the cops were so far behind the criminals they'd never catch up.

I saw one 'security guard' with biker tattoos. He was clearly controlling the dealing inside the club. Others worked as 'bar managers'. Some were former police officers exposed in the corruption scandals who'd left quickly and quietly to save their bosses' blushes. They now milked their corrupt colleagues who were still in the job for intelligence. Their colleagues could hardly refuse. One call and Internal Affairs might come knocking. And so the corruption feeds itself. It's the same all over, I thought, as I entered yet another club, looking for this young waster with the shortest life expectancy of anyone in Perth.

Humans will be humans and bad cops will be bad cops till they die. As one Aussie cop told me, 'UK and Australia? Same shit, different bucket, that's all.'

I forgot about everything else for a total of 30 hours, just searching for Minty. On the second night, Drew and I sat on his mum's house all night and when he didn't show I decided enough was enough. I went inside and spoke to his family. They gave up his girlfriend's address once I'd explained – in loose terms – the kind of trouble he and I were in.

The house, on a square of dead grass, was in a really rough neighbourhood. When I rapped on the screen door, it bounced open. The flimsy MDF door behind it was open. I drew my Glock and stepped into the main room. Drew followed on my shoulder.

Minty was on his hands and knees, searching the filthy carpet for God knows what. My relief was quickly overtaken with disgust at the state of the room. Pizza boxes lying around, pizza slices on the carpet, random clothes scattered, stains on the walls, broken glass, beer cans, burn holes, foil, cigarette butts.

Then there was Minty: red-eyed, rash-covered, hollow face, dirty clothes, wiry arms, bony ribs, collarbones that stretched his paper-thin skin taut. He was smashed on meth, barely alive, barely human.

'Minty,' I said. 'It's all right, I'm going to keep you safe. You need to come with me.'

Minty screamed, got to his feet and paced the room, rubbing himself and yelling. His movements were quick-fire, mechanical, jerky.

'Christ, how much meth have you taken?'

I kept the gun in my hand as Minty whirled past; he picked up a piece of two-by-four.

'Minty, calm down. I'll make you safe.'

'Fucking cops, fucking cops, fucking cops, shoulda never spoke to youse. Who the fuck are you anyway? You've been sent by them, haven't ya? You're in their pay, aren't ya? They all are, everyone is. Why couldn't I be? Why does it have to be me? Why me? Tell me – why me?'

Minty was unmanageable. A bike engine thundered into life a couple of streets away. I called for back-up as it throttled into the night.

When a pair of detectives arrived to help me get Minty under control and in the wagon, he started shouting again.

'It's a conspiracy, man! He's undercover! I helped him get all that meth and now he's gonna kill me!'

'Shut the fuck up, Minty,' I said before turning to the detectives. 'He's para, hopped up on so much meth he doesn't know which way is up.'

'Sure all you want to arrest him for is bail breach?' one of them asked, perhaps wondering whether I really did want to turn this source off permanently.

'Yeah, I just got to get him to jail.'

Finally, Minty was processed and packed away in his own solitary cell. Exhausted, I returned to SID for a sit-down meeting with all the senior officers – detective inspectors, inspectors, superintendents (although Paul Richards was still in the UK).

I told them how worried I was about Minty's safety and the leak in the magazine, and about what M, his Hell's Angels associates and God knows who else already knew.

'Don't worry about that,' I was told. 'We have all the right measures in hand to deal with this and Minty will be taken care of.'

From what I'd seen so far, I didn't believe them, but as a lowly 'two bar', aka senior constable, I had no choice but to accept what I was told.

When I got back to my desk, my phone didn't stop ringing. It seemed as though several police squads had read the article and wanted to talk to my source to see if he could give them any other leads. I actually laughed at this, as I thought about the state of Minty.

'He's not exactly John Gotti,' I told anyone who called about this. 'He's just a bit player who's mashed his head up on meth.'

They didn't believe me and thought I was holding back, keeping all the good stuff to myself.

I heard no more about Minty and so I assumed witness protection had taken over. In the spirit of firewalls, I didn't want to know, at least for now.

I went home and tried to sleep but couldn't switch off. I lay awake at night, replaying the job, worrying about the future, how we were going to get the hell out of this country, thinking about the gun I now kept close to hand, just in case we should receive a midnight visitor. I sat up at every noise and woke with a start, expecting to see smoke in the room and the orange glow of fire on the landing.

A few days later, I was staring at the ceiling when Helen rolled onto her back beside me and told me that her waters had broken.

Helen had been under terrific stress, thanks to her treatment by WAPOL. She'd received an unexpected email from payroll, stating that she would not receive any paid maternity leave. The reason: she was six weeks short of twelve months' continuous service with WAPOL. This was worth about $10,000.

We'd been promised that our UK service would carry over with us to Perth. Another lie. We fought the decision, but it took many difficult weeks before the commissioner himself, Karl O'Callaghan, finally authorised the maternity payment.

Helen had been further overwrought by what had become a medically complicated pregnancy. The fact that her baby might now be in danger from another work-related threat only exacerbated these tensions – as did the fact that her mum had just come over from the UK for the birth.

Helen was in exceptional pain, even for labour. Her agony peaked after ten hours, at the moment of birth – a scream followed by a whimper then silence. We had a son, but, after a brief cuddle, Helen let Angie, the midwife, whisk him to one side. Then Helen fell limp. Her eyes were closed.

'Helen?' The colour rushed from her face until she was white.

Angie frantically started applying dressings.

Then I noticed the blood: a terrifyingly large puddle, growing steadily, second by second.

'What's wrong?'

'She's ruptured an artery,' Angie said and hit the panic button as Helen's legs started to hammer on the trolley: a seizure resulting from the shock of the blood leaving her body.

I stood by helplessly as the nurses applied pressure to the bleeding while they waited for the crash team. Every passing second felt like ten. Helen suddenly stopped seizing and lay still. She was going to die. Doctors finally exploded into the room and set about trying to pinch the artery before rushing Helen to theatre.

A few minutes later Angie told me that Helen had lost five units of blood but had made it to surgery. Our son, Jack, meanwhile, was screaming for his mum as he was put through multiple tests. The docs needed to make sure Helen's blood loss hadn't affected him.

I'd broken bad news to many families before, so knew the routine. Be clear, keep it short and look them in the eye. But telling Helen's mum that her daughter was close to death was one of the hardest things I've had to do, especially as Helen's brother had died just a few years earlier.

My mum hadn't been able to come over because she wasn't well, and I could barely hold myself together as I left Helen's mum and walked outside to call mine.

Once Mum had answered and I'd told her what had happened, she was in tears because she couldn't be with us. After we said goodbye, I looked up at the sky. The sun was rising on a typically perfect, cloudless Perth morning. The sea sparkled, the breeze cooled, it looked as though all was right with the world. As sunlight erased the shadows, I sat on the floor and wept.

20

The Midnight Visitor

I SPENT THE NEXT FOUR HOURS watching over Jack, waiting for news about Helen. I marvelled, as any new father must, at my son's brand-new life and the awesome bond between us; this new kind of love that simply overwhelmed me.

I prayed, pleaded and demanded that Helen would survive; she simply *had* to. I couldn't lose her. I thought about all we'd been through – and the uncertainty of the months, even years, ahead – and determined that I would give my wife and son a safe and happy future – even though I wasn't exactly sure how I'd do this from where we were right now.

When a doctor finally pushed his way through the swing doors, he gave me a serious nod. Helen had survived, he said, but she was still in intensive care after going through major surgery. She'd had 150 internal stitches.

'Can I see her?'

When Helen came to the following morning, she was incredibly weak. She was barely aware that I was there. But she had fought death and won – our new life as parents could begin.

When we finally got to share a quiet moment with Jack at long last, Helen said, 'I want to go home. Home to the UK.'

'We will. Soon. I promise.'

Once we left hospital with Jack, I decided to find out what had been going on with Minty. As far as anyone knew, witness protection hadn't taken him on; instead, he'd been placed on remand for breaching his bail conditions (his massive drug consumption and going AWOL) and was now quoting passages from the Bible to anyone who'd listen.

At the trial a few weeks later, M was found guilty of masterminding the drug shipment and was given 12 years. He was also convicted for the cocaine and methamphetamine and the thousands of Ecstasy tablets we'd found at his home.

'It is clear this was not an aberration,' Judge Wisbey said before he sentenced M to a total of almost forty years on ten counts, with each sentence to be served concurrently. This meant that M would have to serve ten years before being eligible for parole.

Glenn was sentenced to eight years in jail, with six years non-parole for drug possession, while M's brother received four years and four months for being an accessory after the fact.

Minty made it alive through a short sentence for possession but vanished as soon as he was released.

This is harder than it sounds. As I've mentioned before, Perth is an isolated city with limited hideaways for impoverished and brain-damaged junkies. There are also limited routes by which to leave Perth, making it hard to depart without drawing notice if somebody is watching you, and there are certainly no cities close by in which to hide where no one knows your name. Every biker gang is well represented in every major Australian city and, if they were on the lookout, they would be quick to notice a stranger arriving, particularly if they're part of the drug scene.

Minty did not have the financial resources or intelligence to disappear on his own, especially without people noticing, and he certainly wasn't vacuumed up into witness protection.

'I'd bet any money that Minty's skeleton is already bleached white in the bush by now,' I said once I'd learned of his disappearance. No one disagreed.

* * *

A few nights later I was at home with Helen in the lounge while Jack slept upstairs. The dogs started barking. They sometimes gave a quiet 'woof' if someone was walking past our house late at night, as we were on a quiet road and didn't see much passing traffic, but now they were alert, paws scraping at the door.

We both stood up and went to the window.

I hit the light switch for the patio.

A man dressed head to foot in black was climbing over the fence, out of our garden.

'Jesus!'

I ran to the kitchen sink and reached underneath to grab the Glock.

'Go to Jack,' I said to Helen, as I clipped in the magazine and ran outside.

I ran to the spot where I'd seen the figure climbing the fence and jumped over. I could see footmarks on the fence and in the dirt. I circled our house, checking hedges, trees and sheds, but he'd gone.

* * *

A few days later, Helen and I were in a restaurant, planning our now urgent return to the UK, when Helen's mobile phone rang.

'Neddy, is that you?'

'No, you've got the wrong number.'

'Nah, it wouldn't be Neddy Smith, would it? That grassing fucker's still inside, ain't he?'

Neddy was an infamous Australian drug dealer and informant who'd testified against several corrupt police from the Flying Squad, who were later jailed.

When we got home, there was dust on the floor under the loft hatch.

We'd never been up there.

I climbed up and saw scuff marks in the loft. Someone had been in our home.

I needed to talk to someone I could trust.

I called Mike Dean, from the union, and told him what had happened.

'Look, I'm going crazy here,' I said. 'I don't know if it's the cops, the bikers or both, but something very fucking bad is going on.'

'If I were you, mate, I'd watch what you say at home. You might be bugged.'

* * *

I'd just returned to work after Jack's birth but wasn't about to start any more source-led jobs, although we did have a tempting lead into some meth producers to the south of Perth who were tied in with a biker gang from Adelaide. Helen and I no longer trusted the cops, so we hadn't told anyone, apart from Mike at the union, about our sighting of the man in black.

I was at a party at a hotel, what the locals called a 'sun-downer', feeling pretty miserable. The guys from the office had dragged me along. I attacked the bar, but not with my usual good-humoured gusto: I was drinking because I was miserable, not because I wanted to have fun.

Superintendent Paul Richards was merrily pissed, however, and in an ill-fated effort to appear sympathetic, he grabbed hold of my arm and wrote on it with a marker: 'Fuck them all. Signed Superintendent Paul Richards.'

He then wrote on Jason's arm: 'You have a licence to lap-dance naked,' which Jason then tried to do, despite being too drunk to walk straight, let alone gyrate his hips suggestively.

This was fairly typical behaviour for a police do and, although I was extremely pissed off, I wasn't that surprised when someone yanked my trousers down and snapped a photo of my bare behind.

I moved away to the side of the room and started talking to Kev, a fellow UK officer.

'You fucking poms love to stick together, don't you?'

We turned to see Paul Humphries, an inspector who was also the deputy commissioner's staff officer. He'd been making racist remarks about the British all night and it was clear he wanted to start something.

'Paul, you're pissed,' I told him. 'Go away.'

He shoved me.

'OK,' I said. 'That's your free one, now go away.'

'Gimmie a cigarette.'

'No. Go away.'

'You're gonna gimmie a fucking dart or—'

This time I shoved him, hard, and he went over on his backside into a flowerbed.

Paul Richards came over.

'Calm down, mate. He's just trying to wind you up.'

'It's working,' I said.

But I took Richards' advice and bought Humphries a pint to say sorry, which he took grudgingly, spitting out a hate-filled 'Thanks.'

Later, I was talking to Paul Richards when Humphries appeared behind his shoulder, mouthing, 'Fuck off, wanker, cunt,' giving me the universal gestures that accompany such language.

That was it.

I let my glass drop, ran forward and was about to floor him with a clean punch to the chin when Paul Richards grabbed me. Lumpy, thinking Paul was attacking me, smacked Richards.

I walked away before it got any worse, but inside I was raging, fighting mad. I got to the door and stopped.

'Fuck it.'

I took out my police badge and marched back to Richards.

'You can shove this up your arse,' I told him. 'And all of you lot,' I continued, addressing the whole pub, which had now fallen silent, 'you've caused me and my family so many fucking problems, so from now on just leave us the fuck alone!'

On Monday morning, I went into work to talk about what had happened. Paul Richards handed back my badge before sending me home. They weren't going to sack me, he said, but they were doing the next worst thing, which was to send me to Crime Stoppers for the duration of the inquiry into the incident. In my new role, I would take crime reports from members of the public over the phone.

I went to the union, which – to my surprise – was sympathetic, supportive and full of excellent advice. The union's head, Mike Dean, told me that I wasn't alone. They'd dealt with complaints from dozens of other UK officers. Admittedly, most weren't as dramatic as mine, but many had left or had started legal procedures against WAPOL.

A few days later a British dog handler went to the press with allegations of bad practice by senior police officers.

And then Paul came under scrutiny after it was alleged the SID misspent $15,000 – possibly on alcohol, entertainment and accommodation – during a week-long training operation to hunt down drug dealers and seize their gear. At the end of the week, SID had recovered 3.5 grams of cannabis.

Assistant Commissioner (Corruption Prevention and Investigation) Barbara Etter told the *Perth Sunday Times* that she'd launched an internal investigation and that one officer had already been moved to Crime Stoppers. I was the only officer moved from SID to Crime Stoppers. I had nothing to do with the training week incident, having been moved to Crime Stoppers before this incident had occurred.

Someone had been trying to cover their arse, feeding the Assistant Commissioner some bullshit to show the matter was already in hand. Paul left shortly after this and the investigation came to nothing.

There is some irony in the fact that $15,000 was spent to seize 3.5 grams of cannabis and no one was punished, yet I made a few phone calls that led to the seizure of several kilos of class-A drugs and ended up working on Crime Stoppers.

Another article appeared in the *Perth Sunday Times* detailing reports from 125 former police officers who'd left WAPOL in 2009–10. One in five police officers said they were bullied, while one in ten saw improper, illegal or corrupt behaviour, or experienced sexual or racial harassment or discrimination from their supervisors or colleagues. Participants said they'd seen officers commit assaults, and steal and breach traffic rules, while one wrote to say he had seen 'use of excessive force . . . threats, intimidation, inducement' and 'constant bullying on racist grounds' from senior officers. It was clear that WAPOL had some fundamental problems that weren't going to go away any time soon.

After talking to Mike, I decided to do it properly this time and wrote a long letter of resignation, detailing everything that had happened, and sent it directly to the commissioner.

I was no longer a cop.

21

Brave New World

A CHILD'S SWING ARCED SLOWLY BACK and forth in the breeze. The trees were bare, while the grass was patchy and covered in puddles. About 30 metres to the left of the swings was a public toilet. In between was the dead body of a white male in his 30s, the hilt of a large kitchen knife sticking straight up out of his back.

Yes, my first day back at work in the UK had got off to a flying start.

After I resigned, Helen and I sold the house as quickly as we could and at a loss. I then returned to the UK for a brief visit to ask for our old jobs back. It didn't look good, as Surrey were trying to cut back on detectives. Also, a report of my alleged assault of a senior officer in Australia had reached human resources. I explained to Steve Rodhouse what had happened – he was now chief superintendent – and sent him copies of the various reports and emails about the incident and, thank goodness, he vouched for me, while Helen had no trouble getting her old job back as a uniformed response officer.

I'd only been in the UK for 36 hours when Helen called in tears to say Jack had fallen desperately ill with viral meningitis, so I leapt back on a plane. By the time I got there, Jack was full of tubes and needles and had undergone a lumbar puncture. He'd given us a real fright but pulled through and we moved back to the UK as soon as he was well enough.

I'd returned to work in the same office to find it full of probationer detectives. Bill had moved on, but Nick was still there and it seemed as though he and three DCs were running the place, less than half the number who'd been there before.

Oz had left us exhausted, demoralised and hypersensitive. We'd had no time to rest simply because we couldn't afford to. We moved back on 26 January – Australia Day (oh the irony) – found a house, moved in our stuff, got the dogs through immigration, found childcare for Jack and were back at work less than three weeks after landing at Heathrow.

It was difficult to adjust: we'd moved from the wild west of Australia – the open desert, the heat, the bikes and guns, and the freedom to run a series of huge operations – to the towns and villages of Surrey, the enormous bureaucracy of the UK police, and minor social disorders and thieving scrotes – the same old faces.

I had to prove myself as a DC all over again, when I should have already taken the sergeants' exam. While it was great seeing familiar faces, all the old things about the job that used to annoy me seemed to be multiplied tenfold.

I started the job 'cold', with no preparation, briefing or updating on law policy or procedure. One hour into my first shift, on 20 February 2008, I was called to Chelsea Football Club's training ground in Cobham. Chelsea Football manager Avram Grant had been sent a box of white powder with an anti-Semitic note, saying it was anthrax. It contained the line: 'When you open this letter, you will die a very slow and painful death.'

This turned out to be incorrect – unless they ate a few spoonfuls, as the 'anthrax' turned out to be plant food. Mr Grant took it well; he was more angry and concerned about his wife, who'd also been mentioned in the note. The staff at the training ground stood by in amazement as we sealed the area and waited for the Chemical Biological Radiological and Nuclear Protection (CBRN) team to arrive. Once the white powder investigation was under way, I was summoned to a murder near a children's play area.

The witnesses were traumatised parents and kids, some of whom had seen another man running from the toilets a minute after the victim had staggered out. The man was of a similar age to the victim, was scruffily dressed, had blood on his sleeve and looked 'disturbed', as if he was 'on a mission'.

The graffiti on the cubical interiors suggested that this was a place known for gay sexual encounters. A lover's tiff? Unlikely. Perhaps it was a hate crime? Possibly, but the method of killing seemed haphazard, certainly badly planned.

To me, it seemed more like the attack of a madman: the victim had gone into the toilets in the hope of a gay sexual encounter and had instead run straight into a psycho with a knife.

By late afternoon, the office was in chaos, as Major Crimes arrived and joined the hunt for the playpark murderer, while we fielded calls from people demanding to know what the CBRN team was up to. When Steve Rodhouse came in, he said, 'Good to see you, Dangerous. When I saw what was on today, I knew you were back!'

CCTV eventually led Major Crimes and us to 30-year-old Mark Malone. He claimed the stabbing had been an 'accident' and also said he couldn't remember much about attacking the 50-year-old victim, Jeff Akers.

Malone had assaulted a gay man in the same toilets a few months earlier and had a previous conviction for a homophobic attack in 2003.

This time he was sentenced to life, to serve a minimum of 30 years.

The person behind the death threats to Avram Grant was never identified.

* * *

Helen and I found we couldn't switch off outside of work. The stress we'd felt in Australia was there all the time and we were always on alert. Now, after having stayed solid through our Australian nightmare, and having no one to fight in the UK, we started fighting each other. We were broke and couldn't sleep; I drank too much, and once Jack had been put to bed we fought about the same things, over and over again.

I still loved being a detective, but as a team leader of four (a team coordinator, one police constable and two designated investigating officers) my workload was off the scale. I was responsible for dealing with anything from 20 to 70 crimes at a time, everything from theft up to attempted murder.

I also dealt with my team's welfare, training and sickness – and, in an unpleasant development, new things like 'performance development reviews' and 'quality assurance' – and was expected to do so without any training myself.

I spent half my working day writing progress reports on investigations instead of doing detective work. Civilian managers seemed to be everywhere. They were equivalent in rank/payband to chief inspectors, and our head of finance 'ordered' us to address ours as 'Ma'am'. We did not – and when we found out she'd been abusing our data systems to check on her wayward son (who was already on our radar), we were very quick to tell her off.

As I gradually came to realise the police had been transformed into a business model run by civilians and that police officers were the manual labour, I started to joke that our job was to support the support services instead of protecting the public.

In Surrey today, police officers make up less than 50 per cent of the workforce – that's 200 fewer officers than we had just three years ago. Those 200 officers have been replaced by 1,300 civilian staff.

'I've only been gone two fucking years,' I said to Nick after my first week back. 'What happened?'

'It's the Brave New World, Dangerous,' he replied. 'Get used to it.'

22

A Day in the Life

05.40

The LED alarm flashed and screamed. I slapped it off, sat up on the sofa and groaned. Hangover. I stomped through the house like a zombie and shoved my head under a full-speed shower. I staggered downstairs and made a pot of strong, black coffee.

06.20

Vaguely human, I stuck my head into Jack's room. My two-year-old boy was already awake.

'Daddy!' he cried and extended his little arms above the blankets.

'Morning, buddy.' I lived for his smile. The hardest part of my day was tearing myself away from my sweet-souled boy.

'Mummy!' Helen had appeared behind me in the doorway. She smiled at Jack and blanked me. We weren't speaking after our row, the usual 'that bloody job' argument the night before. Our unspoken rule was that we never fought in front of Jack, but I'm sure the sensitive little chap couldn't help but sense the tension between us.

'Come on, Jack,' Helen said. 'Up we get.'

'I've got him,' I said, desperate for a few minutes more of Jack's company before the working day began. I never got to see him in the evenings – although I always held out hope that I'd make it home in time. I lifted him out of the bed and carried him to the bathroom, quietly singing his favourite song as we went.

Twenty-five minutes later I waved goodbye, slammed the car door and started the thirty-mile drive to Staines, making it in just under half an hour, as dawn broke, revealing a grey and windswept summer morning.

07.30

I walked into the office, biro primed, ready to try and move an encyclopedic stack of paperwork from the in-tray to the out-tray. I already had thirty-two open crimes on my desk from the previous day, but as I arrived I was handed another six, including two freshly caught burglars, who were in the cells downstairs. By 07:52, my workload was 38 and counting. By 08:15, I'd reviewed and allocated 32 of them to my team. Just as I thought I was getting somewhere, Nick, the Inspector Clouseau lookalike, slammed down the phone.

'Fuck!'

I stopped writing, turned and looked across at Nick. 'What's up, sarge?'

'Who the fuck stabs someone at eight o'clock in the fucking morning? It's all yours, Dangerous.'

'But I'm 38 crimes and counting.'

'You're up, right? Bill's already out on an ABH, a distraction burglary and a con artist. I'm weighed down with a GBH from last night.' He shrugged. 'The only other detective I can see in this office is you, so off you go, sunshine.'

A stabbing could take all day to deal with. Oh well. Any excuse to ditch the paperwork.

As I jogged down the stairs towards the back door and into the car park, I ran into Jimmy, a black covert officer. Jimmy walked with a 'Shaft' strut and wore a magnificent Afro. 'All right, Jimmy?' I asked.

'Not really, man,' he said, shaking his head. 'I'm fed up with getting challenged every time I come into this fucking building.'

'Jimmy, take a look at yourself. You look like gangster number one.'

'Yeah, but just now I got challenged by a black officer and an Asian one. I showed them my warrant card. But did that reassure them? No! Fuck if it did not!'

'And?'

'They tried to nick me for impersonating a police officer.' He laughed. 'Racist motherfuckers!'

'That's the trouble with working undercover – severe lack of recognition on all fronts. Now, if you'll excuse me, a stabbing awaits.'

08.30

I zipped over to a small shopping centre in Walton so quickly that I beat the ambulance. Sure enough, around the back, a twenty-something bloke in a security guard uniform was sat on a bench with a screwdriver protruding from his flabby stomach.

The PC on the scene consulted his notebook as he read me the facts, out of earshot of the victim.

'The victim works as a security guard. Says he stepped out for a cigarette and was attacked.'

'Description?'

The PC flipped a page. 'White, average height, average build, brown hair, jeans and dark jacket.'

'Couldn't be more generic if he tried,' I said, winking at the PC. Walking over, I whistled, as if impressed, and plastered a sympathetic expression on my face.

'Oh dear, oh dear. That as painful as it looks?'

The guy, who was white, about three stone overweight with rounded shoulders, had tears in his eyes. He looked up at me, nodded and flinched as I bent down for a closer inspection.

'Anyone you want us to contact for you?' I asked. 'To let them know what's happened?'

'We're already doing that,' the PC said. 'There's a girlfriend and we've called—'

'OK, I've seen all I need to,' I said with a sigh, standing up straight and dusting my hands. 'A word please, constable.'

Once we were out of earshot of the victim, I said, 'That young man has faked his own stabbing for attention.'

'What?'

'First off, the screwdriver's gone in side on, into that unhealthy roll of fat spilling over his belt line. It's in the softest part of his body. He's grabbed a nice flabby roll with his left hand and thrust the

Phillips – a wise choice, as the pointed end means it'll do less damage than a normal flat-ended screwdriver – in from right to left. It's just in fatty tissue, there's hardly any blood. If an attacker had thrust in a screwdriver, he would have been far more likely to go in front to back and, once through the skin, the metal would slip through his fatty tissue like a knife through butter and into the muscle below.

'Second, he's had a row with his girlfriend, most likely he's been dumped and this is the only way he can think of winning back her affections.'

'How do you know?'

'He stinks of hangover, hasn't shaved, rings under those puppy-dog eyes. Trust me, I've been there often enough to know.'

'What do you want us to do with him?'

'Well, he's also a pretty hopeless security guard.' I pointed at an adjoining building where a modern-looking CCTV camera covered the car park. 'He hasn't even noticed that there's CCTV up there. Rewind the film, have a look and confront him.'

Then, thinking of all the paperwork yet to be gone through on my desk, I added, 'Once you've done that, nick him for wasting police time and give him a fixed penalty fine.'

09.30

Back at the station I allocated my two burglary suspects to Marisa and Nicki. Marisa was an ex-army Royal Military Police (RMP) sergeant who'd served two tours in Iraq. She is one of the best investigators I've been privileged to see in action. Nicki was an ex-Territorial RMP who'd been on one tour of Iraq and was an extremely good researcher. Many of the best police officers and investigators came to us from the army.

I then allocated the remaining crimes to my team before reviewing the disclosure reports to be given to our prisoners (that's so they can see what evidence we have against them) and OK'ing them.

Our prisoners included three Section 18 GBHs (that's Grievous Bodily Harm with intent, as opposed to the more common Section 20 GBH without intent, i.e. 'I didn't mean to crack his skull open, officer'); a serial paedophile who'd sexually assaulted an eleven-year-old boy, and nine house burglaries, for which we'd nabbed two suspects.

10.00

More crimes were coming in all the time: my workload was now at 43. I reviewed the new crimes and put down two as 'no crimes' (severe lack of willingness on the part of the victims in an assault case), then allocated the remaining three: a Section 20 GBH, racial vandalism and – the current flavour of the month – a Facebook insult, which, believe it or not, constitutes a harassment and communications offence. As mad as this seems, someone will ring the call centre and say that their ex has posted a nasty message on Facebook about them. While all police officers would wish the operator would tell them we had more important things to deal with – such as rape, racially motivated assaults, murder and so on – the call taker will create a crime report of 'harassment' and two officers will be sent around to take statements. This could well end up taking anything between ten and twenty hours of police work and result in an encyclopedia-sized folder over the following weeks and months. Arrests and interviews will be conducted, laptops will be seized and very expensive research will be carried out to prove that the message was indeed posted by the accused. After all that, the CPS will take a look at it and say, 'No thank you very much,' and we'll caution the offender. Alternatively, it could turn into a job, in which case Facebook will decline to give us any information without a United States Federal Warrant (which we won't get) – until a teenager commits suicide because of online bullying, then we get loads of cooperation.

10.38

I was bent over a pile of forms when the open channel crackled into life. 'Anyone available for a human foot in a wheelie bin?'

My pen hovered. We got plenty of calls like this, but they were always mannequins.

'Yeah, this is Nick from Staines CID and we're monitoring, 2300.'

I looked up. Nick 'the Genie' smiled at me pleasantly.

'What the fuck, Nick?' He'd given them my collar number. Bastard, he knew I was up to my eyebrows and didn't have time for this crap.

'Do you see another detective in this room?'

A few minutes later I was on the phone to Kelly, the PC on the scene.

'Are you *sure* it's a human foot?' I asked.

'Well, it certainly *looks* like one,' she replied cautiously. 'Except it's green and purple.'

'How does it smell?'

'Smell? Erm, I don't know.'

'Have a sniff. If it smells of a cloying, all-enveloping sickly sweet odour that sticks to your nose, clothes and breath, then it's a dead body.'

There was a pause and then: 'Oh God, yeah, that's exactly how it smells.'

'Do us a favour, cordon the estate, we'll be there as soon as.' After I hung up the phone, I called across to Nick. 'Got any ibuprofen?'

'Breakfast of champions,' Nick replied as he lobbed a white plastic bottle.

As I drove, I got a call from a very experienced uniformed sergeant who'd arrived on the scene. 'Yeah, that's definitely a ripe one.'

'OK, I'm calling it as a murder. I'll get onto Major Crimes.'

A few minutes later a detective inspector from the Major Crime Investigation Team called me back to give me an earful about why I couldn't call it a murder until I'd assessed the scene.

I 'uhuh'd' my way through the call, keeping my thoughts to myself. A rotting body in a wheelie bin not a murder? What was it, then? A suicide by wheelie bin? Accidental? Did the victim fall in with their rubbish, break their neck and then fold himself or herself up so the lid fell shut behind them?

11.00

I was the first detective on the scene. It was an ordinary street in Cobham containing thirty smallish council houses that were overlooked on two sides by council flats. Cobham – a prosperous commuter town, home to about 10,000 people – was hardly a crime blackspot and there was no obvious reason why a body should have been dumped in this street. Murderers tend to dump their victims' bodies in woods or simply leave them at the scene. Sometimes, keen to show the world what they've done, they set fire to the body in a prominent location. The more determined ones bury their victims in woodland or chop them into little pieces, scattering them far and wide. It was the first time in over ten years of policing that I'd encountered a murderer who'd tried to recruit the bin men to help dispose of an intact body.

The foot was poking out of a wheelie bin that had fallen on its side. The skin was indeed green and purple, as Kelly had said; the nails were a bloody black. Definitely not a mannequin.

The bin men hadn't emptied the wheelie bin for three weeks because it was too heavy – good old health and safety. I had no idea what had caused it to topple over, but the impact had caused the cadaver to burst and it was now releasing an all-too familiar sickly sweet, thick and heavy cloying odour that clung to anyone within range. It was already in my clothes and on my skin. The odour would still be in my nostrils tonight, and the strange, unpleasant taste that went with it would still be in my mouth whatever spirits I might choose to pour down my throat at the end of the day.

The smell of human decay takes days to fade and isn't budged easily by soap or washing powder – they should make a special detergent for detectives: 'New Improved Blazzo: Removes the Stench of Death'.

I rubbed my eyes. I was still waiting for the painkillers to kick in. I spotted Kelly, the 22-year-old bright-eyed, bushy-tailed WPC who was first on the scene.

'You all right?' I asked. She looked a little green. This was her dead body premiere, her first taste of the smell of death. She nodded.

'Hang in there,' I told her. 'You get used to it.' Words of small comfort, really. You don't. I didn't, anyway.

I looked up at the sky. Heavy grey clouds were rolling over the flat countryside. For once, the weatherman was right; the predicted summer storm was brewing. I had to move fast. I needed to grab as much forensic information as possible before the crime scene changed further. As people get on with their lives, vehicles start to come and go, and witnesses leave a scene, it becomes harder to piece together a picture of the incident. Other factors – the wind changing direction and picking up speed, and rain washing away fibres, stains and prints – also make a huge impact on evidence.

The residents of a block of low-rise flats had a 270-degree view over the scene. I ordered cordons to go beyond the flats and started door-to-doors while waiting for the forensics to turn up.

11.15

'It's my neighbour's bin,' the man told me, peering over my shoulder at the crime scene as he spoke.

'And where's your neighbour?' I asked.

'Pete? He moved out a few weeks ago. His wife died three years back, but he met a new sort recently and they went to live abroad together.'

'What did he do with all his possessions?' I asked. 'Did he take anything with him?'

'He hired a van to move out all his gear.' The neighbour remembered it had an orange logo and a circle on the side. Luckily, I had three detectives back at the office to call upon – Nick, Dave and Adele – who quickly found that this description matched the insignia of the vans from a hire firm in Kingston, Surrey. Sure enough, the suspect – as I now considered him – had rented the van and had driven it to France and then Malta about three weeks earlier.

11.30

Katy, the senior Scenes of Crime Officer, rolled up. In her early 30s, she was dedicated, professional and, best of all, quick to get a crime scene under wraps.

'So, how do you want to get the body out of there?' I asked.

'Well, once we've put a tent over it, we can lift it and try to slide it out. We just can't let it slip, that's all, otherwise it'll be kersplatto on the road and we'll lose evidence, not to mention give the locals a gruesome display when the bodily fluids stream downhill towards the cordon.'

'And there's press on three sides of the cordon, trying to photograph it,' I added. 'So let's not give them anything for the evening edition.'

In the end, we decided that if five of us took the wheeled end of the bin and up-ended it slightly, we would be able to gently slide the body out onto the body bag, which had raised edges to trap any fluids. Katy really needed the best preservation possible. Things like fibres, maggots and insects are crucial in putting together the story of a murder – they can tell you everything, from the approximate date of death to whether the body has been moved from one location to another.

11.40

Once the forensic tent was up and over the scene, Katy, poor Kelly and two other uniformed officers prepared to lift the bin. The smell was incredible. Having given up on Vicks, I'd come to rely on only breathing through my mouth to avoid the smell and sucking Extra Strong Mints, but the thought of putting anything in my mouth only made the queasiness worse.

'Anybody feels like they're going to vomit, you've got to run as far from the scene as possible, OK?' Katy said. 'We can't risk contamination and I don't want to have to work around whatever you had for breakfast.'

We nodded, took a deep breath. 'On my count. One. Two. Three!' We heaved the bin up and started to tip it over, and out the decomposed remains slid, along with a load of fluid and countless maggots.

Less than a second later, the crowds gathered around the cordon saw four of us scramble outside the tent and make for the bushes behind a nearby house at top speed. Katy was the only one able to stay inside.

11.43

Just as I was getting myself back together, the phone rang. It was the CPS and they were refusing to charge my burglaries. I couldn't believe it. The burglars in question were my old friends the Blythe brothers, Gary and Derek. As I mentioned before, Gary, the older brother, was a 30-year-old junkie and alcoholic who looked double his age, while 18-year-old Derek was a nice kid who'd been led astray by Gary. I still held out a small and naive reserve of hope that Derek could be 'saved'.

Gary's record of past crimes was extremely thick (he once confessed to carrying out thirty-five burglaries in just two weeks). Looking at the evidence, I'd assumed that the hapless pair was bang to rights and that we'd have little trouble placing him on remand and giving the law-abiding residents of Surrey a brief respite. According to the CPS, we needed more proof. Fingerprints on stolen goods; matching footprints at the scene? What else was there?

'Look, I've caught a murder, let me get back to you.' I hung up and went back to work on the body in the bin. Still no sign of Major Crimes, so I pressed on with the help of the sergeant, Kelly and Nick back at the office. By the time the DI from Major Crimes finally rocked up, I was done and dusted.

'Looks to me as if a good bet would be Peter Wallner,' I told her. 'He recently left the UK to live abroad in Malta with his new girlfriend. Melanie, the old one, died suddenly three years ago.'

'OK, we'll take it from here.'

A thank you would have been nice. That was the end of my involvement in the case; it was frustrating not to be able to join Major Crimes to see it through to the end, but this was very much part of the life of an on-call detective.[27]

13.20

The CPS still couldn't get their heads round the fact that we had the Blythe brothers bang to rights. This quickly spiralled into an argument and so, after referring them to an identical case from six months

---

[27] Peter Wallner was jailed for life in June 2010. He'd murdered Melanie by hitting her on the head with a cast-iron griddle pan while she was sleeping. Wallner slept with his new girlfriend in the same bed the very next day. He then bought a £99 freezer from Argos and kept the body there for three years. Wallner had held a memorial service for Melanie and took her 'ashes' (from his barbecue) to her family in South Africa, telling them that she'd died of an aneurysm.

After he put Melanie's body in the wheelie bin, he gave the freezer to his neighbours. The officer who was sent to tell them that they'd been keeping food in a container that had been used to store a dead body for three years did so with ill-concealed glee.

earlier, when they'd had no trouble remanding the suspect, I told them to take it up with my detective inspector.

'I just don't get how they think,' I told Nick once I was back in the office. 'It's like talking to someone with schizophrenia.'

I took out my biro and started to hit the mass of paperwork with a vengeance. If I motored through it and nothing else happened, please God, then there was still a chance I'd get to leave on time and see Jack before bedtime.

14.40

My phone rang. It was the CPS. I made the time-honoured hand signal to Nick, who nodded sympathetically. Despite talking to the DI, they were still refusing to charge and remand the Blythe brothers. 'Look,' I said, struggling to control my temper, 'these are two of our county's most prolific burglars.'

'We don't think the evidence warrants charging. There's room for reasonable doubt.'

'So, all we're going to tell them is that even though we've got them bang to rights and they know it, they're free to return to the wilds of Surrey. They're drug addicts, so that means they'll go straight back to work over some poor citizen's home this evening and those goods, those valuable items that those good citizens have slaved, like you and I, to purchase, will disappear and be sold at 20 per cent of the market value so the money can be spent on supporting our local drug dealers.'

'I'm sorry but—'

'You can talk to my superintendent. Good luck with that.'

I hung up and sighed. 'Jesus.'

'You know what?' Nick said. 'We should do like the Swiss. They had a massive heroin problem in a town the size of Guildford and they took all the addicts to an airbase out of town and gave them all the heroin they wanted for free. The burglary rate dropped to sweet fuck-all overnight.'

'Then we could do some real police work,' I said.

Nick made like he was smoking a joint and passed it across to me. 'Yeah, dream on, Dangerous,' he drawled in a stoner voice.

15.00

The door flew open. Uncle Bill marched in and sat down. 'Eyes down, lads. Tarzan's on the war path.'

Nick and I both swore and then tried to look busy. 'Tarzan' was Chief Superintendent George Hampton and he was under pressure to meet targets. He was ex-Royal Marines and still behaved like he was in barracks.

The door crashed open. There he stood, wild-eyed, red in the face, his low brow furrowed in anger. We all looked down. 'Please don't pick me, don't pick me,' I repeated over and over in my mind, thinking of Jack.

Tarzan thrust out a fat finger, pointed at me and screamed, 'MY OFFICE!' Then stormed off.

I looked at Bill and Nick. 'What the fuck did I do?' I asked. They shrugged.

As I got up from my desk, the sound of the funeral march came from Bill's computer. He and Nick made the sign of the cross as I passed.

'Very funny.'

It turned out that Tarzan was ready to wrestle a crocodile over a recent surge in our robbery rate. I could have screamed, if Tarzan wasn't busy doing it already. I sat in the chair and took it, resisting the urge to speak my mind.

Tarzan wanted Bart and me to find and nick some crack-addicted robbers who were terrorising the community. We would have preferred to have found and closed the crack house, but no – raiding crack houses is expensive, dangerous and suggests to the good people of Surrey that we have, horror of horrors, a drug problem.

16.00

I emerged from the meeting to hear that the superintendent had taken the head of Surrey CPS to task over the Blythe brothers and, thank God, they'd finally agreed to prosecute. I went down to custody to charge them and had them remanded by 17.30. There was still a chance I could get away.

18.00

I got back to my desk to find a rape and a playground happy slap had come in. I allocated these crimes and prepared to leave, thinking of a bedtime story to read Jack.

'Hang on, Dangerous,' Nick said as he put down the phone. 'A report has just come in of a drug dealer, name of Thomas Stubbins, stabbed and run over in Chertsey. One of yours, isn't he?'

Drugs crime was my specialist subject, and Tom's name was all too familiar.

The case was mine.

So, that's it. Game over. No chance of seeing Jack before bedtime. I rang Helen and reignited our ongoing argument over my working hours. Once again, I wouldn't see Jack in the evening and he'd go to bed without hearing a story from his dad.

The stabbing had been carried out by a crack dealer, 'Bucky', who was already known to us. I quickly got an address from an informant. Bucky was a gun-carrying Yardie. His standard MO was to intimidate local drug users and set up shop in their house, where he'd rule by fear.

After making a few calls, I discovered that an officer was already up on Bucky as a TP and he confirmed Bucky was in the house. Game on. Once the raiding party had been organised and the warrants sent off, we sat down with a pizza at 20.30 to wait for the paperwork to come back for the arrest of Bucky and another five suspects for the stabbing.

22.30

The warrants arrived. This being Surrey, we didn't have the luxury of an armed squad to call on at short notice at this time of the night, so we crossed our fingers that none of us would get shot when we steamed into the house. We knew we wouldn't get the necessary authority for a firearms team based on this loose intelligence, so it was simply better to do the job and ask forgiveness later if any problems cropped up. There's nothing quite like the feeling of plunging into the unknown, unarmed; it certainly gets the pulse racing.

Luckily for us, when we matchsticked the door with an enforcer, we were inside, screaming, 'Police!' and up the stairs before Bucky could extract himself from the embrace of a local prostitute. We didn't find a gun, but a hunting knife was under his bed.

00.15
All the targets bar one were in custody.

02.30
Finally, they were booked in and bedded down in the cells, ready for some searching questions in the morning. A good night's work. Time for me to get the car and head home.

03.10
My key finally found the lock. I tiptoed up to Jack's room for a look at my sleeping boy, then straight down to the fridge for a beer, and bedded down on the couch.

I closed my eyes. The day replayed itself: bodies, burglars, dealers, handguns and happy slappers.

Five minutes later (it felt like) the alarm went. I looked at the flashing green legend:

05.40
Welcome to life in the modern CID.

23

From Facebook to Special Branch and Back Again

I LOOKED AT THE BULGING RING binder and sighed in utter despair. Just a few years ago, this job would have come nowhere near a CID office. In those good old days, an experienced PC (if only there were some left) would have bound this lot of timewasters over to keep the peace at a Magistrates' Court in one swift ten-minute hearing.

Instead, 'Mandy', 'Tracey' and 'Ricky' were mine, all mine. After six months, I knew their lives better than they did. After all, they spent most of their time with one another drunk and/or stoned and could hardly remember who did what to whom and when. I, on the other hand, had to deal with them while sober and write everything down to boot, so the details really stuck. Honestly, instead of writing this book I could have written a novel starring the three of them that would have rivalled one of Trollope's grand literary soap operas.

Mandy and Tracey had been assaulting each other for months – texting, swearing, shoving and Facebooking the hell out of each other, all because Ricky couldn't decide which one of them he wanted to impregnate (but he seemed to be enjoying practising with both).

Ricky was hardly GQ Man of the Year. For him, high fashion involved baggy, low-low-slung pants, which helped him to walk as though he had a bowling ball between his legs – a cross between Charlie Chaplin and MC Hammer.

Eventually, Tracey discovered the broad police definition of 'assault' and thanks to new buzz-terms such as community reassurance, 'robust' policing, duty of care and the need to maintain public confidence (ahem) in policing, this debacle had to be sorted out by an experienced detective constable, i.e. me.

When the file landed on my desk, I was forced (practically at gunpoint) to seek charges for Section 4 public order, common assault, harassment and the sending of offensive messages (instead of wasting police time).

So, I set about proving the case against Mandy, only to discover that a detective on the other side of the office was trapped in a parallel universe where Mandy had made a raft of counter allegations about Tracey.

Alas, unlike Stephen Hawking's theory (where two parallel worlds cross into co-existence, they cancel each other out), Ricky, Mandy and Tracey did not disappear in a puff of logic but instead led to the formation of a new universe made entirely out of paperwork.

Eventually, some weeks later, both files were sent to the local CPS office based in our nick. The prosecutor, bless him, wasn't able to make his little mind up, so sent me away for a map of the offences (this is a map with little red dots on it, with short explanations detailing the sequence of events).

This same prosecutor always did this to me as a delaying tactic until another, wiser prosecutor with Solomon-like abilities was on duty, who would be able to weigh the two mighty files and decide who should be charged with what and why.

This case eventually bounced around the CID office for six months, with endless, pointless inquiries and procrastination from the CPS – during which time, encouraged by our 'interest', Mandy and Tracey had been reporting further crimes committed by one against the other.

If we'd dealt with this immediately by binding the three of them over to keep the peace, they would have either gone away and stopped bothering us or if one, or both or, heaven forbid, all three of them together had given us any further trouble, I could have taken them and locked them away for a few weeks, during which time Mandy and Tracey would have dumped that idiot excuse for MC Hammer and married each other instead.

I was in the middle of all this, begging the CPS to please, please, just make a decision so I could go and solve some of those troublesome rapes, burglaries and drug-related stabbings that everyone had been getting so worked up about lately, when something really rather interesting came up.

A woman – whom I'll call 'Rebecca' – reported that her husband had beaten her up. I called her as soon as I received the PC's report, but as there were no bruises or witnesses, it was a case of he-says-she-says and I wasn't hopeful that my investigation would come to much.

This feeling was reinforced when I discovered that her husband happened to be a powerful European businessman with a platoon of expensive lawyers at his command.

'Well, there is something else I can tell you,' Rebecca said, clearly seeking revenge.

'Yes?' My pen was poised in hope.

'He keeps an unlicensed handgun in the house.'

Aha. Now, that's more like it.

'And do you happen to know where he keeps it?'

'Under the boiler.'

Of course this could be a plant, an effort on her part to serve her husband a cold slice of revenge. But possession of an illegal firearm can add up to five years inside, so, whatever the case, this was definitely worth checking out.

As was normal procedure, I ran the name of the accused through our database and a very interesting note flashed up. I was to call Special Branch immediately, which I did.

'Stay put. Don't do anything until we get there.'

A few hours later I was driving alongside some very smart and well-spoken gentlemen from Special Branch, that unique and noble part of the police that is devoted to combating terrorism. With Russian assassins, Irish Nationalists and extremist Muslim groups, not to mention animal liberation groups and the English Defence League, they'd never been busier.

We rolled up to the address – after cruising down a mile-long drive in the Surrey hills. It was dark, but the house – mansion, stately home – was well lit.

We were met at the door by a foreign, ex-military bodyguard with two of the largest and most well-behaved Rottweilers I've come across – and I've seen lots. Criminals seem to love them; I think they see something of themselves in these dogs and that's why they're drawn to them. The animals sat by his side, alert but still. It was clear that one word and these chaps would have our throats in their jaws before you could say, 'Down, boy.' The man's head was shaven and he had military tattoos. He was about 5 ft 7 without an ounce of fat on him and was trying very hard to pass for a 'handyman'.

'My employer is not here now,' he said. 'He's away on business. You cannot come in.'

I explained that I had a warrant. He refused again and we were soon locked in an uncomfortable stand-off. I'm sure he was spooked by the Special Branch chaps, who were hanging back, or perhaps he had good reason to be worried about what I might find.

I refused to budge and explained patiently about UK law and authority. I hoped he wouldn't force me to say something like, 'I'm going to have to call a senior officer,' as no guv'nor was going to touch this job. It was clear that something bent was about to happen and no one wanted his or her name anywhere near it in case it all went horribly wrong. Thankfully, the 'handyman' finally decided to take the dogs away and let us in.

Inside everything was velvet red or gilded in gold. Huge portraits by Old Masters and a few newer ones filled the hallway. As we passed through a giant library with sliding ladders, a painted ceiling and ancient-looking books, I realised it was going to take me hours just to find a boiler, and the right one to boot, let alone find the gun.

As I began my search, one of the Special Branch chaps took me to one side.

'Any chance you could distract Mr Handyman for us?'

I nodded. I didn't ask any questions, thinking Official Secrets and all that, and asked the handyman if he could show us where the cars were, as we'd like to check the gloveboxes.

The 'garage' was more like a museum. The amount of money this man had to hand must have been obscene. I wondered where he'd started from, perhaps as an entrepreneur who was in the right place at the right time, and ruthless and smart enough to defeat his competitors.

You almost had to admire him, but I couldn't help but think that an awful lot of people must have suffered for one man to become so incredibly rich in such a short space of time. You don't get *this* wealthy by helping others less fortunate than yourself.

Mr Handyman struggled to find the keys and, while he continued his search, I sought out the boiler room and found the gun, which turned out to be nothing more than a BB gun – a realistic-looking plastic toy that fires plastic pellets.

I returned to the house to see how the SB boys were getting along. I found them in the study, systematically photographing and scanning documents, including bank statements, using a portable scanner. They'd also opened a few laptops and had inserted pen drives that were downloading the laptops' contents.

One of them looked up as I came in.

'Everything OK?' he asked.

'What are you up to then?' I asked, with a slight smile.

'Well, we got to really, don't we?'

This was data theft – very, very illegal. We were in there on the power of a warrant granted under the Firearms Act 1968. We were most definitely not empowered to sift data. But I was hardly going to stop them. If I'd grassed on them, chances are nothing would come of it, except I'd earn myself a reputation as someone not to be trusted. Sometimes rules are broken and it just makes more sense to accept that.

As I'd been hunting a firearm, I had to inform an inspector about what I had found and he'd now joined us. When I got outside, he was getting into his car.

'Well?' he asked. 'Did you find the gun?'

'BB gun, guv. Nothing for us to worry about. His wife may have planted it there, a case of attempted revenge.'

'I see,' he said. 'Well, no need for me to stick around then, is there?'

'Sir?'

'Well, my dinner's on. Mustn't keep the missus waiting. I've hardly been home this week.'

'But, sir—'

'Yes?' he replied testily.

'Well, Special Branch are still here.'

'So? They're big boys, aren't they? They don't need me here to hold their hands. If you need me, I'll be—'

'Having dinner, sir?'

'Correct.'

When Special Branch had finally finished, they thanked me, said goodbye and drove back to base, where their analysts were waiting to go through their booty.

I went back to the station to write my report. Still on my desk was Mandy's enormous file. I wanted to open the window, throw it into the street below and erase all memory of their pathetic disputes.

The next day assault charges were finally brought against Mandy, who then made a complaint against me for breaching 'me 'uman rights, innit', for being out on bail so long and taking 'that bitch's side, innit'.

At Magistrates' Court, Mandy elected for trial by jury at Crown Court so the whole world (estate) could witness her tribulations. So, off to Crown Court we went (removing me from real work again) and after about 30 minutes of toing and froing, the judge saw through Mandy's not guilty plea and delivered a very polite but menacing admonishment, detailing the long list of evidence against her (text messages, Facebook postings, eyewitnesses, etc.).

Mandy stood firm and refused to change her plea, so the file, now three lever-arches full, came back to me for an upgrade, which took me another half-day and involved more paperwork, adding full interview transcripts, exhibit lists, unused material schedules and so on.

We went back four weeks later and this time Mandy copped a plea to Section 5 public order (a far less serious offence) and a breach of the peace. She was conditionally discharged for 12 months (this is the same as being bound over to keep the peace) and fined a mighty £150.

Cost to the taxpayer? Between £10,000 and £15,000, taking into account my time, the barristers' time, the court process and other legal and support services' fees.

Oh, and next week it was Tracey's turn.

Now, where's that Special Branch application form?

24

Nobly Corrupt

THE SPECIAL BRANCH OFFICERS IN THE previous chapter were engaged in what is known as 'noble cause corruption', a technique favoured by TV character Detective Inspector Gene Hunt[28]: you know scrote is guilty of said crime but can't prove it in court, so find another way of either sending scrote down for a long stretch by fitting scrote up for said crime or another, similar crime. It's sometimes referred to as the 'Ways and Means Act'.

The milder form of this could be 'bending' the rules to ease along a charge. My old man, for instance, had been bumped up from detective sergeant to an acting detective inspector for one job.

The paperwork putting him back down, however, wasn't issued for some weeks afterwards. In the meantime, Dad used his DI rank to authorise searches on other jobs.

Did I ever abuse authority and position to ease a job along? Yes, I did. I was nobly corrupt and there are many, many others.

For example, if you were to obtain from BT the phone records on the call box closest to Surrey's CID offices, you'd probably find the most called number was 0800 555 111 – Crime Stoppers. Once we were certain there was drug dealing in a property, say, we'd go to our boss for a warrant. Every now and then he would

---

[28] A deputy chief constable banned all reference to Gene Hunt in Surrey police stations, including any news articles, books, pictures and quotes. Seriously.

say, 'There's not enough evidence here to justify kicking their door down. We need corroboration.'

'Fair enough, guv.'

One of us would leave the office, stroll down the road, pick up the receiver, dial Crime Stoppers and say, 'Yes, I'd like to report drug dealing taking place at X Address . . . Yes, I've seen them selling crack and heroin and people have been coming and going all day. I'm sick of it, I'm going to call the local paper.'

By the time the 'mystery caller' was back in the office, we'd have our warrant. We were never wrong because we only used this method when we were absolutely certain but simply lacked the proof for a warrant that would allow us to smash our way into the property. That doesn't make it right, of course.

'Verballing' is a type of noble cause corruption, not used so much these days, thanks to PACE, but variations still exist. Verballing takes place when a police officer puts words into a suspect's mouth. A favourite variation on verballing is to wind the suspect up so that they're spitting and swearing in the interview and when their anger is at its zenith you drop the line, 'The judge ain't gonna like this, pal.'

What usually follows from the irate client is something like: 'Fuck the fucking judge. Fucking old cunt!'

At the time, the drunken lout will think he's successfully stuck two fingers up at authority, but nine months later when the arresting officer delivers that quote in front of a jury in his best court voice, dressed in suit and tie, the judge's eyebrows will arch as if to say, 'Oh, so that's what he thinks, is it?' The results can be devastating for the accused.

Verballing also takes place in the pre-PACE, after-arrest interview. Once you're nicked and cautioned, we can't interview you outside of a custody environment and without your being able to exercise your rights. We can ask questions to save life and limb, or to recover property, but that's all. However, on many occasions with a certain DS – who is now a senior Met officer – I had entries in my notebook that started:

On day/date/time, I was with DS ****** and we spoke with John Smith. I said to SMITH I am arresting you on suspicion of robbery x 5 and burglary x 6. He was cautioned and made no reply. He was placed in a police vehicle and conveyed to custody. During the journey SMITH made the following unsolicited comments, to which he signed for accuracy in this PNB [police notebook].

What followed next was a full and frank confession to said crimes. Why? Had he decided to turn a new leaf or suddenly felt the urge to unburden? No. It's because we threatened to take his wife into custody – which would lead to his kids being taken into care. This section of the conversation would not find its way into our notebooks. It's a very common ploy; so common, in fact, that it has its own term amongst police officers. It's called 'taking a hostage'.

Sometimes we would just be having a 'casual chat' in the car and, before he knows what he's done, the suspect has dropped himself in it and, realising it's too late to backtrack, feels compelled to sign. This technique was most successful if the suspect was out of his head on gear. By the time he got his appointed solicitor, he'd be straight and no one would be any the wiser.

And it goes further than this. Once, a burglar was brought in. He knew he'd done it and so did we. Trouble was, we had no evidence. Or did we?

Ask any proper criminal if they've had clothing seized at the time of arrest and the answer will be yes. Those brown paper bags of clothing usually get taken upstairs to our office, often unsealed. In this instance, a DS had a much smaller brown paper bag, one filled with minute glass fragments from one of the burglaries. Guess where the glass was discovered? I only found out later, but by that time the conviction was in. The burglar and I spoke some years later and he accepted it as fair play for all the others he had got away with.

Now, whilst this might be a 'successful outcome', what if the same DS was convinced a rape suspect was guilty but had no proof and that other bag of broken glass or evidence from the victim's home could be used to send him away for ten years?

* * *

Then there's being bent for yourself or 'straight corruption'. This could be knowingly committing an offence for personal gain. Did I do this? Yes. I drove to work whilst over the limit from the night before to work overtime, as did many others, and many still do.

And, of course, every police officer has a warrant card or, as they are more commonly known, an IDT.[29] Any cop who says they haven't badged their way into a nightclub at least once is lying. A few clubs even have a sign-in book for cops, to make queue-jumping easier. I made use of those – on several occasions, accompanied by inspectors and above.

There is a much darker side to corruption, of course: taking bribes, or using confidential information for your own benefit, or committing offences for financial gain (e.g. drug dealing). I know a few officers who fall into this category, some of whom are still going strong.

They see these as perks – privileges of the game. I was once offered £30k in cash for information on drugs warrants. I turned it down, reported it and nothing happened.

Corporate corrupters are officers who have rank, influence or both and use their position, for example, to post their mates on cushy jobs or obtain overtime payments. I've taken advantage of both, seen both happen and have suffered from the negative effects of both.

Let's say you're a DCI and want a specific DC for your unit, but your opposing DCI on the same unit doesn't want to lose the DC for the same reasons you want that DC. What do you do? Simple. You make an offer to bypass normal resource bids and do a favour with your other resources/political acumen if the DC is released to you.

This happened to me, and an entire recruitment – diversity and equal opportunities policy was bypassed. I was right for the job and had the necessary skills, but the way I was transferred broke every rule in the book.

You can apply a similar technique if you're a PC trying to get into CID or another unit. You've enough experience and show immense talent, but for some reason you're just not either getting a chance to

---

[29] International Disco Ticket

appear before the promotional board or passing the paper sift.

The key to success here is to ask who the DCI is on the team you want to move to and find out what they like. In one case, tickets to an important cricket game secured a job in CID.

Remember, I finished number two out of the dozen or so PCs who applied to CID. I sent a bottle of malt to the man with the final say. The PC who finished first sent a case. I doff my policeman's helmet to you, ma'am.

* * *

Police officers have immense power and access. If a senior officer decides to use this power for personal gain, to disrupt someone on a personal level or do a 'favour' for someone, then the system really does fall apart.

This kind of corruption can be noble, too. The most important decision maker in a surveillance application form is the authorising officer. This officer, of superintendent rank or above, is supposed to carefully review the 28-page application before signing off his approval.

One authorising officer trusted me enough to give me blank, pre-signed authorities. Suddenly, I (a lowly detective constable) had the power and authority to have a surveillance team invade someone's personal life for three months. This was totally illegal and against the Human Rights Act. Today, this authorising officer regularly briefs the Prime Minister and government ministers.

Then there are those senior officers who step in to save themselves by making a phone call – the public foots the bill, as junior ranks sort out the mess.

I suppose the question here is: would you do the same thing if you had that power? You suddenly find yourself drunk and upside down in a brand new car on a straight and remote country lane after leaving a big police party. Do you:

a: turn yourself in, get fired, lose your £80k index-linked pension and £90k leaving bonus?

b. call the AA and hope nobody notices?

  c. phone a friend? (i.e. call a trusted junior officer and explain how grateful you will be if they could see their way to sorting out your unholy mess without breathalysing you.)

This actually happened and the answer is, of course, c.

Other senior officers were just as bad. One alcoholic assistant chief constable was caught driving several times over the limit. He resigned, kept his pension and no mention was ever made in the press.

There is an understanding in the police that once you reach a certain rank you're 'in the club' and safe; you'll be looked after, no matter what you do wrong – everybody's got one another's back. If you're below that rank, then it's a different story entirely.

Then there are the sell-outs. The police are supposed to be politically independent. When I was still in uniform, I was invited to an informal meeting with our then new chief constable, Ian Blair, where we were able to ask him any question we liked about the job. He'd just told us that he'd committed to five years' service in Surrey and so my question was:

'What are you going to do for Surrey over the next five years?'

'I'm going to do all I can to reduce crime,' he replied, before adding, 'Don't you worry, I'm here for the long haul, five years and beyond.'

Blair left Surrey to become commissioner for the Met police eight months later. And the rest, as they say, is travesty. Blair did little to rein in his support for Tony Blair's Labour Government (for example, he let Labour politicians campaign from Met police cars sporting a red Labour rose and the slogan 'Vote Labour').

When that government lost the election, Boris Johnson, the Conservative Mayor of London, forced Blair out of the top job. In response, Blair's Labour supporters forced through a life peerage for the former commissioner, for all his good work as a police officer.

Corruption that occurs in the lower ranks can often only occur thanks to senior officers who think that the crimes of others will reflect badly on them and their promotional chances.

Arresting someone for possession of a controlled substance is supposed to be a good thing, right?

Not if he turns out to be the poster boy for your police force, it's not.

Tarzan was under pressure to meet targets and told us, 'Don't bother with these long-term ops, it's too late for that this year. We need' – he consulted a file on his desk – 'another 20 drug arrests to meet our targets.'

Right, then.

Drugs had gone missing from our evidence stores, so we called the Professional Standards Department, who set up a surveillance camera and, lo and behold, a PC came in, fiddled about for a bit and vanished again.

When we checked the stash, we discovered he'd take a small amount of crack. He said it was the only thing that helped his headaches (which suggested he'd been trying other drugs). The officer was gay and happened to have a very influential partner, who wrote directly to the chief constable and the court, pleading for clemency.

The officer received community service and he quietly resigned from the job. This after abusing his position to steal class-A drugs for inter-couple enjoyment.

* * *

Take one handsome family-oriented officer and make him the police representative for the local neighbourhood. It's a PR dream. A little while later several female officers, female residents, victims of crime and a couple of – ahem – ladies of the night complain that this officer is a sex pest and *voilà*, you have a PR nightmare.

Especially when you check his record and discover that the same officer had previously been arrested as part of a sting operation targeting kerb crawlers in a neighbouring police force.

For some reason, this rather crucial fact was not uncovered during the vetting process when he applied to become a constable. This man was eased out quietly, while the harassed females were denied a full explanation and compensation because the vetting failures were never disclosed to them.

A one-off mistake? Sadly not.

* * *

Another one of our officers was found in possession of and admitted downloading child pornography. He too was allowed to resign with just a caution, with no mention in the press. It was too embarrassing for those responsible to admit that they'd allowed child abusers to join their police force.

At least 24 officers in Surrey (that I knew of) had criminal records for offences including perverting the course of justice, grievous bodily harm, theft, drug taking and drug dealing.

One night, a probationary PC was out on the town and so drunk he was unable to stand straight. On being refused entry to a club, he racially abused the doorman, who was of an appearance that does not inspire confidence in airports these days. The police were called and the probie was arrested.

So just to re-cap:

Male PC
Probationer
Drunk
Racist
Arrested

I'd love to tell you that the following also happened:

Charged
Went to court
Convicted

But I can't. A close relative happened to be a staff officer to the chief constable. So what happened to our racist, violent, alcohol-abusing friend?

Nothing. In fact he's since left the police of his own accord and the reference he received from Surrey Constabulary helped him to get into the Royal Military Academy, Sandhurst, from where he's recently graduated and is about to start a tour abroad – commanding a platoon.

* * *

For me, it suddenly seemed as though every time I tried to do my job I was stepping over corruption and cover up. This is partly because it was usually the CID officers who were trusted enough to deal with scandals 'quietly', so we got to know about, if not experience up close, most of the goings-on.

Everyone breaks the rules, from PC to commissioner. The only rule you shouldn't break is: don't get caught. Unless you have friends in high places or secrets the powerful would prefer kept quiet.

After dealing with our crack-thieving policeman, I flipped out at Bart and Nick.

'If only those fucking chief inspectors didn't want to be superintendents and collect their fucking end-of-career bonuses and meaty fucking pensions; if only they had the guts to just for once be a fucking policeman, then the police wouldn't be full of fuck-ups like poster boy and we might be able to spend more time policing than covering our own fucking arses! But no, once you're above the rank of chief inspector you're in the club where everybody stays fucking friends, everybody gets looked after if they fuck up and everybody still gets paid.'

'I don't think *you're* going to end up on any poster any time soon, Dangerous,' Nick replied.

25

The Crime Factory

CRIME REPORTING AND RECORDING IS ANOTHER way we regularly manipulated and abused the system – because we had to, to get any work done.

We used to have something called 'discretion', where some piffling matter – for example, a passionate disagreement over who saw what parking space first – was dealt with on the street by a copper, saying, 'No harm, no foul. You go that way and you go the other.'

Then Labour hit us with onerous reporting, creating a new word, so now absolutely everything we encounter has to be 'crimed' according to the Home Office Counting Rules (HOCR). We're also measured on detection rates, so as long as a crime is 'undetected' (unsolved), then it counts against us.

The rise in crime reporting was so dramatic that there is no way that we could caution, charge or summons every offence and therefore detect every crime. To cover this, the police came up with something called a 'detected, no proceedings' or 'effective resolution', which the Home Office accepted. This is designed specifically with minor crimes in mind and can result in a non-paperwork jamboree for an officer if:

It's not in the public interest to prosecute (there are many ways
    to manipulate this)
The Victim does not want to proceed (ditto)
The Suspect has died

The Suspect cannot be prosecuted because of a medical condition, but if they *were* well enough there would have been a reasonable chance of conviction

How would I talk a victim out of proceeding?

'Look, let's have a cup of tea and talk through the process of statements, court appearances, days off work for court, witness care. Too much hassle? I understand your concerns. Well, if you're sure you don't want to. Sign here, please. Thank you.'

Once a local drug addict is sectioned (detained under the Mental Health Act), detectives and police officers alike immediately release an avalanche of 'no proceedings applications'.

'Guv, he's gone mental and we know he nicked a car stereo. Look how many other thefts of car stereos we've got over the past five years. Surely, he must have done them all?'

The same applies for dead scrote. Any crime that can be linked to them, whether stone-bonker or the subject of a detective's wild fantasy, it gets attached to them and cleared.

This method of binning jobs is mostly used for volume 'petty' crime that would otherwise sit undetected. No one gets a record, so they aren't looked at too hard and we bank large chunks of crime stats by doing this. Detectives don't want to do this, but clearing 'shit jobs' is an absolute must, so that we can keep up with more serious offences.

Reclassification is another neat way of binning a job. A house owner who'd reported a burglary had departed on a holiday before giving us a statement. I waited a week before approaching the DI and telling him that despite phone calls and a calling card I'd had no response.

Without a statement or any further information we can't establish whether the crime fits the definition of a burglary, so we reclassified it as a trespass and I sent them a letter letting them know this was what we'd done. Nine times out of ten you'll never hear from the victim again, and therefore instead of an undetected burglary on the divisional sheet, you're left with a trespass, which is something the Home Office isn't interested in.

'One-on and one-off' is another popular method of stat cooking. Detectives are measured on how many crimes they detect. So if a detective ends up with one job that has several different offences, they 'crime' every one of them and charge them all individually, which takes an inordinate amount of time and duplication, but gets them several detections out of one incident.

As an extreme example of this, I once dealt with a fraudster who'd conned about 50 different people in something known as a 'Ponzi' scheme, named after Charles Ponzi, an infamously successful American scam artist from the 1920s. Basically, a Ponzi robs Peter to pay Paul. Usually, by the time people realise, it's far too late – the money is gone and so is the fraudster.

Shaun Hayes was a former Guards soldier who'd married the socialite daughter of a rich family. His marriage meant he was introduced to the wealthy set and he came to mingle amongst celebrities and footballers at their favourite Surrey haunts.

He'd wait until he was in a group of five people or so before starting his pitch, which ran something like: 'I've got an uncle in Customs who can get hold of cars, computers and luxury goods that have been seized. He'll sell them to me so cheap that you wouldn't believe it and I sell them on for a profit. Tell you what, if one of you gives me £50,000 today, I'll give you back £100,000 on Monday.'

He was extremely believable – he was married to the right woman, espoused the Guards code of honour, spoke like a king and had fake letters of introduction and invoicing that were so convincing that even the shrewdest people ended up falling for him.

Hayes would then actually give back the £100k to the punter – making sure he did so in front of the same group. Then everybody wanted in. This £100k had come from another conned individual, of course.

Hayes didn't count on Sue, however, a genuinely nice person with a kind heart. Hayes spun a story that preyed on her good nature after they met through a mutual contact. He told Sue a fantastic story about a simple business idea that would ensure his son's future, if only he could get the £30k he needed.

Sue loaned him everything she had: £26,000, interest free. Her recently deceased mother had left it to her. Sue wanted nothing in return except to feel as though she'd helped someone.

Then repayment dates were missed, and missed again, and again. As Hayes' excuses became more and more outlandish, Sue started to make enquiries. She soon found several people in the area in similar situations and called us.

Thanks to Sue's initial enquiry, we started to trace dozens of people that Hayes had conned, including:

> an army colonel for £15,000 for IT equipment
> a car dealer for £70,000 for 15 high-end cars
> a solicitor for £25,000 for IT equipment
> a former SAS captain for £70,000 for two Aston Martins
> a Met copper and former colleague of Hayes, who'd accepted a £20,000 Audi TT from him as a gift
> a fireman who subsequently bought the same TT from Hayes for £10,000, intending to sell it on to fund a wedding
> a prison officer for £5,000 for a van that never materialised
> a builder for £300,000 in cheques for a boat

I ended up with around 35 victims who were prepared to make statements. There were many more who refused to put pen to paper out of sheer embarrassment that they had been caught out through greed.

All up, Hayes took around £1.8 million in cash, cheques and money transfers. After his initial charging, a press release went out and then my phone didn't stop ringing. People called from all over the world, from Hong Kong to the USA.

The file grew into a monster, until Bill and I were working every rest day just to keep on top of it, as well as our day-to-day caseload of rape, burglary, assault and robbery. Bill eventually roped in two retired coppers as statement takers and dedicated investigators to help us.

Just as we were in the middle of all this, our new chief constable decided to show he meant business by demanding 360 more detected crimes for the division by the end of the year. It was October. I was called into a meeting between Bill, the DCI and two detective inspectors. After the meeting, I crimed all 126 offences separately and wrote them off as detected individual crimes. This meant we culled a third of our 'quota' in one swoop. Hurrah!

This story has a curious footnote. When we arrived at court for Hayes' remand hearing, Bill and I noticed something wasn't right. There were quite a few blokes around us who just did not fit: they looked very 'military'. Bill rang the surveillance DI and asked if a job was on. There wasn't. Bill then ran some other checks and no other agency was recorded as having teams out in that area.

We had to find out what was going on, so I marched up to one of them. He was fit, aged 25–30, well-dressed and had a military bearing. He was extremely evasive, so I demanded to see his MOD90, which, unless he had reasons of national security for not doing so, he was duty bound to produce. And produce one he did. I handed it to Bill, who made a few calls.

Bill came back and pulled me to the side. 'Something's not right here. RMP at Colchester confirm it's a valid card but won't tell me where this guy is from or even confirm his name.'

Just then Martin, a PC I knew quite well, called me from inside the court.

'Hayes is yours, isn't he? I only ask because there's two right hard-looking bastards asking about him at the usher's desk.'

I asked Martin to spin them and, again, MOD90s were produced.

Bill then made some more calls and a few minutes later the area was flooded with uniforms, at which the fit-looking gentlemen started to disappear.

This was the work of the former SAS captain. He was the real deal and not 'the second guy on the balcony' that every pub in the UK seems to have. He was inside the court and was well-spoken, well-dressed in off-duty officer attire and very pleasant. Nevertheless, I found that just being in the same room as him was unnerving.

Bill put the whole army surveillance team scenario to him and he replied: 'Gentlemen, hypothetically speaking it would not be hard for someone in my position to hypothetically speak to some former colleagues who might hypothetically seek to assist me in the return of my money. Do you see my position?'

We could, but we made him promise there would be no more

appearances like this during the trial. However, this guy was out £70k and not at all happy. Good luck for the rest of your life, Hayes.

We only recovered the Audi TT, an A-Class Merc worth about £6,000 and a few hundred pounds in cash. The rest, about £600k, disappeared. Hayes got five years and served three, so not a bad return for him.

All victims are equal, but some victims are more equal than others. Take anti-social crimes. Scrote goes on a bender and smashes up two bus shelters, urinates on the town hall steps, bashes the copper trying to nick him and then assaults six other coppers trying to place him in a cell without hurting him.

There are ten separate offences there.

Q. How many recorded crimes?

A. Two.

The council is the victim for the bus shelters and the town hall and the Queen is the victim for the seven assaults on police. One victim equals one crime no matter how many offences.

TP and UC officers spend months in danger, buying drugs on countless occasions whilst witnessing all sorts of offences, from money laundering to prostitution.

On 'hit day', we end up with eleventy thousand scrotes in custody for crimes that occurred on a daily basis over six months, all witnessed by police officers.

Q. Surely this should be a bonanza of recorded-crime clear-ups?

A. Not quite.

A criminal network on a job like this will be broken down into two-three conspiracies, with players overlapping throughout each conspiracy. This is because it takes the same amount of work to prove that there was a conspiracy to sell drugs amongst a group of people (even less if you managed to do it properly) than to prove that each individual was supplying drugs.

So three conspiracies = three recorded crimes, not several dozen recorded crimes of supply, which would indicate that you have a serious 'drugs issue' on your patch – and no commander wants that.

So, apart from the fact that they're breaking the law, why do we go after so many drug dealers? Every force and division (Borough Command Unit, BCU) has a set target of Organised Criminal Networks (OCNs) and individuals to charge for supply of class-A drugs offences each year. In my division's case, the magic number was 50 individuals for the financial year.

So by using conspiracy, recorded drug crime is kept low and OCN dismantling figures are achieved while enough individuals are charged. *Voilà.*

Hit days usually always coincide with the end of the last quarter and the beginning of the next, and the same for the financial year, with phases one and two of the operation on either side of those dates. This means the finishing period ends on a high, while giving the police a running start on the next, ensuring that all our funding is spent so we get the same amount for the next budget, if not with an increase.

The Home Office Counting Rules are constantly being bent in these ways so we can meet targets. The HOCR's are dull and extremely complicated and anyone who claims to know them inside out is lying. If you lined up two forces who had exactly the same number of incidents and crimes, I guarantee you that their stats would not match.

I also guarantee that if you ask any supervisor or manager if they have ever manipulated stats to suit their needs and they answer 'No,' then they are lying.

Similarly, if someone tells you they worked in the police and did not break any of the rules as described in the last two chapters, at the very least by association and knowledge, then they are lying out of the top of their chief constable's cap.

26

Occupational Who?

BY 2009, I WAS STARTING TO struggle, but I didn't feel as if I could talk about how I felt. Such a move at work would be fatal in terms of promotion and the types of postings I'd be given. I'd seen for myself how those police officers who confessed they were struggling were quickly disowned. I felt sorry for them but also thought they were weaker than I was – that there was no way I would ever feel the same.

Doing so would also open me to ridicule. In Australia, those who showed sensitivity in traumatic cases were told to 'drink a glass of concrete and harden up'. In the UK, we used a different expression but the sentiment was the same: 'Detective work too tough? Put the big hat back on and walk the streets.'

My outburst in Australia was a symptom of stress. I'd been in similar situations before, with drunk and aggressive police officers, but had never lost control like that. It was a sign – an early clue that the file in my mind into which I'd packed all the bad cases was ready to burst.

Another indicator was that I was hardly sleeping: my photographic memory simply wouldn't shut off at night, even if I drank. If I had a quiet moment, deaths, post-mortems, murders, fights, amputations filled my thoughts.

No one likes to talk about upsetting events or feelings – especially police officers – but staying silent only made the goings-on in my mind more unbearable. I think I knew I needed to unburden, but I couldn't explain how I felt to Helen, who was also suffering, and so our arguing got worse.

We were working at the same police station but on opposite shifts – even though we'd suggested several alternative rotas to our unsympathetic bosses. This meant we had just one weekend together each month and almost no evenings; even when we were together, our body clocks ran counter to each other, something that was especially obvious in the evenings. While one of us was exhausted and wanted to relax, the other was just waking up and preparing to start another long shift.

I'd come home and ask Helen how her (previous) day was.

'Fatal RTA,' she'd reply. 'Yours?'

'Another stranger rape and I spent the afternoon staring at a dead junkie.'

Even worse, I hardly got to see Jack, the one person who made me smile and forget everything. I always worked past his bedtime and invariably missed breakfasts and trips to the park.

I began to suffer from flashbacks, night sweats, nightmares and hyper-alertness. I was jumpy at work and snapped whenever I thought someone was challenging me – which was often – and over the smallest point.

I started to find it hard to get up and go to work in the morning. I used to love my job because of its demands; now I resented them. So much had happened to me in the last three years: I'd got married, lost my father, moved to Australia, where I ended up with a price on my head, my wife had nearly died, my son had been seriously ill and we'd moved back to the UK, making a crippling financial loss of £50k on our property sales.

I desperately wanted to get our lives back on track, but I felt as though I was falling into a void with nothing to catch me.

In desperation, we bought a house, simply because the price was right and I thought we would be able to sell it for a quick profit, enough to make up for the money lost in Australia. It was too expensive for us, however, and, combined with the £1,000 monthly childcare, we struggled to make the repayments. On top of this, I started to use all my free time to study for my sergeants' exams. If I could get my career moving, I thought, then life would naturally improve.

OCCUPATIONAL WHO?

At work I was a boisterous DC in a confusingly politically correct and policy-driven world. Too many of our superiors seemed to be young and inexperienced officers with a hatful of degrees who'd never laid hands on a criminal. I'd been bred to fight crime; they'd been taught to manage it, something I saw being constantly reinforced.

For example, an informant revealed that a Surrey branch of Thomas Cook was going to be robbed of its travellers' cheques later that day. We did a bit of research and it looked as though this was part of a series of similar hits, so we got excited at the prospect of a good nicking.

This excitement proved to be premature. Once the senior managers became involved, cost took priority. Plus, they said that the firearms team had been 'very busy lately', with some officers on leave, while others would need overtime payments, not to mention the genuine legal risk of breaching the robbers' human rights. (Thanks to the short notice, there'd be no time to fill in and authorise all the pre-planned authorities for the use of firearms, so if we shot them they could sue us.)

The robbery was still going to happen, so how did we stop it? We parked a marked, unoccupied police vehicle in front of the shop for the day and, *voilà*, no robbery.

Senior officers said, 'Peaceful conclusion, with no expense or bad publicity.'

Instead, the robbers drove to another town, where they robbed a bookmaker. They came back to the same Thomas Cook much later, when the informant hadn't been able to warn us. *Voilà*, one very happy band of robbers, enjoying their easily won riches, when we could have nabbed them red-handed two robberies earlier.

Even harder to bear was the incompetence.

Sharon, a 20-year-old student, returned home from a night out with her friends. She had just put her key in the lock when her ex-boyfriend, Connor, jumped her. He pushed her through the door and held her prisoner in her own home, raping her repeatedly, before defecating and urinating in her underwear drawer.

Hours later, he threw her in the back of his van. They drove past the scene of a serious road traffic accident. Connor was forced to slow the van as he passed. Sharon saw blue lights and thought she was saved.

'HELP!' she screamed, fighting to get her head to the window. 'I'm being kidnapped. He raped me, he's going to kill me!'

The inspector at the scene heard Sharon's desperate cries but chose to ignore them, thinking she was 'having a laugh'. Connor drove Sharon to a multistorey car park, where he told her he was going to rape her and then throw her off the roof.

Soon after, a security guard emerged from the stairwell, causing Connor to flee.

The police don't always take accusations of rape seriously. The worst example (apart from the one above) I knew of was when two male DCs told a rape victim: 'Come on, luv. The way you dress, you were asking for it, weren't you?'

The reason for this attitude (although it's no excuse) comes from the dozens of cases at the other end of the scale we end up dealing with: regrettable sexual encounters.

For example, a girl gets drunk with her friends, sleeps with a man, wakes up the next morning, realises her boyfriend's going to find out, so cries rape and calls us.

The first time I arrested a young man after what turned out to be a regrettable sexual encounter, he couldn't stop crying. The girl later confessed to lying, but I don't know if he ever got over it. Imagine trying to explain to your friends and family: 'I've been arrested for rape – but I'm innocent. No, really, I am.'

He'd been put through a terrible experience – publicly arrested, then brought into custody, where he'd had to strip, standing on a large white square of paper in order to catch forensic evidence such as hair and skin tissue, before being swabbed and given a grilling in the interview room, wearing nothing but a white paper suit.

Rape is a very emotive term. People think of rape as an alleyway attack. Most rapes reported to police are not like that: they occur in nightclubs, at a party or at home and feature ex-boyfriends and girlfriends, or wives and husbands. The question of consent is a delicate one.

In training school and on the CID course, recruits are given a scenario where they're chatting up a girl in a nightclub. She asks what you do. You don't want to say 'police officer' because that makes you sound like you aren't much fun, so you say you're an airline pilot and, bingo, she's into you and you end up spending the night together. If she wakes up the next morning and sees your police uniform hanging in the cupboard instead of an airline pilot's, then it's very likely that she's going to be extremely annoyed with you for lying.

She might even say, 'If I'd known you were a cop, I wouldn't have slept with you!'

If so, she's not given true consent and therefore you've (technically) raped her.

Proving rape is extremely difficult. If the male party claims it was consensual and there are no marks or bruises on the woman, no evidence of injury or a struggle, and perhaps they'd had a few drinks, there are no witnesses, no CCTV, then, well, we will take the case to a logical but extremely unsatisfactory conclusion.

Once we found and arrested Connor we thought we had a rock-solid case. It wasn't to be. One of the key witnesses, who had seen Sharon immediately after the attack, destroyed the prosecution when the defence said she was lying.

'Oh no,' she said. 'I would never lie. You can ask my friend, who's over there in the jury.'

'Your friend?'

'Yes, she's also my neighbour. We've known one another for years now.'

The case collapsed and the CPS didn't give us another chance. Budgets had to be met. This was one of those outcomes that spooled around and around my photographic mind. 'If only . . .'

I wasn't the perfect detective, but I was passionate about the job and it was this that pushed me ever closer towards the edge. I knew I wasn't myself, and that I was going to have to do something if I wasn't going to go totally mad, so, very reluctantly, I made an appointment to see Occupational Health.

'Try and relax,' they told me. 'These feelings will pass. You could always see your GP if you feel it's getting too much.'

Brilliant.

So I went to my GP and he offered me addictive drugs.

I looked at him in amazement. 'You know that I'm a cop! I spend my working life trying to prevent the spread of addictive drugs. Surely there must be something else.'

'A holiday?'

I had no holidays left to take; I'd used them all to study for sergeants' exams and I simply couldn't afford unpaid leave. I also needed the £2,000 Special Priority Payment awarded to detectives at the end of each year – but it is partly dependent upon not taking sick leave or extra time off. Not fulfilling your Attendance Criteria also affects your promotion prospects and I had put in so much work for the sergeants' exams that I simply couldn't afford to mess it up.

I didn't tell the doctor this. Instead, I said, 'Taking some time out to sit around and think about my life and career is not the answer. When I stare into space I see – well, you don't want to know what I see.'

'Then you have no choice,' the doctor said, as he wrote a prescription. 'Twenty milligrams of fluoxetine a day. It's an antidepressant. It will help.'

I took the slip of paper and left. The doctor was right. What choice was there?

27

Falling Down

I SALUTED MY TWO COLLEAGUES FAREWELL as I left the restaurant and started to walk to the train station. I was on my way back to the section house after a night out – a meal with two detectives to celebrate my success in passing my sergeants' exams and being accepted onto the Met's elite murder squad, the dream job for a tech like me.

But I wasn't happy.

Helen had a first-class maths degree and so had resigned from the police for a regular 9 to 5 job as an actuary near our home in Leatherhead. Her career change drove us further apart. As a civilian, she worked shorter hours for more money in a pleasant and professional environment, staffed by mature and sensible workers who didn't swear at and insult one another or play childish jokes that eventually got out of hand.[30]

The police, she felt, was nothing but bad news and I was part of that, with my long hours and horror stories, and the job's impossible demands. I'd considered leaving the Job, but all I knew was police work – plus, the recession was under way and I'd just passed my exams.

We were still broke. My hours were as crazy as ever, while Helen worked all the overtime she could to pay the bills. We were both exhausted, hardly talking to each other and drinking to relax.

'What are we doing this for?' Helen asked one day. I couldn't think of

---

[30] One of my colleagues set my stapler in jelly, so I glued his stapler to the desk. It escalated to the point where he welded my locker shut and I removed the wheels from his car, leaving it on a set of bricks.

an answer. Emotionally, I felt flat and found it increasingly hard to express myself. Helen focused more and more on Jack, overcompensating for our failing relationship. I wasn't there for my boy as much as I should have been, but the job, the job . . .

Then one evening Helen said, 'We can't stay together.'

Jack was at my mum's and this gave us the space to have the mother of all rows, which resulted in me packing a bag and moving into the section house. As I left, I passed Helen without a word. She was already on the phone, seeking support from a female police friend.

It happened to a lot of us at the same time. Two days later another guy in our office announced he was getting a divorce, followed by another young DC called Giles. Another officer in our team, whose wife was expecting their first child, had also just been kicked out.

Helen and I split up. I moved out of our four-bedroom house into a tiny 8 ft x 7 ft room in Egham's police station's section house. It was about the same size as our nick's prison cell. This was the worst possible location for me in my state of mind, but I really didn't have anywhere else to go or anyone else to turn to – and it was cheap.

I had given 12 years of my life to the police and nothing else, and it showed. I always thought total commitment was necessary for someone like me, who wanted to achieve everything possible and be the best in his professional life. To an extent, I had lived my dream, but now I was spent and alone.

I was a decade older than most of the people in the section house and, as friendly as they all were, I didn't particularly want to spend time with them, especially not a night out on the town.

As I sat in my 'cell', listening to their action-packed evenings, I silently swigged anything from four to eight cans of beer, one after the other, or if it was my day off, maybe eight or twelve cans and a bottle of wine.

I smoked 40 a day and, although I was already quite slim, I started to lose weight, eventually dropping two stone. I rarely slept more than four hours. Every moment I spent alone was a moment too much: every time I closed my eyes, unpleasant thoughts and images flashed through my mind. My body would tense, the adrenalin would flow and my muscles would twitch at the memory of dealing with dead junkies . . .

the accident victim with amputated legs . . . the baby in the morgue. When I shaved in the morning, I saw hollow eyes looking back at me. A cold, dead stare.

Some days, when I came into my horrible cell after work I literally ripped the shirt from my back, an expression of inexplicable frustration and anger and my bitterness at not being able to see Jack. My love-to-hate feelings grew towards Helen and I smashed my mobile more than once after we rowed. I regularly punched the wall before clutching my hands together between my legs, tears streaming, the physical pain blanking out my mental agony for a few seconds.

I was at work when an email circular arrived, giving guidance on what to enter on the police computer as a suspect's occupation when inputting their details.

One of the office staff typed 'burglar' as a joke. Someone else put in 'police officer'.

She was laughing but then stopped and turned to me, saying, 'Is this you?'

It was. The shock was incredible.

'*I* have a crime report? *Me?*'

It was right there on the screen, in an unlocked file, for all to see. Helen had reported me on the night of our row. I didn't access it myself, but my colleagues certainly wasted no time and told me I was listed as 'High Risk', with a drink problem.

After this, my nickname was changed from 'Dangerous' to 'Domestic'. During one office discussion, a senior officer pointedly said, 'Well, at least I'm happily married,' causing much knowing laughter. I left the office, walked to the sick room and cried.

Then I raised a grievance against the inspector who had filed the report (she was the friend Helen had telephoned the night I moved out) and Surrey Police for leaving it open and unlocked, and for not telling me I was the subject of a complaint from a member of the public.

A short while later I was in the station car park having a smoke when a police officer I barely knew made a snide remark.

'I see Helen's getting all pally with the firearms unit on Facebook.'

'What's that supposed to mean?' I asked.

'You'll find out.'

When I asked Helen about it, she flipped.

I couldn't wait to get out of Surrey. To this end, I'd applied to join the Met Police's homicide command. The Met refused me at first, as, contrary to their requirements I'd lived outside of the UK for more than twelve months over the previous five years. I'd pointed out that I was already back at Surrey with no problems after having worked as a security-cleared police officer in Australia. I'd also been totally transparent and disclosed the 'sun-downer incident' in my paperwork. Eventually, nine months after I'd first made the application, they agreed and I was vetted. I resigned, as is normal when moving between forces, giving my bosses 28 days' notice.

I also tried to 'man up'. I cut right down on my drinking, dealing with the mental pain as best as I could. I was determined to get myself sorted, so I could focus on my new job and on getting back together with Helen.

To that end, I hardly drank during the meal to celebrate my success at being accepted into the Met. I was due to see Jack the following day and there was no better motivation than that to stay sober.

My thoughts were interrupted as I got on the platform at Chertsey. A large gang of young men were on the opposite platform, being a bit boisterous. I could see it wasn't the 'fun' kind of boisterous. They were nasty and aggressive.

One of them came over to my side of the platform and, to impress his mates, started trying to intimidate me. He marched up to me with a gorilla-like swagger, mouthing off, until he was a couple of feet away. To show him I wasn't about to be bullied, I shoved him firmly away.

'Right!' he yelled. 'You wait and see what happens when I get to my pals.'

Damn. As he went round to the other platform, I left the station and hid in the car park, waiting until the next train had gone through, then walked back to the platform as the next train arrived.

Unfortunately, as I climbed in, I saw the same lad get in with six mates. They stood, staring directly at me, serious now. It was clear what was going to happen. I could either wait until I got off at the next station and get beaten in front of no witnesses and no CCTV, or here on the train, with witnesses and CCTV.

So I got in their faces and shouted at them. 'Just back the fuck off and behave yourselves!'

When this had no effect, I upped the aggressiveness a bit more. 'Don't you fucking try it on with me. You better back the fuck off if you know what's good for you!'

When the train arrived at the station, they still hadn't attacked, so once again I yelled at them to back off. Four of them came out straight away, immediately surrounded me and started to throw some punches. I spotted a gap, threw out my arm and caught one of them a neat blow to the chin. This would be my only shot.

While they kept me busy, the three other youths came running at me from behind; one of them took a flying jump and landed a huge punch to the back of my head. I went down hard. The moment I hit the floor, the kicks began. I pulled up my arms and legs, too late to save a pair of ribs, which I felt bend and then crack. Then, as I fought to get some air, a heel went down on my head. My eyes blurred and dimmed as my body jerked with the kicks and stamps from the seven youths.

I came to alone. As I lifted my head, pain rattled over my face, then head, then shot down my spine. I coughed and cried out in pain. I tried to stand up. I'd been kicked in the back and my spine wouldn't straighten. I staggered as I got to my feet, blood dripping steadily to the floor. My shaking arms and hands were covered in defensive injuries.

I collapsed on a bench and a few minutes later the cops turned up. They wanted to interview me, but I just wanted to go home. They refused to let me leave.

'But I'm the victim,' I said, 'not a suspect, and there are plenty of witnesses to that fact. I just want to get home; I'm supposed to see my son tomorrow. I just want to leave it for now.'

I tried to move past the sergeant, who grabbed my arm, restraining me. I swore at her. (I apologised later – I wasn't in the best frame of mind.)

Once the British Transport Police turned up, I gave them my coat for forensics and then told them I was going back to my room at the section house, which I did, on my own.

The next morning it was clear that I'd underestimated my injuries. Blood had dried and stuck my face to the pillow. I could hardly dress myself. I exclaimed at my reflection in the mirror. I couldn't let Jack see me like this; it would terrify the poor lad. I called Helen, who said she didn't believe me and hung up.

I called work and an inspector came to take me to hospital. He quickly made it clear that he didn't want to do this and only did so because our welfare policy obliged him to do so. He said the attack might be turned against me. 'You're not exactly flavour of the month in Surrey,' he said, referring to the rumours about my marriage, Helen's crime report and my drinking. 'And the CCTV shows you confronting those lads.'

I explained what had happened and that I'd attempted to use pre-emptive action to get them to back down, that it was obvious they were planning to attack me and there were witnesses on the train who could support me. Anyway, even if I had shouted at them on the train, there had been no need for all seven of them to kick me into unconsciousness.

The inspector dropped me at the hospital and left me there to get fixed up. The doctors confirmed my broken ribs, along with dozens of severe bruises. They sent me home with a bottle of painkillers.

From the start, the response from my supervisors and senior officers was underwhelming – normally when an officer is down, everybody drops whatever they're doing to help. The exception was the uniform Neighbourhood Team based at Egham. They pursued the people responsible for so long and with such passion that they were eventually told to back off by the inspector, who said that I'd asked for the kicking by confronting the seven lads.

The sergeant told me he would have done the same thing in that situation. 'Whatever the case, *you* did not assault *them*,' he said. 'Seven men attacked you and beat you unconscious. They could have killed you.'

They discovered that this same gang had been beating up and robbing students from the local college, the Royal Holloway (the dean had complained to the chief constable), and had also been responsible for several racially motivated attacks. The MO was identical, as were their descriptions.

My mental state took a big dive after this. I felt so helpless and out in the cold. I went back to see Occupational Health, who quickly confessed that they didn't know what they could do to help me. After five days off to recover from my physical injuries, I returned to work.

Once back, I went to see a chief inspector about my leaked crime report. 'Women are bitches, aren't they?' he said. 'Now, let's see what this is about.' To my amazement, he showed me Helen's report. Showing a suspect in a crime the details of the report made by the victim is illegal.

I was doubly stunned when he showed me another file, which I did not know about. Helen had alleged that I'd installed bugging devices in our home. She thought that's how I knew about rumours (which were false) about her relationship with a firearms officer. My shock was compounded when I saw that Surrey Police had swept the house for surveillance devices at Helen's request (of course, they found nothing). This was crazy, a waste of time and money. Sweeping someone's house for listening devices is an exceptional and expensive thing to do. The last time Surrey did this was for a judge involved in reviewing terrorist cases.

The chief inspector asked me not to mention this, as by showing me the report he had broken the law and police regulations to the point of gross misconduct. I said I was going to talk to Helen, so he was going to have to tell Professional Standards what had happened.

He tried to get me to calm down and offered to take me for a night on the town, including a trip to a casino.

We'd just read a report together which detailed my alcohol problems.

I called Helen and explained that I knew about the crime report. We talked for a long time and things started to turn. We still loved each other. Helen told me she had already withdrawn her report. A dinner date was followed by more visits to see Jack and soon I was staying two or three nights a week. The most healing thing I could do was play footie with Jack in the park. Finally, I had an active part in my son's life again.

I took Helen out for her birthday and we talked about me moving back in. It was all coming together and I was determined to keep us on track. After all, I had passed my exams and was about to join the Met, so we could leave Surrey for a fresh start. I was still suffering from nightmares and irrational thoughts, but I kept them to myself. If I could just hang on, get out of Surrey, get back with my wife and son, then in time I was sure I would heal. I was underestimating the strength of my mental problems, however, and had no idea how close I was to breaking down.

It was March 2010. Helen rang me to say that a senior colleague of mine had called her and asked to meet her in a coffee shop, which she'd done.

He apologised to Helen for the crime reports being shown to me and apologised on behalf of Surrey Police for betraying her confidence. He stated that he was personally looking into the matter and was considering this to be a case of gross misconduct. He asked Helen for evidential support in possible future hearings against the chief inspector involved and myself, and was visibly surprised when Helen replied that we were back together.

I called the officer, obviously worried about what might happen to me and why a deputy chief constable had become involved in such a 'minor' case. I also said I was worried about upsetting the delicate balance of my recent reconciliation with Helen.

He replied that he kept his 'radar low' on such matters, hence his involvement; he felt Helen was owed an apology, he said, reassuring me that I was in no trouble and he would not ask Helen for evidence against me.

In 12 years of service, I'd never heard of a DCC contacting a former PC, now a member of the public, to have a one-to-one meeting to discuss a domestic issue and a betrayal of confidence.

Not long after this, on a Friday, five days before I was due to start in my new job, the Met called me.

'Your security clearance has been withdrawn, so we won't be offering you the post. Sorry.'

'Why on earth not?'

They said they'd received 'new information' about the sun-downer incident in Western Australia in 2007. I explained that all the relevant reports about this had already been passed to the Met and dealt with during the vetting process. I had not been charged with anything or accused of any crime in Australia. I demanded to know what had changed. They wouldn't say.

I had five days before I'd be homeless and jobless. I tried to find out what had happened and soon, to my amazement, I found myself talking to the DCC *again*, on the phone.

He confirmed that updated information had been sent to the Met about my time in Australia and my crime report. Since receiving it, they'd decided I was high risk.

'Well, whatever the case, I'm in a blind panic here. I need my job back.'

'I'll review it next week and let you know,' he said. 'But it doesn't look very favourable.'

I was stunned. I reminded him of my excellent service record. I'd received three commendations since coming back from Australia. I'd worked damn hard to pass my sergeants' exams and get through the boards for the Met's world-class murder squad.

'Is there something more going on here I don't know about?' I asked.

'I'll look at this and, depending on what I find, you may or may not get your job back.'

Suddenly, all the frustration boiled over. I was a good and loyal detective. How dare he leave me hanging like that?

'This is my life you're ruining. Who the fuck do you think you people are? If I find out there is something untoward going on here, and frankly the timing stinks, I will go fucking mental and you can all go fuck yourselves with the consequences!'

I hung up. Not the smartest move I've ever made, I admit, but my mind was reeling. This couldn't be happening.

It was the weekend. I went to my room, turned off my phones and didn't move for two days. On Monday morning, I switched on my phone. It rang almost immediately.

It was the DCC, asking, 'DO YOU STILL WANT A CAREER?'

I refused to speak to him unless someone from the Police Federation was present. When we finally did get to talk, he was much calmer and said that I was a valued and respected officer and that I had a lot of 'fans' in the police, 'including him'.

The DCC went on to say Surrey was a disciplined organisation and that if I wrote a letter of apology within two days I would be reinstated. If I did not, then we would part ways.

My Fed rep then questioned the timings of the disclosure of information to the Met. The DCC confirmed this: 'A report came across my desk relating to the crime reports and Helen. It included what had happened in Australia and I asked someone in Professional Standards if we were sure we had disclosed this to the Met as a way of double-checking. I can only think that this person then sent it off their own bat.'

'Came across his desk'? 'Sent it off their own bat'? What the hell did he mean?

I wrote the letter and was reinstated, but I had since been 'replaced' by another detective, so I was given a job 50 miles from home, £7,000 a year worse off, in a role that saw me performing the work of a uniformed constable. There would be no promotion or any move to the Met. This posting was designed to make me turn in my resignation.

I called Helen and told her what had happened and that it looked like I had a fight on my hands if I wanted to stay a detective. She was shocked and sympathetic but said, 'I can't face any more battles with the police. I can't face what it might do to us. I can't be with you any more. I want you and Surrey Police out of my life.'

We started to argue and by the time the call was over we were rowing over my visiting rights to our son.

I felt suicidal. The emotions associated with the dreams, thoughts, fears and memories I'd been struggling to contain burst free. I couldn't hold on. I'd lost. Within a few days, I'd gone from having it all – getting my wife and son and my home back, along with a promotion and a new, better-paid job outside of Surrey – to losing everything.

That was it. Game over. I sat in my tiny room, opened a can of beer and started to sob. My legs started to shake; my head felt as though it was going to burst in grief, anger and despair. I felt something wet on my face. I touched my nose; my hand came away covered in blood.

Then everything went red.

28

My Worst Nightmare

I SAT UP. I WAS IN bed. My head hurt. My hands ached. My knuckles were bruised and bloody. Where was I? A small box room. A bright strip light. Not the section house. Then I saw the door. Metal. A grille window. No handle on my side.

A cell. I was in a prison cell.

I stood up, felt dizzy and sat down again. What had happened? For once, my reliable memory had failed me. Flashes came and went, followed by pain and dizziness. I could feel my stomach knotting; the feeling I got when I'd lost control of a situation. I tried to force myself to remember – anything. My head throbbed with pain.

I remembered I had wanted to kill myself.

I looked around. My clothes were beside the bed; my shoelaces and belt were there. If I was suicidal, then why hadn't they taken them? Did they *want* me to commit suicide? This had to be a nightmare. I had to wake up, I had to. *I* didn't belong in a prison cell. It was impossible.

The door opened. A detective inspector, Sean, was there.

'What the fuck did I do?' I asked.

Sean sat down and he took me through the day. It was a nightmare; I simply couldn't recall any of it.

I'd called the station from the section house and said I had a gun, that I was going to kill myself and take someone from the firearms team with me. A few minutes later, Steve Rodhouse, who'd been a guest at my wedding, had overreacted and called out the armed response team, who'd arrested me with weapons drawn.

'You were like a zombie,' Sean said. 'Until they tried to put you in here, then you tried to knock out an unlucky PC.'

I'd been charged with assault and threats to kill, a custodial offence.

I couldn't understand why they wanted to send me to prison. I was a good officer. Of course, I shouldn't have threatened anyone, but I'd had a breakdown. Surely, what I needed now was help, not to be arrested by the firearms unit and put away with all the people I'd spent my career chasing.

Fortunately, I had a great solicitor (one who normally represented the scrotes we tried to put away) and he got me out on bail. As part of the bail conditions, I had to reside outside of Surrey, so, after being smuggled out of the station in the boot of a car to escape waiting press (someone leaked my name and overexaggerated the details of my arrest), I jumped on a train to Brighton. Once there I got drunk before deciding to call Helen from a phone box (the police had seized my mobile). This was in breach of my bail, but I had to speak to her. She called me back once my change ran out and we spoke for an hour. I told her I loved her, but I still couldn't control my temper and we fought.

My best friend, Paul, a former cop turned successful businessman, called me once I was back at Mum's house (he was the Paul I was with when my dad gave us his 'welcome to the police' speech). I hadn't talked to him for ages, partly because I knew he would see through the weak defences I was using to hold back my recent mental troubles.

'What have you done?' he demanded.

'I know, tell me about it.'

'You don't understand, do you? They're coming for you. You're going to go to prison.'

'What?'

'Helen's just called and told me what's been going on. She's reported you for breach of bail.'

I hung up. I was going to be arrested and this time I'd be taken to prison. I wouldn't last 24 hours. Death was preferable. I looked at the picture of Jack in my wallet. I didn't want to leave him.

The only way to avoid remand was to prove that I needed urgent medical care. I called the Priory, told them my story and described my mental state. They said I was very welcome, but that it would cost me £750 per night, so even if I maxed out my credit card, I wouldn't be there for long.

Mum was a trained nurse and said we should go to hospital, so a few hours later, after convincing a doctor that I would kill myself if I ended up in a prison cell, I was admitted on a voluntary basis to Langley Green intensive-care psychiatric unit.

I was placed in a small room on my own and was soon diagnosed with severe depression. When the doctors found out I'd been on daily 20 mg doses of the antidepressant fluoxcetine, which had been upped a week before my breakdown by a junior doctor (who was in the presence of and being assessed by a senior practice doctor) from 20 mg to 60 mg overnight, they told me this was dangerous and contributed greatly to my loss of control and grip on reality.

Gradually, despite my drug-induced haze (I was fed a diet of very strong antidepressants), I got to know my fellow inmates and wannabe suicides. Adam had just sliced the artery in his forearm after smuggling in a pencil sharpener. He was in his 20s, suffering from cannabis-induced psychosis and depression. Keith, the speed freak, talked to himself and attacked people at random.

Nicky was a thirty-something former stockbroker who'd lost his wife to a younger, wealthier model. He'd tried to kill himself several times in several different ways. He'd spent £65k on cocaine, snorting away his bank account, credit cards, possessions and home.

It seemed as though everyone in that cuckoo's nest was there because of drugs. This was one of the many tragic consequences of our failure to do anything to slow the illegal drugs trade in the UK. We just let the dealers get on with it and pick up the pieces as best as we can.

Learning that wasn't exactly conducive to my recovery – I felt like the job, the very thing that defined me, had been futile; that I'd given 12 years of my life for nothing.

Alcohol had definitely helped play a big part in my downfall, but it was the job that had led to my mental breakdown. Even so, the thought of never again being able to deploy, never again to enjoy the teamwork and extraordinary challenge, never to feel the power of arrest and the right of justice was too much to bear.

Although I'd used the system to get into hospital so I wouldn't be sent on remand, I really was suicidal. My desire to kill myself was much stronger than I or anyone else had realised.

The drugs turned me into a zombie. When my family came to visit, I'd zone out, forget they were there and then when they got up to go I'd realise what had happened and would beg them not to leave. They had to go eventually, of course, and then no drug could stop me from falling into a hollow and agonising despair.

When I zoned out, my mind played warped dreams over and over of all the things that had happened to me, all spliced and jumbled – the bodies, the witnesses, the interviews, the threats, the violence, the weapons, the tears, the pain. Everything came rolling towards me at once, after more than a decade of repression, doing everything I could to stop the memories hurting me; now, they were stampeding out of the darkness and refused to go away. I could see every detail, every shoelace, every dropped cigarette, every speck of blood, every bruise on little old ladies who'd been mugged, every fibre, hair, cutting implement, drug, swollen limb; all the scrotes laughing, laughing, laughing.

'No more.'

'No more.'

'No more!'

This was the end. I wrote no note. No last goodbye. The act would be message enough: I couldn't live without Helen and Jack. I couldn't live inside my skull with my nightmares. I waited until I was alone. I placed the noose over my head and let myself fall.

I woke up inhaling, as if taking my first breath. The air hit my lungs like a spear. My neck hurt like hell and I could barely move my head. A male nurse was sitting on a chair beside me.

'The name's Sonny. Pleased to meet you. The only way from here is up, my friend.'

I frowned. I couldn't speak, but my expression clearly said that I wasn't happy to be here.

'That was a good try,' he continued, his voice soft, friendly, a gentle Nigerian accent. 'Another minute and we wouldn't have got you back.'

I saw Jack's picture on the bedside table.

'A boy needs his father,' Sonny said.

It took me four weeks to come to terms with the idea of trying to recover, that there was a possibility of getting better and leading some kind of life in the outside world. Therapy consisted of strong antidepressants and talking to Sonny and Anne, a pair of non-medical nurses who were the first to admit they weren't trained counsellors.

Whenever I closed my eyes, I saw my history in dead bodies, overdoses sitting in armchairs; I could see the blood that had settled into their lower halves seeping through their pores like sweat. I saw the autopsy of the six-week-old baby; I saw police officers and criminals screaming at me until I couldn't tell the difference between the two. At night I flinched from violent blows, from drug dealers pointing guns. Each of these events had come with a cost: they had taken a piece of my strength until there was nothing left to replace it.

Even more painful were the scenes and memories of family life, happier times – getting married, then seeing Jack walk, speak and run into my arms with invincible trust and unconditional love.

Someone from the ward was always there for me when I woke up screaming in the night and we talked it through. Anne saved my life after I tried to kill myself a second time.

'You're going to make it,' she told me time and again. She spoke with such conviction; I didn't know where her certainty came from.

She was right. It took a while, but once they judged I was no longer a serious suicide risk, I was moved into the 'normal' part of the ward – which was anything but. The other patients immediately invited me to join them on various 'breakouts', when they'd sneak out to the pub, where some of them bought drugs.

Life in this part of the ward was almost as unpredictable as police work. Keith was extremely paranoid and every now and then he attacked one of the nurses. Invariably, I would end up pulling them apart.

* * *

While I was recovering, some facts about what had happened to me emerged. 'Selectively worded' reports, which I later obtained under the Data Protection Act, had been sent to the Met, effectively halting my transfer.

> *Information from XXXX Risk Assessment Unit, Australian Police –*
> *Perth:*
> *On 12/10/07 OFFICER A attended an intelligence Social*
> *Function at the Brisbane Hotel. He allegedly became involved in a*
> *physical altercation with another officer and was subsequently*
> *removed from the hotel by a senior officer. Once outside the premises he*
> *allegedly continued with his abusive language and aggressive*
> *behaviour. Furthermore, it was later ascertained that he bared his*
> *buttocks at the hotel in the presence of others.*

I'd already been cleared by the Met vetting unit following checks with Surrey Police and the Australian government. This is an altered, more harshly worded version.

The Met had also been sent one further report, it was extremely misleading and hadn't helped my case. It read:

> *Information from Superintendent XXXX, PSD, Surrey Police*
> *OFFICER A is currently under investigation by BTP in relation*
> *to a fight in Egham. It has been alleged that he was not helpful to*
> *BTP and that CCTV footage indicates that OFFICER A was the*
> *instigator of the said fight. Investigation is ongoing.*

I hadn't been treated as a suspect, arrested or invited for voluntary interview. I'd never been issued with any notices of discipline regarding this incident and so there had been no reason to pass it on to the Met. I had left the train, having assaulted no one, and was then attacked by seven youths and beaten unconscious. It was true that I was unhelpful, thanks to the late hour and the pain I was in. This is a typical and understandable reaction of victims. Very often, in similar circumstances, the police officer will record in his notebook: 'Statement not taken due to time of night and condition of victim.'

I did later help the British Transport Police by allowing them to seize my coat and the next day emailed them a statement from a Surrey Police computer.

I couldn't understand why I was being punished for having a harmless argument with my wife, a disagreement that even Helen agreed had simply got out of hand and was not worthy of complaint. Yet, not only was nobody prepared to investigate, let alone discuss the matter, nobody cared that my career had been destroyed as a result and that it was this incident that had helped tip me over the edge.

I would still face a trial, however.

It was another two and a half months before I was ready for the outside world and Madame Justice was waiting – as were the press. Someone had leaked the story, along with my real name, and sensational stories about the 'shaven-headed cop' who'd caused 'an armed siege' appeared. I had to be snuck into court to avoid photographers.

In true CPS tradition, the original assault and threat-to-kill charges were dropped, but the police were determined to convict me of something, so I was eventually charged with 'misuse of a communications device'.

I should have contested it, but I was still too weak to fight. I pled guilty to make it all go away. I'd asked several senior police officers for supporting statements. None of them agreed, until I called DI Brendan Collins.

'I've pled guilty and I'm in the shit,' I said.

'Yes, you are.'

'I didn't want to have to ask you. I've been ostracised and I imagine anyone who sides with me will be too, and I don't want to put you in it this close to your retirement. I suppose you have to ask for permission, but—'

'I suppose I do,' he said. 'In my old age, that seems to have slipped my mind.'

When Brendan read out a statement on my behalf, it broke my heart. 'Over the past few years, Officer A has suffered domestic and emotional problems that would challenge the very strongest of us. To his credit, he continued to perform very well, providing first-class service to me and to the people of Surrey.'

A crew of scrotes laughed and jeered from the gallery, adding to my shame. Nick Beer, who'd worked alongside me on the body in the freezer case, also came to support me. He was ready to tear the gallery to pieces to get to them.

Brendan was forced out of his job when the next round of compulsory redundancies arrived. He's now working in Afghanistan to pay for the remainder of his daughter's education.

The magistrates could not agree what to do with me. I had to wait as they retired three times to debate whether to send me to prison or not. Finally, as I stared on, hopeless and helpless, they gave their verdict and then sentence.

Guilty.

A fine, plus costs.

No custody, thanks to my ongoing psychiatric treatment.

I stepped out of the court and into the sunshine. I was divorced, penniless, jobless, homeless and, worst of all, hadn't seen my son in months.

There really was nowhere else to go but up.

29

In the Line of Duty

THE POLICE HAVE A ROLL CALL of honour that immortalises those officers who have fallen in the line of duty over the years. My great grandfather is on it. He was shot dead in an IRA ambush at the age of 46.

But there are many other officers who have fallen in the line of duty whose names are not on that list.

After my own experience, I searched my memory for all the officers I knew who had broken down at work and it turned out I could think of dozens – not only that, there were several suicides.

These include a DC who walked into the sea and vanished; a DI who left a note on his door for his family, saying, 'I'm sorry. Don't come in. Call the police.' He had hanged himself in his front room.

My dad once told me about a DC who was sitting in the passenger seat of a light aircraft and who, without a word, stepped out into 15,000 feet of nothing.

These officers and many more besides (ongoing legal cases and investigations prevent me from citing many more names here) have given everything to the job that finally destroys them, but they are not honoured.

Then there are those still alive, a chief inspector who cut his wrists after his wife falsely reported him for domestic violence and he lost his job; a DS I know from a gun crime unit who wakes up screaming in the night; a pregnant DC who worked on my team as hard and as long as the rest of us and who suffered a miscarriage four months in. Many officers I knew from Major Crimes, various covert units, CID, fatal accident investigators and so on had the same symptoms as me and were on the verge of breaking down.

DCI Paul Feast, who helped me deal with Maxine's suicide (see *Problem Families*), lost his mind two years later. After a marathon drinking session, he choked his girlfriend, telling her he was going to kill her. Once she'd passed out, Paul took her car and drove the wrong way up the motorway, ramming a total of eight cars, including police cars, causing several injuries. When he finally crashed, he was bundled to the floor and later weighed off for five years by a judge. When officers searched his house, they found a big plasma TV with a police exhibit label on it and a property store docket.

That kind of behaviour doesn't just spring up overnight. I don't know Paul well, but DCIs do attend every suspicious death on their patch. If he'd been able to talk about how he felt with a professional, to talk through his demons, then maybe he wouldn't have ended up spending five years in prison.

Another DC had split up with his wife and they were going through a nasty divorce, rowing about kids and money, when she suddenly welcomed him back into the family home, slept with him and the next day accused him of rape. He lost his job and went to prison. She confessed – 18 months later – but there was no way back for the DC.

These are real tragedies: good people destroying their careers and taking their lives. They aren't 'cries for help'; cops don't know how to cry for help. When they kill themselves, they mean to do it, just like I did, because they believe there is no other option to stop the torment.

One thing unites us all. We love our job with a passion and believe in it totally. We're the type that's hardest hit when things go wrong. I believe that in all these cases the officers concerned were suffering from post-traumatic stress disorder (PTSD).

It wasn't until I was released (after three months) that – still feeling lost and suffering the same feelings – I went to see a different doctor. She passed me a questionnaire to fill in. When I handed it back, her jaw dropped. I was off the scale for PTSD, which is treatable through counselling by teaching the brain how to think 'normally' again, without the use of drugs.

PTSD was why I was in a constant state of hyper-awareness – 'danger mode' – and couldn't switch off. It was why I yelled at people for the stupidest thing, why I exploded every time I spoke to Helen.

It was in that moment that I realised so many other detectives I knew had exactly the same symptoms, although most of them to a lesser degree.

Research in the UK into PTSD in the police is non-existent, as is treatment. The British Army, after decades of seeing sorrow as a weakness or nightmares as a sign of cowardice, has recently acknowledged that PTSD is a serious problem and now provides its officers with treatment for this disorder.

In 2010, for the second year in a row, more American soldiers – both enlisted men and women, and veterans – committed suicide than were killed in the wars in Iraq and Afghanistan.[31]

Twenty-four British soldiers died during the 1991 Gulf War, but the Ministry of Defence disclosed in 2010 that 169 veterans of the conflict had died from 'intentional self-harm' or in circumstances that led to open verdicts at inquests.

Likewise, an estimated 264 Falklands veterans have committed suicide since the conflict ended, compared with 255 soldiers killed in action.

David Hill, director of operations for the charity Combat Stress, said it took an average of 14 years for veterans to ask for help with post-traumatic stress disorder. Many suffered in silence – often harbouring suicidal thoughts – because they were reluctant to admit their vulnerability.

Of course, soldiers have a much more dangerous job than police officers; after all, we don't spend our days dealing with bullets, missiles and roadside bombs. But that doesn't mean we don't get to see sights

---

[31] Excluding accidents and illness, 462 soldiers died in combat, while 468 committed suicide. In 2009, there were 381 suicides, which also exceeded the number of combat deaths.

that are just as disturbing, from dead babies and children to people horribly wounded in traffic accidents.

There are no up-to-date figures for UK police officers, but I personally know six officers who have killed themselves in recent years and many more who have had breakdowns that have led to their own arrest.

Cops are trained to ignore the natural human instinct to flee and instead are programmed to run towards danger. There is nothing quite like the terror of being the first to arrive at an horrific accident and having to assess the situation, knowing that you are about to see indescribable suffering.

I'll never forget pulling up to an accident where Steve, a road traffic officer, was already there performing mouth-to-mouth and CPR. Not that remarkable, apart from every time Steve came up for air he had to spit the victim's blood out of his own mouth. That was after his crew mate, Nicola, had scooped the victim's broken teeth, blood and mucus out of his mouth without gloves because they'd been shredded from pulling the man out of the mangled mess of oak tree versus small hatchback at 50 mph. The victim died.

Afterwards, once they'd cleaned up and written their reports, they went home. The emotions that hit you as you walk through your front door after watching a young man die on the ground in front of you, while you can taste their blood in your mouth, are indescribable and unmanageable. You want to unburden but at the same time how can your family hope to understand, and why should you force them to visit that trauma with you? It is not down to our families – who weren't there and don't deserve to be dragged to the scene by us – to pick up the pieces and put us back together again.

Time is needed for officers to decompress after an incident like this; they should be given the opportunity to talk with colleagues who can share their stories and sympathy, followed by a professional who can put the incident into perspective and will be there on the end of a telephone when they're still awake at three in the morning.

There is very little research into PTSD among UK police officers. The studies I've seen are outdated and, to my eyes, inaccurate. The latest figures for the number of officers suffering PTSD date back to

1993 and claim the rate is 15 per cent. I think the rate is much higher, but, even so, the public should be very concerned that a significant number of officers are policing the streets while suffering from some of the symptoms of PTSD.

There are many causes of PTSD but they're easily missed. Friends and family could not understand what had happened to me. To them, it looked as though I had lost my mind overnight – but it was the accumulation of years of damage.

During my 12 years as a police officer, I arrested over 400 suspects and dealt with many hundreds more. I have attended dozens of training courses, which have helped me make these arrests and obtain the correct evidence.

As with many police officers, these arrests have involved weapons, firearms, violent injuries, personal injury, confrontation with criminals and high-stress covert situations.

I was trained to deal with all of this.

What I was not trained to do was process the aftermath.

I was vilified in the press and bullied by my own organisation before and after the meltdown. I hope that those people who took advantage and called me a 'nutter', a 'window licker' and so on never see a loved one go through what I did or suffer it themselves (although these sorts of insults and lack of empathy are a sign of stress and PTSD).

I was a taxpayer, I received no pension and I worked for 12 years in the service of Queen and Country. I was a good police officer. I simply became mentally ill with depression, PTSD and alcoholism. Too many people assume that 'mentally ill' means 'dangerously psychotic'. This is rarely true and now I can say I truly understand the stigma that is attached to mental illness.

All too often, when the press publishes stories about police officers who have badly messed up, blogs and comments from the public flood in. They call for the dog handler to be hanged by the neck because of his terrible mistake, or cheer on the suicide of a divorced sergeant, or that of a DCI caught drink-driving, who, after finding his name in the press, hangs himself.

For everyone out there, whether you hate or love the police, if something happens to you or your family, it will be us you call or who come running to help. Of course, you have no idea what is going on in the attending officer's life. If that officer is later arrested in similar circumstances to me or breaks down, will he still be a disgrace if he was the one who found your missing child, solved the rape of your sister, caught the man who burgled your home and returned your property, or saved you from a gang of yobs? Keep in mind that almost every police officer has the noblest of intentions (and certainly starts out that way) and does his or her absolute best, often overcoming fear and running towards danger at great emotional and mental cost.

Just as there are no figures for PTSD, there are no figures for police suicides in the UK and there are almost no avenues for help. Officers who finally admit that they are struggling at work are told to go to Occupational Health, but often find them lacking.

When these officers finally suffer a breakdown, they find themselves hit with the full weight of the law. Police officers aren't tried as citizens but as police officers. This is right and proper if they are corrupt, but if the officer has been caught shoplifting from M&S or has smashed his wife's car up with a crow-bar, then while he should pay for the mistake, he also needs help and understanding – and if he had felt able to ask for help sooner, then the crimes would not have been committed.

As Bill once told me, 'We're great at sorting out other people's mess, but when it comes to our own, we're bloody useless.'

Police officers can't sue their employer for the effects of stress and their failure to deal with it. They are not covered, in the normal sense, by Health and Safety legislation because much of what they do is too dangerous to legislate for and, incredibly, they are not 'employees'. They are 'appointed'.

A civilian friend of mine recently questioned why I had such an explosive end to my career.

'Well, imagine you wake up tomorrow and your wife's gone, your son is gone, your career is over and you're dependent on alcohol. How would you feel? You're in the ice-cream business; I used to chase the *very* bad guys, pick up the pieces after murder, suicides and rapes.'

'Fair one,' he replied.

Today, after several months of the right treatment – not involving drugs – I am getting there, although it is difficult and requires a great deal of work and effort on my part. Clare, my psychologist, would agree that I have been (and continue to be) one of her most challenging cases, but she has seen me through the worst.

I am still struggling and I have to thank my co-author, who has helped steer me in a vaguely organised way through this book, which I hope might go some way to helping others who find themselves in a similar position to myself.

Paul, my best friend, and now also my business partner, spoke to me on the phone whilst I was locked up. 'Tomorrow is the start,' he said. 'Forget what happened today. This time next year we will be laughing about this and on the way to making a fortune, building a successful and sustainable business.'

He was right.

* * *

I had three-year-old Jack this weekend for the first time in a year, so I could have Christmas with him and give him his presents. He sprang out of the car and ran to me, arms outstretched, yelling, 'Daddy!' It's wonderful to see him so fresh and full of life. It's very, very infectious and makes me want to live. That lad is a miracle. A happy, intelligent and sweet-souled person.

Last night he and I just fooled around playing cars in the lounge. He asked about whether I was getting a new house and if his room would have a Rory Race Car bed. Then he saw a photo of me in uniform that Mum had put out.

'Are you still a policeman, Daddy?'

I looked long and hard at that picture, taken – it seems – a lifetime ago. If I knew then what I know now . . .

'No, not any more.'

'Why not?'

What could I say? I was stuck for words. Perhaps I should have made something up, but I just couldn't answer.

Out of the blue, Jack grabbed me round the neck in a big cuddle and whispered, 'Daddy, I love you.'

Suddenly the weekend was over and, as I handed Jack back to Helen, I realised I was unlikely to see him playing with his presents again before he grows out of them.

The long slow ache that stays with me through the night is still there, strong as ever. Until the day I die I will miss making an arrest, but not as much as I miss my wife and son.

I can think of no better profession in the world and I will always miss the buzz and common purpose. I will miss those 3 a.m. moments in the office, when the day is done, the prisoners are in the bin, we're nursing our bruises and rubbing our wrists after finishing reams of paperwork, sipping on a beer and savouring the peace.

My heart wants to go back but my head says (very strongly) that I can't (not that they'd have me back anyway). For me, there will be no more fear, no more adrenalin rushes and although the nightmares still come, now I talk about them – I put them out in the open where they can't hurt me.